Benedict in the World
Portraits of Monastic Oblates

Linda Kulzer, O.S.B.
and
Roberta Bondi
Editors

THE LITURGICAL PRESS
Collegeville, Minnesota

www.litpress.org

Cover design by Greg Becker. Walker Percy photo: Rhonda Faust, Maple Street Book Shop, New Orleans. Dorothy Day photo: courtesy of the Marquette University Archives. Raïssa Maritain photo: Alcuin Photo Library.

1   2   3   4   5   6   7   8   9

Library of Congress Cataloging-in-Publication Data

Benedict in the world : portraits of monastic oblates / Linda Kulzer and Roberta Bondi, editors.
    p. cm.
    Includes bibliographical references.
    ISBN 0-8146-2571-1 (alk. paper)
    1. Oblates of St. Benedict—Biography. I. Kulzer, Linda. II. Bondi, Roberta C.
  BX3055 .B45 2002
  271'.1'—dc21
  [B]   2002067641

Contents

Foreword:
On Being a Benedictine Oblate

Roberta C. Bondi

I am an oblate of St. Benedict's Monastery, St. Joseph, Minnesota. I am also a historian of the early Church and spirituality. I teach in a United Methodist seminary. I am a wife, mother, and grandmother, the owner of a cat, and a Protestant. Though it sadly has been lost to the tradition in which I grew up, I have had a strong attraction to monasticism since graduate school days when I first studied its Egyptian, Syrian, and Latin founders. There, in my first exposure to those early folks, I discovered a love of God, of prayer, and of neighbor combined with a kind of freedom of spirit that was breathtaking. In them I seemed to be seeing a loosening of the hold of the destructive values that shape "everyday society," especially the lives of women, as well as an affirmation of what it meant to be a human I had only encountered once before in my Christian experience. This was in an Anglican English women's community I visited back in the sixties.

It was twenty years later before I came to St. Benedict's for Sunday Mass and lunch with the sisters. Even in those three hours, however, I was nearly certain that what I had first met in those ancient texts and seen hints of in the English convent was still alive here. Subsequent visits and especially the time I spent on a sabbatical leave several years later confirmed my suspicions about the place.

I wasn't a fool, however. Never for a moment did I think the sisters were "perfect" or even "saintly" in the popular, sentimental way we often use those terms. Because they are human beings, as were their predecessors in this life, as a realistic adult I knew very well that they were and are now subject to the myriad stresses and temptations that plague any group of people who live in such near proximity to one another. So what? With their love of God and each other, in their lives of prayer and work, in their commitment to a vision of society in which people truly flourish, in their freedom from the social values and judgments that destroy or wilt the lives of women, in their extravagant hospitality, in their support of and pride in each other, I could see for myself that the sisters of St. Benedict's monastery really did embody what was best in the ancient monasticism that drew me.

I considered becoming an oblate, but I was not sure it was possible for me. How could I, as a *Protestant married* woman with a nice home and a good job, find a meaningful way to relate to this community and to their Benedictine identity? Would I have to become Roman Catholic, live as a celibate in my marriage, or give up my home? With respect to the Roman Catholic question, conversations with the oblate director reminded me of and confirmed for me what I already knew: Benedictines precede the present divisions of the body of Christ by many centuries, so that monasticism is really the common heritage of all God's Christian people.

As for living as a celibate or giving up my home, there was certainly no demand for that. Indeed, though the monastics as well as the hierarchy of the early and medieval Church often spoke as though monastic life were a higher Christian calling than lay life, Benedictines don't seem to talk this way now. Rather, equally pleasing to God, monasticism and lay life are two different routes to the same end—continued growth in love of God and love of neighbor. Indeed, as I think about it now, I realize how much closer my husband seems to me at St. Benedict's than he does in all of the other places I travel with my work, as well as how much easier the transition from home to monastery, monastery to home. In other words, far from threatening my marriage and family life, as I once feared, I have discovered that my relationship with St. Benedict's has grounded it and blessed it.

My fears and ignorance laid aside, recognizing that St. Benedict's really was and is my spiritual home in a most fundamental way, I became an oblate. I recommitted myself to do my best as a lay person to live according to the values embodied in the ancient Rule of St. Benedict, to cast in my regular prayers with those of St. Benedict's Monastery, to love it, and be supported by it. This was my public commitment.

At the same time, I made some private vows of my own. I was terribly aware both how much the world needs communities like St. Benedict's with all they are and stand for, and how very endangered places like it are in our modern society. In my heart, therefore, I also promised to use my skills and gifts to support St. Benedict's and Benedictine monasticism with the best of what I have, to "spread the word," so to speak, about them as they really are. And I promised, too, if I could, to do whatever it was my sisters asked me to do. Indeed, this is why I gladly said yes when I was invited to be a co-editor for this book.

This is a part of my story as an oblate, and it will have much in common with the stories of many other ordinary and extraordinary men and women who have been or are also Benedictine oblates. At the same time, even the quickest reading of the essays of this book will make it clear that, apart from a commitment to the Rule of St. Benedict and a life of prayer shared (sometimes at a long distance) with a particular community, there has never been one kind of person who becomes an oblate, one single way or even one single reason to be one.

In the fifteenth century, Frances of Rome, for example, would have chosen a cloistered life if her mother and the confessor selected by her mother hadn't insisted that she marry. An ascetic visionary who spent her time and resources in the care of the poor, she eventually made an abortive attempt to set up a kind of monastery for oblates. St. Henry II, ca. 973–1024, became an emperor of the Holy Roman Empire in 1002. As a strong supporter of monasticism and a religious person himself, he is one of the patron saints of oblates. Then, in the seventeenth century, there was Elena Cornaro, of very different disposition and life from Frances and Henry. She became the first woman in the world to receive a doctorate. Caring for the poor as well as engaging in on-going learned conversation with the scholars of her time, she died at thirty-eight of tuberculosis.

As for the modern oblates included in this book, some lived very public lives and, like Dorothy Day, the Crowleys, and Carolyn Attnaeve, spent a great deal of their energy on social concerns. Some, like Walter Percy, Rumer Godden, and Joris-Karl Huysman, were novelists. The Maritains were philosophers. Like most of us, however, not all of these people are well known. For example, Emerson Hynes was a professor, Eric Dean a Presbyterian minister, Edith Gurian a librarian, Rita Sorg a journalist and mother of nine children, and Evelyn Davie a school teacher.

I am convinced that Benedictine monasticism is a very significant resource both for the renewal of the universal body of Christ which is the whole Christian church, and for the modern world. A major way we can share in its work today is by participating in it as oblates. Whether or not you are an oblate, however, Sister Linda and I hope that you will find things both useful and inspirational in this book.

Roberta C. Bondi
Candler School of Theology
Emory University

Acknowledgments

It is not possible to mention everyone who helped to compile these nineteen biographies of prominent oblates. Roberta Bondi and I are particularly indebted to St. Benedict's Monastery for providing the Studium as a space, an environment, and the source of the many kinds of support needed to complete an enterprise of this nature. As co-editors we want to express deep gratitude to those individuals whose oblate biographies make up the body of this work. Their willingness, hard work, and enthusiasm for this project are gratefully acknowledged.

I wish to acknowledge the help provided by the American Benedictine Academy in the form of a research grant. I am most grateful to my prioress, S. Ephrem Hollermann, and our community for adding to the grant from ABA so that it was possible for me to do research in England, accompanied by my sister, S. Marilyn Kulzer. I can never thank Roberta Bondi, my co-editor, sufficiently for her assistance in the many details that needed attention and for her lovely "Foreword." S. Mary Ann Stuart, o.s.b., of Mount St. Benedict Monastery, Crookston, Minnesota, gave truly valuable assistance as a proofreader. I am grateful to Barbara Fahnhorst of the College of St. Benedict for all she did to make possible the invaluable help of student employees of the college. Most prominent among these is Rina Shockman, whose cheerful attention to all the aspects of this book kept me going. I thank Karen Huot, another student employee, who assisted in so many ways with this project. I am also grateful to Meg Colleton, who lived in our monastery for a time as a Benedictine Live-In. She did much-needed research and, in addition, contributed a chapter on the Crowleys. Last, but not least, I thank the members of my community (particularly housemates and friends in Evin Hall) for their interest and support through these many years while this project was coming to completion.

Linda Kulzer, o.s.b.
January 22, 2002

Introduction

Linda Kulzer, O.S.B.

In 1994, a friend of mine asked me to recommend a book on the lives of Benedictine oblates. When I could not suggest even one title, this friend, Peg-Emmet Corcoran, asked me to consider putting together such a collection. I was intrigued by this challenge. It seemed to me that oblates have a right to look for support and inspiration in the life stories of others who have loved their oblate journey. I was delighted when Roberta Bondi, an oblate of our monastery (St. Benedict's, St. Joseph, Minnesota), agreed to be my co-editor. I thank Peg-Emmet for the invitation that has led to this book.

This volume begins with an introductory chapter on oblates today and then presents a collection of the life stories of nineteen significant Benedictine oblates. Over a period of two years (1999–2001) nineteen authors have been at work to help make possible this collection of lives of Benedictine oblates. One of the stipulations for inclusion here was that this volume would feature only lives of deceased oblates. Several other writers have indicated to me their hopes for editing a collection on living oblates.

While most of the oblates in this book lived in the time span between 1875 and 2000, some earlier oblates have also been included because of their particular historical significance. St. Henry II, one of the patrons of oblates, was born around 973. St. Frances of Rome, also a patron of oblates, lived from 1384 to 1440. Sir Oliver Plunkett, the Tyburn martyr, was born in 1625. Elena Cornaro, the first woman in the world to be awarded a Ph.D., lived during the late 1600s.

This volume details the lives of eight women oblates, seven men oblates, and two oblate couples. Seventeen of the subjects were Catholic, one was Presbyterian (Eric Dean), and one Anglican (Denys Prideaux). The first oblate chapter features the life of Carolyn Attnaeve, a Native American of the Delaware tribe. Evelyn Davie was an African American convert to Catholicism. She was a charter member of the oblate group of Sacred Heart Convent in Cullman, Alabama.

Dorothy Day, a woman featured in this book, has been named one of the most outstanding lay Catholics in the world during the twentieth century. Others who were nominated for this honor were the two oblate couples included in the collection: Patrick and Patricia Crowley and Jacques and Raïssa Maritain. Three of the oblates in this collection have works that are listed among "The 100 Best Spiritual Books of the Century." They are Dorothy Day's *Long Loneliness,* Raïssa Maritain's *Journals,* and Walker Percy's *Lost in the Cosmos.*

In looking over the collection of oblates featured here, I find it impressive to note the variety of individuals one meets. I found myself thinking of them under a variety of descriptions. Among a group I might regard as "Oblate Scholars and Teachers" are people like Eric Dean, Jacques and Raïssa Maritain, Emerson Hynes, Carolyn Attnaeve, and Elena Cornaro. Patrick and Patty Crowley would certainly be worthy of the title "Oblate Leaders." There are two chapters on the Crowleys. One is a touching, first-person account of Patrick Crowley's life written by his wife Patty Crowley. A second chapter has been added featuring both Patrick and Patty in order to give additional information about the contributions these two Benedictine oblates have made to the American Catholic world. St. Henry II would also fit well into this category, "Oblate Leaders."

"Oblate Women and Men of Unusual Courage" is a classification that would describe people like the martyr Oliver Plunkett, Dorothy Day, Evelyn Davie, Denys Prideaux, and Frances of Rome. The accounts of their lives demonstrate impressive heroism. Two persons who seem to fit into the category "Oblate Women of Daily Faithfulness" are Edith Gurian and Rita Sorg. I believe many of us would find this a description to which we aspire. Finally there is a fine group of "Oblate Authors." Many will recognize Walker Percy, Rumer Godden, H. A. Reinhold, and Joris-Karl Huysman. It was Huysman's novel, *The Oblate,* which influenced Dorothy Day's decision to become an oblate.

The chapters have been arranged alphabetically according to the last names of the oblates featured. A glance at the list of the nineteen persons who wrote these life accounts shows thirteen women authors and six men authors. Nine of the persons who contributed these chapters are themselves Benedictine oblates and eight are professed Benedictine monastics. Among the professed Benedictine monastics is S. Mary Anthony Wagner, who passed into eternity on September 18, 2002, before this work could be published. She was the Oblate Director at St. Benedict's Monastery, St. Joseph, Minnesota, for thirty years and was considered a guru in the world of American Benedictine Oblate Directors.

It seems very significant to have this mix of both oblate and professed monastics as authors. Here they are working together in bringing to light the lives of these lay monastics. You are invited to proceed now to the life stories of these outstanding Benedictine oblates.

Linda Kulzer, O.S.B.

1

Monasticism Beyond the Walls

Linda Kulzer, O.S.B.

While the chapters that follow are all devoted to oblates of the past, it seems helpful to devote this first chapter to an exploration of the state of Benedictine oblation today. The current influx of oblates (read also associates, affiliates, co-members, etc.) into our monastic communities is both a welcome and an unexpected phenomenon. It might be viewed as the most significant development in monasticism in recent times. Could this happening be related to the statement by Alasdair MacIntyre in the very last paragraph of his well known book, *After Virtue*? Looking for ways of healing the moral ills so obvious in our culture today, he ends the book by saying "we await another—doubtless very different—St. Benedict." For the last two decades Benedictines have been puzzling over the implications of this unusual claim. I would like to suggest that it may indeed be the swelling ranks of Benedictine oblates who are the "very different" Benedictines able to carry into our culture the insights of monastic spirituality—insights that can help heal the ills that seem to be crippling our society.

It is not clear just when this vibrant oblate movement began. The *National Catholic Reporter* ran an article in the May 26, 2000, issue entitled "Survey Reveals Growth in Orders' Associates." It points out the unusual growth in the number of men and women who affiliate in one way or another with a religious community. The statistics given indicate that there are 25,400 associates or oblates in America today. That figure is a 75 percent increase over figures tabulated in 1995.

Looking specifically at Benedictine oblates, we find their number has been growing especially fast in the last ten years. In many cases today the number of oblates affiliated with a Benedictine house far exceeds the number of professed monastics in that community. In the paper "Monastic and Oblate: Mutual Blessings," given for the 1999 North American Oblate Directors' Meeting, Norvene Vest reported that in her home monastery (Valyermo, California) about 25 monks support and are supported by some 300 oblates. In a visit to Elmore Abbey in England (Anglican Abbey of Benedictine monks), this writer found 350 oblates affiliating with an abbey of 10 monks.

Defining the Oblate State

Do the interests of those affiliating with monasteries today differ from the interests noted in oblates of the less recent past? One way to examine this question might be to look at the changes in the way in which oblature was defined in the past and the manner in which it is described at the present time. In the 1953 *Manual of the Oblates of St. Benedict,* the oblate is described as one who

> spiritually affiliates himself with a Benedictine monastery and its community, in order to thereby lead a more perfect Christian life in the world according to the spirit of the Rule of St. Benedict; to share likewise in the spiritual treasures of the Benedictine Order and enjoy the special privileges granted by the Church to Oblates; and to promote, as far as lies in his power the good of the monastery to which he is attached and of the entire Benedictine Order.

Here we find the oblates pictured at a certain distance from the monastic life itself. In some ways they appear as an appendage rather than an integral part of Benedictine life in the monastery.

A definition that begins to express more closely the current longings of oblates comes from Bethlehem Priory, an Anglican Benedictine community in Lexington, Kentucky.

> Oblates are those who discern that God has called them to more of a life of prayer and study and who have turned (for advice, help and direction) to the experience that monasticism has developed over the centuries. They are those who keep the monastic ideal before their eyes, even though they are not monks.

Within the last few years a breakthrough seems to have occurred in regard to the way in which the oblate state is defined. Oblates are coming to us with the realization that they have a calling, a monastic vocation— not, however, one that will be lived out in the monastery, but one to be lived outside the walls of the monastery. We now hear oblates referring to themselves as "lay monastics" and their form of life as "monasticism beyond the walls." Those of us who are professed monastics find we have to expand our vision of vocation and monasticism.

There are a number of persons who are helping to develop this new understanding. Among them is Mark Plais who wrote an article for *Cistercian Studies Quarterly* (34:3 [1990]) entitled "Lay Monasticism." Janet Buchanen has written a fine doctoral dissertation entitled "Monks Beyond Monastery Walls: Benedictine Oblation and the Future of Benedictine Spirituality." She points to the influence of Raimundo Panikkar's *Blessed Simplicity* and Marsha Sinetar's *People as Monks and Mystics.* Panikkar claims that there is a monastic archetype innate in every human being and that ultimately everyone is called in one way or another to be a monk. It is Panikkar who has coined the term "new monk" to refer to the lay person longing to live the monastic dimension of life. Panikkar sagely notes that the challenge lies in providing the facilitating structures that open the way to this monastic dimension and support it. Marsha Sinetar has presented case studies of lay people who live what she would refer to as authentically monastic lives. She would likely define the "new monk" as someone who responds to an inner call and reinterprets his/her way of being in the world.

Ecumenism among Oblates

What seems to have happened concomitantly, or perhaps as a result of the breakthrough of the lay monasticism concept, is the very sizeable influx of Christians of other traditions who are joining the oblate ranks. This ecumenical inclusivity is appropriate because the Benedictine world itself is ecumenical. St. Benedict wrote the Rule long before the conflicts of the Middle Ages and the Reformation. Thus the treasures of Benedictine spirituality are the heritage of all Christians. Some particularly insightful writings on the Rule and Benedictine spirituality have come from the pens of oblates of Christian denominations other than Catholic: Kathleen Norris, Norvene Vest, and Eric Dean.

There have been many indications of how happily this gathering of all denominations meeting together at the home monastery is working out. Gilbert R. Budd Friend-Jones, in an article in the *ABA Proceedings 2000,* testifies: "Without asking that we give up our own denominations, families, or places in our communities, they invite us to share in their life together. They offer us places in their choirs and their table, in their libraries and among their gardens."

This author had the opportunity recently to do some research concerning ecumenical oblates in England. In visiting Stanbrook Abbey (Catholic), Elmore Abbey (Anglican), and Malling Abbey (Anglican), much the same situation was found in regard to a revitalization of oblate life. There was a clear beginning of a more ecumenical mix among oblates, but it was not as pronounced as is currently found in the United States.

Our oblates appear to have a new and dynamic concept of themselves and their longings. Jerome Leo Hughes, o.s.b., a claustral oblate at St. Mary's Monastery, Petersham, Massachusetts, and a frequent contributor to an Internet list called Oblateforum, states this new outlook very clearly (2/23/2001): "The Benedictine vocation is not just, or even primarily cloistered, celibate monastics. The vast majority of Benedictines are Oblates, married men and women from many different Churches. Therein lies the greatest treasure of the Benedictine family, one that is often undervalued, even by Oblates themselves."

Perhaps all this discussion of the "new monk" and the monastic dimension of the attraction that has brought so many oblates to our doors can tend to promote an unreal picture of the actual dailiness of the life of the typical oblate. We need to remember that oblates go on with their ordinary lives. They continue to face the usual frustrations of loneliness, challenging marriages, separation and divorce, worries about children, job loss or job insecurity, and the pettiness that is the lot of the human condition. While being an oblate brings a longed-for sense of direction it in no way removes one from the human condition.

What is it that makes Benedictine spirituality so appealing to those who encounter it? Perhaps it is the invitation to a mysticism of everyday life, a very ordinary way by which our sacred yearnings are wedded to the secular necessities of our lives. This spirituality of the ordinary has been an extraordinary leaven creating a milieu in which attitudes of prayer, peace, justice, and love have not only permeated communities of monastics but whole societies over the past millennia.

Expectations of New Oblates

What might be some expectations these new oblates have of the professed members of our monastic communities? How do we tend to regard this new influx? The most honest answer seems to report a mixed reaction. Not all professed monastics are ready to agree with Jerome Leo Hughes' assessment of the situation. It would seem, however, that the majority of professed monastics view this influx of oblates and their new outlook on monasticism as a great gift displaying again the wonderful mercy of God. It is God's generous blessing to those of us within the walls who have been struggling with the meaning of our diminishing numbers.

Turning again for a moment to Janet Buchanan's dissertation, we find a reference to the problem of the diminishing numbers of professed monastics. She believes that the staying power of monastic communities in the future is very dependent on "their ability to transmit their monastic charism in such a way that it will continue to transform those who receive it." She becomes quite explicit when she makes it clear that her project addresses "Benedictine Oblation as a primary response to the question, how will monasticism live on?" (38).

At times, we professed monastics do feel challenged by this influx of new oblates. We find ourselves meeting oblates who have come through a long search and have developed a sound and deep spiritual life. These same oblates have come upon monasticism as the treasure for which their hearts have been longing. They already have a deep grasp of and appreciation for Benedictine spirituality. When they look to us as the monastic guides they have been waiting for, some of us feel not only challenged, but also deeply humbled. As we share life based on the Rule of St. Benedict with oblates, we find ourselves inspired to live that life more fully and generously within the monastic walls.

Antoinette Purcell, O.S.B., has made some helpful observations about what we professed monastics are being invited to do in her presentation "A View from Inside the Walls," in *ABA* [American Benedictine Academy] *Proceedings 2000*. She believes that one change we need to consider within the monastery "is to keep before the eyes of those seeking as well as the community receiving that being an oblate is about a way of life not a program." She recommends a mindset that sees oblates not as second-class monastics, but as part of the same community lived in a different lifestyle. She goes on to observe:

> It is only that mindset which will allow us to receive from monastics outside the walls the treasures they have for us. I expect that monastics outside the walls can provide, for me personally and for my community, benefits and challenges that will help to shape me and us as monastics for the twenty-first century. I believe that we can nurture and support one another so that together we give witness to people of this time a hope for today and tomorrow.

In an article referred to earlier, Norvene Vest has suggested ways in which monastics and oblates can learn to become mutually supportive of each other. She sees us as having a shared vocation to be a witness and challenge to our society as a whole.

Summary

This chapter has explored the new calling experienced by today's oblates. It is likely that the concept of the oblate's monastic vocation has drawn additional Christians from a variety of different faiths to become a part of this movement. This unusual ecumenical mix has enriched the experience of the oblate groups and the monasteries to which they belong. Many professed monastics are seeing the influx of these "new monks" as both a gift and a challenge. It is also becoming increasingly clear that not only will the oblates and the professed members be a source of mutual blessings for each other, but the new oblates could be the likely way for monasticism to live on. Thus it seems possible that the prediction of Alasdair MacIntyre that "we await another—doubtless very different—St. Benedict" could actually be a description of the many Benedictine oblates who are already transmitting the monastic charism to our present society.

2

Carolyn Attneave: Catcher of the Light

Paschal A. Morlino, o.s.b.

First Impressions

I first met Carolyn at a symposium hosted by St. Vincent's Archabbey and St. Vincent's College in 1979 to honor award-winning children's television programming pioneer Fred Rogers, a native of Latrobe, Pennsylvania. Carolyn was one of the main speakers and also a discussion panel member. She was bubbling over with enthusiasm for the event and thrilled with the turnout of eight hundred participants. My involvement with Carolyn at this time resulted from my assigned tasks to look after her, keep her accommodations in order, and make sure she had all the materials she needed for the symposium. She actually needed very few materials since she herself was an abundant source of ideas and was continually introducing new and unique ideas into play, whether in formal settings or during walks along the roadway to and from sessions. She was very active in networking all segments of the symposium by interrelating and coordinating the various disciplines represented.

Over the next few years Carolyn and I had the privilege of working together frequently on a project I had begun in 1971, namely Adelphoi Village, an institution that houses and cares for troubled youth. She organized several workshops for our staff. This common interest also led me to visit with her occasionally in Seattle where she was professor of psychology, psychiatry, and behavioral sciences at the University of Washington. She invited me to speak in her psychology classes as a consumer of the services which psychologists can provide. As a result of her many visits to the St. Vincent campus during these years, Carolyn fell in love with the monastic community of the archabbey. She came to feel very much at home both with the community and also with the land where the community was located.[1]

Heritage and History

But Carolyn's had not been an easy journey. She made her first visits to St. Vincent principally for professional reasons. The 1979 symposium was the beginning. She also was at St. Vincent as commencement speaker at the college in May 1981. At that time she received an honorary degree of doctor of science and spoke on "Interdependence Unbound by Time and Space," which concerned people's need to contribute to one another in harmony and mutual satisfaction. She referred to family ties, intergeneration relationships, and interactions among groups of peoples. Hence she touched on a theme which was not only professional but personal. Speaking of her heritage as a Delaware Indian, she referred to the role of one of her ancestors, known in English as "White Eyes," who participated in the Pittsburgh Treaty of 1778. This was the first treaty with another nation signed by the newly formed United States of America; the other nation was the Delaware tribe. In it the Delaware agreed to leave Pennsylvania and never to claim it again. The Delaware people had been first encountered by Europeans in the area along the great Delaware River, which forms the eastern border of Pennsylvania. This tribe, or Lenni Lenape as they call themselves, had established good relations with William Penn. But because of pressure from the increasing number of new settlers and following repeated victimization at the hands of Penn's successors, they moved to Western Pennsylvania about 1720. Amid the escalating difficulties between England and France and the inevitable disputes among the tribes that were drawn onto either side in the armed conflicts of the eighteenth century, the Delaware attempted to maintain their traditional buffer role as peacemakers. After the American War of Independence, the geopolitical scene had greatly changed. The 1778 Treaty of Pittsburgh was part of the attempt to establish a new order free from European interference. The United States promised that a separate Indian

---

[1] St. Vincent Archabbey, the first Benedictine monastery in the United States, was founded in 1846 from St. Michael's Abbey in Metten, Bavaria. Soon after Father Boniface Wimmer arrived here he began the community by investing eighteen newly-arrived monks. The community grew rapidly and began to make other foundations, many of which became independent abbeys. Currently, its main apostolates include the operation of St. Vincent College and St. Vincent Seminary and the staffing of twenty-five parishes. The community also has foreign missions in Brazil and Taiwan, and staffs a priory and military preparatory school in Savannah, Georgia.

state would be formed where Indian people would be an equal part of the new nation. However, that promise was deferred and never fully implemented. Eventually remnants of the Delaware, after a series of westward relocations through the nineteenth century, were settled in Indian Territory. This land was established as the state of Oklahoma in 1907; as a result, all Indians living there were made citizens of the United States.

Carolyn was born in El Paso, Texas, on July 2, 1920, to James and Carrie Florence (Adams) Lewis. She spent many of her childhood summers in Oklahoma with her grandparents, where she learned the bitter history of her people and was shaped by their traditions. She married Fred Attneave in 1949. They had a daughter, Dorothy, and a son, Philip. Her studies and work took her across the United States: to California, Oklahoma, Chicago, Lubbock, Philadelphia, Boston, and Seattle. She was on the board of the American Family Therapy Association, served on a panel of the President's Commission on Mental Health, and was a delegate to the 1980 White House Conference on Families. The 1981 St. Vincent College commencement program noted, "Her expertise in family therapy has led her from the classroom to the White House, from Indian reservations in the West to Harvard School of Public Health in the East, from Alaska to London." The commencement program added, "Her knowledge of the American Indian family and its traditions has provided her with insights into the use of the extended family as a tool in therapy." Her contribution to community mental health was exercised in practice and documented in a long list of publications.

Reflections

At this commencement address Carolyn spoke of the attraction she experienced in returning to the ancestral homelands of the Delaware in Pennsylvania, but she also admitted the powerful inner difficulties which several earlier attempts to connect here had occasioned. She said she had tried twice to move back to Philadelphia, "but could never manage more than a year or two without the loneliness and ghosts haunting me, making it unbearable." She spoke of a tightening of the chest, and a tensing of the muscles when she crossed the Delaware River, and "I could not drive the Pennsylvania Turnpike fast enough to get away from the sense of doom." Then she referred to her accepting the invitation to participate in the 1979 symposium: "It took all my willpower to get on the plane and get off it at Pittsburgh." This event turned out to be a changing point in her life.

> But here I experienced something new—a feeling of mutuality, of acceptance, and of shared commitments. This year I have been looking forward to coming for this occasion as one might anticipate joyfully coming home. . . .

The honor extended to me is not purely an individual or personal one—but a return to the spirit of 300 years ago for my tribe as well.

Understanding Benedictine Values

Perhaps the most ambitious professional visit which Carolyn paid to St. Vincent took the form of a study of coeducation as it was introduced into the previously all-male St. Vincent College. Her activities included collecting baseline data in 1982–83, both prior to and immediately after the announcement of the decision to change to coeducation, and conducting a comprehensive study throughout the first year of coeducation, 1983–84.

Carolyn undertook the study with the help of a National Science Foundation Grant of a Visiting Professorship for Women, and she was assisted by several members of the college faculty and staff as well as by four college students and two outside consultants. (One of those assisting her was Fr. Warren Murrmann, O.S.B., who collaborated and provided considerable help and expertise in preparing this article.) The project enabled Carolyn to analyze seriously the Benedictine values, which underpin the academic enterprise at St. Vincent. Her study addressed a concern as to whether the Benedictine values are human values rather than gender specific. She stated in her results, measuring what the report called the college's social climate, "the application of these values to women as well as men [was] the occasion of minimal strain."[2]

Her research led her to delve into Benedictine history and the role of women's education in it, as well as the presence and role of women at St. Vincent before the start of coeducation in 1983. She was impressed particularly by the role of the Benedictine sisters in the history of the Catholic Church in the United States, especially in the area of education. She became fascinated by the community of Benedictine sisters associated with St. Vincent since 1931. She wrote lovingly of this community of women who were at the time still actively engaged in preparing and serving meals to everyone on campus.

After her year-long stay at St. Vincent working on the coeducation report, Carolyn seems to have reconciled with her Pennsylvania past. She had multiplied and deepened personal ties with personnel in the college and especially with members of the Benedictine community. Also, she found welcome and comfort in the land itself. One day on an automobile ride she was taken to a place near the town of Ligonier, where there had been a Delaware Indian village in the early eighteenth century. She looked

---

[2] Final Project Report, p. 1.

around, mused, and simply drank in the surroundings. She said it was a good place for a village, a protected valley with clear water. There she felt a strong sense of being in touch with her ancestors. The ghosts she encountered at that time were no longer the kind that haunted her earlier visits to Pennsylvania.

Growth in Benedictine Spirituality

Part of the closeness that Carolyn felt with the Benedictine community arose from the traditional Benedictine reverence for the land as belonging to God and as used by him to show his goodness to his children. Carolyn had the ability to see everything as God's handiwork. She found consolation and a source of strength in the Benedictine tradition of reverence for the things around us: air, water, sky, trees, animals. She spoke often of finding a kindred spirit in the wisdom of Benedict, who taught that monks are to hold things in common (RB 33) and receive according as each one has need (RB 34). Being the stewards of God's world, we are responsible for taking good care of it (RB 32). She read in Benedict's injunction that the cellarer looks upon all goods of the monastery as though they were the consecrated vessels of the altar (RB 31), a sensitivity to God's revealing himself in the ordinary items of life and giving us the added task of supporting and sustaining one another through these items. In the web of life, all are afflicted when one member is afflicted, and all benefit when one member benefits.

During her visits to St. Vincent, which became more frequent with the passing years, she became increasingly serious about her spiritual involvement in the monastic community and its spirituality. She communicated with Archabbot Leopold Krul in July of 1983, reminding him he had stated earlier that he had recognized in her "the spirit of an oblate." At first, she associated the compliment with historical and literary references of earlier centuries, but subsequently she discovered information about contemporary forms of affiliation with various Benedictine monasteries. She had spoken with several fellow parishioners of St. Bridget in Seattle who were Benedictine oblates associated with St. Martin's Abbey in Lacey, Washington. Consequently, she asked Archabbot Leopold whether in the "archabbey's complex tapestry of relationships" there was also an association of oblates and, if so, inquired whether she could use her upcoming sabbatical year at St. Vincent "to best advantage in relation to it." She did take advantage of this opportunity and made her oblation in affiliation with St. Vincent Archabbey on August 20, 1984.

Although she was an active member of St. Bridget's Church and served as a reader, a special minister of the Eucharist, and a member of the liturgy committee, she increasingly spoke of St. Vincent as her spiritual home. She felt that, just as one had a physical home and a physical family, one also needed a spiritual home and a spiritual family. While regarding her true home as in heaven with the risen Lord, she came to consider the archabbey and its physical environment as her spiritual home on earth. She used the term "spiritual" not to describe merely a mental or idealized notion of reality. She employed it in the sacramental sense of finding the spirit in the physical, the heavenly within the earthly. Her view was that while religion must speak of God and heavenly things, it also must be down to earth. Christianity is not an abstract idea; it is a way of life.

She saw in the Benedictine way of life, moreover, the key to relating to her Christianity the lives of her ancestors, their history, and her involvement in their world. The "social network" of which she was a part clearly included those who had gone on before. She had a lively understanding of what Christian theology calls the communion of saints, enriched by her perspectives as an American Indian, a psychologist, and an oblate within the Christian monastic tradition.

Carolyn was proud that she was a member of the Turtle Clan of the Delaware tribe. In tribal Indian lore, clan members share in the characteristics and virtues of the particular spirit represented by the animal associated with that clan. For many tribes of northeastern North America the story of the creation of this land tells of its formation at a time when everything was water. The spirits wished to build land and so various animals were sent down into the water to bring up mud. A few of them were able to do this, but then they discovered they had nowhere to put it. The turtle volunteered its back for this purpose, and thus it became the foundation of this "turtle island" which we now call America. Characteristics of the turtle include longevity, durability, slowness along with steady reliability, and willingness to support others. The turtle's offering of its back is thus a symbol of life lived in mutual support and of hope and confidence offered to others. Her quip, "We Turtles might be slow, but we have strong backs," reflects this symbolism. Thus Carolyn perceived the web of interrelationship and mutual enrichment among her Indian heritage, her Christian faith, and her professional work as teacher and therapist.

American Indian religions reflect the awareness that God is revealed and discovered through nature. Carolyn found that the monastic tradition shared this spirituality. Her long and difficult journey back to the land of her ancestors in Pennsylvania became a symbol of her own spiritual journey, which joined her Delaware Indian heritage with Christianity, so that they mutually reinforced each other. In 1982 her journey had led her into full communion with the Catholic Church, and in 1984 to her full status as a Benedictine oblate.

In her later years she encountered the writings of Hildegard of Bingen and other medieval monastic mystics who contemplated the revelation of God in two complementary bibles, in the book of nature and in the book of God's word. Particularly in Hildegard, she found a glimpse of her own perception of the close connection, interrelatedness, and harmonious balance existing among all things. She pointed out, however, that such balance and harmony often come about only after bitter difficulties and long periods of imbalance. This process characterized her own search, often over circuitous byways. But eventually she was convinced that her steps had brought her to a sure and well-worn trail. As a Benedictine oblate, she rejoiced that she had found a healthy merger of the various paths she had trod. All her roads led to St. Vincent, she said, and in her vocation to be an oblate she found the best way for her to follow Christ.

The words of the prologue to the Holy Rule may well be applied to the final years of her life:

> Do not be daunted immediately by fear and run away from the road that leads to salvation. It is bound to be narrow at the outset. But as we progress in this way of life and in faith, we shall run on the path of God's commandments, our hearts overflowing with the inexpressible delight of love (Prol. 48–49).

Her Legacy

Carolyn Attneave died in Seattle on June 21, 1992, at the age of seventy-one. She was buried in the cemetery at St. Vincent Archabbey in Latrobe. At the news of her death, she was honored with a special talking-drum ceremony by American Indian psychologists meeting in Colorado. Those who knew her well spoke of her accomplishment in succeeding in mainstream society as an internationally known mental-health theorist while still keeping her feet planted firmly in the traditions of her native people.

She was an unassuming intellectual who introduced her professional peers to an original approach of dealing with people with mental-health problems by consulting a wide network of family members, friends, and associates. The approach was considered innovative when she first advocated it. However, we can perceive in it the wisdom of the native peoples, for whom each person is not merely an individual but primarily a member of a family, a clan, a tribe. We recognize in this approach the teaching of St. Paul, who proclaims that though there are many members, all are one in Christ (1 Corinthians). We likewise hear such a communitarian vision in St. Benedict's Rule, contained in such teachings as, "No one is to pursue what he judges better for himself, but instead, what he judges better for someone else" (RB 72.7). In her own quest for light, Carolyn caught it in the dewdrops sparkling on the fine webs of social networking. She brought this light down to earth and she taught it to others.

3

Oblate and Heroine:
Elena Lucrezia Scholastica Cornaro Piscopia (1646–1684)

Ann Kessler, O.S.B.

Can one woman simultaneously be a Benedictine oblate, a rebel, a prima donna, a heroine, and a patron saint of educated women?[1] Could this same oblate also be a wealthy young aristocrat who, in life as well as death, defied her parents by rejecting the suitors her father and brothers accepted as potential grooms, by leaving the convent they chose for her after a very brief stay, and by selecting a monastic burial site instead of the parental choice of the Basilica of St. Anthony or the Cathedral of Padua?

Could she be a woman whose application for a theology doctorate was vetoed by the same prelate, a cardinal, who later acceded to the young woman's wishes regarding her funeral and interment?

Elena Lucrezia Cornaro Piscopia, who added Scolastica (Italian spelling) to her name at the time she became a Benedictine oblate, is indisputably the first woman in the world to receive a college or university degree. This wealthy and brilliant Venetian aristocrat is finally becoming better known for what she did—and did not do. She is extolled primarily as the first to break the barrier, which for centuries barred women from

---

[1] *Kappa Gamma Pi Newsletter* (November 1974) headlined a short biography titled "Patron Saint of Educated Women." An article in Montana's *Missoulian* (June 25, 1978) was entitled "First Female College Graduate Caused Big Furor 3 Centuries Ago." Dom Francesco Ludovico Maschietto, presently (2001) an elderly monk of St. Justina, called his biography *Elena Lucrezia Cornaro Piscopia: Prima donna laureata nel mundo* (Padua: Atenore, 1978). I was fortunate to have the kind assistance of Dom Stefano Visintin, a monk of Praglia Abbey (near Padua) as translator, host, guide, and source of current Italian abbey history during and after my research tour. (A publisher is currently considering a recent English translation of Maschietto's definitive work.)

achieving a university degree. Although the seventeenth century boasted almost 150 institutions of higher learning, a twentieth-century survey of these institutions showed that not until 1678, when Elena graduated, had any institution conferred a degree on a woman.

In earlier centuries some scholarly Benedictine nuns had certainly deserved the same recognition, but no Hilda of Whitby, Roswitha of Gandersheim, Hildegard of Bingen, Mechtild of Magdeburg, or Gertrude of Helfta, women clearly qualified to receive a liberal arts, philosophy, or theology degree, ever applied for one (some having lived before the rise of universities), nor would any degree have been granted, had they done so.

Parental Testimony

When Elena's coffin was opened and her gravesite restored in 1895, reports circulated that her body was incorrupt. More reputable sources maintained that, although the bones had turned to dust, her Benedictine oblate garb had not disintegrated. During the re-interment a leaden plate (apparently designed by her father) found inside her coffin was transferred to the new sarcophagus. It reads in part:

> Here rests Lucrezia Cornaro Piscopia, a Venetian noble woman of famous name, virgin, dedicated to God and St. Benedict, most skilled in the ancient classical languages of Hebrew, Latin and Greek, and the modern languages of Spanish, French, and Italian which she spoke flawlessly. Excelling in all branches of learning, publicly granted a Doctoral Laureate at Padua in the year 1678.

It also related the fact that "moved by her fame and writings," she had received visits or messages from famous persons such as Pope Innocent XI; John III, King of Poland; Emperor Leopold I; and Charles III, Duke of Lorraine. Also highly commending her were King Louis XIV of France and "other princes" who bestowed upon her the highest honors. It concludes that on July 26, 1684, she "commuted this mortal glory for an immortal one, to receive the double aureole of virgin and doctor in the 38th year of her age. Her surviving parent, Gianbattista of San Marco, mourns her most sorrowfully."[2] Actually, both parents survived her, but apparently only worthy of mention was the Procurator of St. Mark's in Venice, the official in charge of the treasury and superintendent of the Cathedral, second only to the chief magistrate, the royal doge (duke).

---

[2] Two reports of the plate's inscriptions are combined here. See Nicola Fuso, *Elena Lucrezia Cornaro Piscopia, 1645–1684* (Pittsburgh: Tercentenary Committee, 1975) 106; and Jane Howard Guernsey, *The Lady Cornaro: Pride and Prodigy of Venice* (Clinton Corners, N.Y.: College Avenue Press, 1999) 228.

The Gifted Woman

It was her father, Gianbattista Cornaro Piscopia,[3] who was determined to control all aspects of his daughter's youth and adulthood and whom she strove to please in recompense for his not forcing her to marry. His daughter's final gift to him was her agreeing to study diligently for a university doctorate. Had she been a man, she might have become a Benedictine monk—a member of the renowned intellectual group of savants of the Maurist Congregation, perhaps even a priest like Mabillon, the Maurist's greatest light, who came to visit her during her lifetime and her father after her death. She was always able to hold her own with the renowned educated men of her day, impressing Mabillon and other scholars who appeared at her home in order to dialogue with the most famous feminine intellectual of her century.[4]

Genealogy and Spirituality

The Cornaros could boast of many prominent ancestors including three popes, eight cardinals, four Venetian doges, several procurators of St. Mark's, ambassadors, scholars, military heroes, and a queen. Titian, Tintoretto, and Veronese all painted portraits of the fifteenth-century Cornaro Queen of Cyprus whose family members added Piscopia to their name—taken from the title of the palace and estate on Cyprus deeded to the Cornaros by the king in lieu of the repayment of a loan from his queen's parents.[5]

Elena was an heiress of the Cornaro-Piscopia branch of the family, which was independently wealthy, the result of preceding generations who had succeeded in various merchant and real estate ventures. The family had, however, for some time lacked a famous individual, something Elena's father was determined to rectify. Certain biographers claim that Gianbattista used his daughter to bring honor to the family in lieu of her unremarkable brothers. Not only did they lack Elena's gifts, but because their mother was a commoner, Elena's father gained noble status for his sons only after payment of a fee of thousands of ducats. Actually, it was only in 1654, when Elena was eight, that a formal wedding, earlier forbidden by the Council of Ten, recognized the long-standing union of her parents.

Elena's mother entertained lavishly at the palatial lodgings allocated to the Procurator on the Piazza San Marco. At times Zanetta, who loved

---

[3] Maschietto consistently names him Giovanni Battista, but the plaque uses Gianbattista—which, for the sake of clarity and brevity, I prefer.

[4] *Revue Bénédictine* 13 (1896) 5

[5] Anne Stuart Bailey, "A Daughter of the Doges," *American Catholic Quarterly Review* 21 (1896) 821, n. 1.

playing duchess, lost patience with her modest and reserved daughter who would join her reluctantly in what Elena considered frivolous pursuits, such as being elegantly garbed or spending precious time observing from their windows the frolics of the carnival actors and spectators in the Piazza or at the Rialto along the Grand Canal.

San Giorgio Abbey

A concession Elena had to make was agreeing to use the family's richly outfitted gondolas to travel to her favorite spiritual refuge, the Benedictine Abbey of San Giorgio Maggiore. Here, surrounded by Benedictine statuary and art, she participated in the eucharistic liturgy and prayed the Divine Office with the monks. She frequented the abbey's island also, because "like all Benedictine monasteries it was comparable to a small town where the poor were tended and fed, sick people were nursed, kings and prominent personalities were entertained."[6] Her friendship with Abbot Cornelius Codinini would eventually make it possible for her to call upon him when she had need of his support in the rejection of family-promoted marriage proposals. Elena always found time daily for the spiritual, for the Benedictine Liturgy of the Hours or the Office of the Blessed Virgin, the rosary, the Litany of the Saints, Scripture, and Mass at a private chapel, a parish church, or one of the monasteries.

The Young Scholar

When she was only seven, a friend of Elena's father, Gianbattista Fabris, a pastor at nearby St. Luke's church, as well as a renowned Aristotelian scholar, became aware of her spiritual bent, her intellectual talents, and her clear logical reasoning. He offered to tutor her in Latin, Greek, and philosophy, an offer her father readily accepted. When she made astoundingly rapid progress, the proud parent engaged more tutors who instructed her in other languages, modern Greek, Spanish, English, Hebrew, French, and Arabic. Tutors were also engaged to teach her theology, geography, literature, mathematics, astronomy, rhetoric, dialectics, and the fine arts. Although some argue that Elena applied herself to study only to please her father, the Lady Abbess Pynsent, author of a nineteenth-century biography, insists that Elena "set herself to her new studies with great pleasure and diligence. She felt that in pursuing it she was cultivating the gifts God had given her."[7]

---

[6] Nicola Ivanoff, *Venezia: San Giorgio Maggiore* (Venice: n.p., n.d.) 26.

[7] Mathilde Pynsent, *The Life of Helen Lucretia Cornaro Piscopia: Oblate of the Order of St. Benedict and Doctor in the University of Padua* (Rome: n.p., 1895) 15.

During this time she had constant access to her father's magnificent personal library, considered one of the finest private collections in Venice. It included not only rare books of every kind, but the complete works of Aristotle with various commentaries, Roman philosophers and literati, valuable Greek and Latin manuscripts, as well as more modern histories and literary works on the Venetian Republic. Elena grew up surrounded not only by these many volumes, but also by mathematical and astronomical instruments, globes, navigational charts, and maps. Open to the public as well, this young scholar's favorite haunt eventually also provided her first encounter with a renowned professor who became her mentor and sponsor and eventually did the ritual garbing of Elena with the insignia of her doctorate after her exam. As Carlo Rinaldini later recounted, he arrived unannounced at the palace library one day to examine some of the rich Cornaro holdings. After leafing through some works of Archimedes, he was silently reflecting on one of that great mathematician's theories, when a young, dignified, and beautiful girl appeared and began elaborating on the complex theorem. The awestruck professor was speechless, but soon recovered enough to ask her name. It was the beginning of a lifetime friendship between Elena and Rinaldini, later chair of the department of philosophy at Padua's university, a person she often designated as her "cultural father."[8]

Gianbattista also maintained a private art gallery housing works inspired by Titian, Veronese, Bassono, and other great European artists. Elena studied the paintings and gradually became something of an authority on art. She was also an accomplished musician, naturally gifted with the ability to perform by ear as well as to sight-read some of the most challenging compositions. Her music instructor, Maddalena Cappelli, became Elena's closest confidante and lifelong companion. She was engaged to live with the family, providing Elena with a broad musical background while guiding her composition of a number of musical works. Elena's God-given gifts included a pleasing soprano voice, which she was often called upon by her parents to display after some of the dinners for dignitaries at the palace.[9]

Elena's Oblation

Although she had studied Scripture since she was eleven, as an adolescent Elena was even more taken with it, preferring theology and scripture over the study of philosophy. She relished reading the lives of the saints. Two of her favorites were the Italians, Benedict of Norcia and

[8] Guernsey, *The Lady Cornaro,* 52–3, 100–1.
[9] Ibid., 49–50, 80–1; Bailey, "A Daughter of the Doges," 822.

Aloysius Gonzaga. In imitation of the young Aloysius, when Elena was eleven, she secretly made a vow of virginity, an action which later brought upon her the fury of her parents and brother who had plans for her marriage to one or the other of her numerous suitors. These included a nephew of the doge and a German prince. The family tried every ruse to convince her that her vow of virginity was invalid because she was so young and because it was private. A dispensation from Rome was secured to support the family's claim but tearful and defiant Elena would not relent. She sought help elsewhere.

While a certain suitor waited for her acceptance after he had completed arrangements with her father, the nineteen-year-old Elena secretly sent for Abbot Codanini of San Giorgio. After hearing her story, he allowed her to renew her private vow of virginity in his presence and accepted her commitment as a Benedictine oblate. It was at this time that she added Scolastica to her name and began to include with her signature "Oblate of St. Benedict." With the abbot's permission, as often as she could secretly do so, she wore the contemporary Benedictine oblate scapular under her clothes.[10]

Convent Interlude

The frustrated family finally, but most reluctantly, gave up hopes of her ever marrying. However, when it came to permitting her to enter a monastery or convent, it was the parents, not Elena, who made the final choice. They and Elena agreed to exclude the Benedictines and even the Augustinians where one of Gianbattista's younger sisters was a member.[11] According to Lady Abbess Pynsent, the Benedictines were not an option because, in Elena's day, Benedictine nuns in Italy were all strictly enclosed, "and this appeared to Helen Lucretia [*sic*] an obstacle to devoting to the service of God the talents which He gave her. In her mind the consecration of herself to God meant the dedication to Him of all she had received from Him."[12]

---

[10] Maschietto, *Elena Lucrezia Cornaro Piscopia,* 177–85, best explains the Italian oblate history of the period. He also indicates that oblates had the right to wear the habit and to be buried at a Benedictine monastery. According to William Brickman, in *Western European Education* 16:3 (Fall 1984) 95, Elena was "deeply religious and retiring, always wearing the garb of a Benedictine oblate under her outer feminine clothing."

[11] Maschietto, *Elena Lucrezia Cornaro Piscopia,* xvii.

[12] Pynsent, *The Life of Helen Lucretia Cornaro Piscopia,* 42–4. See Elizabeth Makowski, *Canon Law and Cloistered Women* (Washington, D.C.: Catholic University Press, 1997). Trent did little to change the papal *Periculoso* of 1298.

After selecting four possibilities, with Elena's consent, the parents placed the names of the convents in an urn and chose one at random. Thus, Elena briefly became part of a community loosely affiliated with the Franciscans—one whose apostolic mission included teaching religion to children and caring for poor women in hospitals. Genuinely happy at first, Elena soon discovered that discord and political intrigue divided the community, and that it was lacking in real religious fervor and the contemplative atmosphere she had hoped to find. It was not for her. After receiving assurance from a spiritual director, Venerable Maria Felice, foundress of a Capuchin community of women in Venice, Elena was convinced that it was evident that God wanted greater things from her and that she was to shine in the world as a beacon of evangelical perfection. Elena returned to her family home to resume her studies and her participation in the abbey liturgy.

Her fame continued to spread, however. Seven of the major Italian academies, groups of intellectuals who regularly gathered to debate scientific, theological, and philosophical issues, vied for her membership. In her early twenties, no longer reserved, now a confident, articulate young lady, she was elected president of several academies. Her interest in these groups also stemmed from the fact that several of them supported projects for the needy and supplied educational assistance to poor youth. In response to one invitation, she did go to Rome to lecture to an academy there. She also gave a series of talks about the social and political problems of the Venetian Republic, drawing upon her experience of caring for patients in four Venetian hospices, the orphaned, the elderly, and other marginalized groups such as courtesans and poverty-stricken prostitutes. This compassionate noble woman, implementing the corporal and spiritual works of mercy delineated in chapter four of St. Benedict's *Rule,* made sure that those in need whom she encountered had sufficient food, money, and health care as well as spiritual counsel.[13]

Venice to Padua

For health reasons, Elena's father would, on occasion, send her with a staff to the family mansion in Padua.[14] He scheduled a long sojourn there for her so that she might also benefit from the educational and cultural opportunities in the university city. About this time (1672), when Elena was

[13] Guernsey, *The Lady Cornaro,* 101–4.

[14] The residence, now owned by the Commune of Padua, is at 37 Rue Ceasaretto in modern Padua; the Venetian palace "The Loredan" (changed from Cornaro when it was inherited by Loredan nephews of Elena) is in the Rialto area on the Grand Canal. Its main mode of transportation is still the gondola.

twenty-six, following the recommendations of several of her mentors and admirers, her father began the process of application for a theology degree for his daughter from the prestigious University of Padua.

Initially, Elena was most reluctant to consider applying for a degree, feeling it was not a necessary move toward obtaining sanctity. Finally, convinced by Professor Rinaldini and his peers that it would bring great honor to her family, the cities of Venice and Padua, as well as Padua's university, Elena reluctantly relented. The process, however, was fraught with obstacles. Initially, the Cardinal Chancellor vetoed Elena's application on grounds that theology degrees were only for those preparing for priestly ordination. (He is reported also to have stated that women were made for motherhood, not learning. The Roman Curia was also critical of the application.) However, a year later, after many more petitions, the cardinal relented, on condition that Elena seek a degree in philosophy, not theology. The family and her mentors reluctantly accepted the verdict.

The Famous Oral Examination

For six years Elena prepared for the exam. The Cornaro mansion was not far from the university or from the Benedictine Abbey of St. Justina (the Italian Giustina) where she attended religious services and frequently joined the monks in chapel and other spiritual, charitable, or educational activities. What thrilled her most was the fact that her friend from San Giorgio, Abbot Codanini, was transferred to St. Justina only a year after she took up her prolonged residence there.[15] In Padua, Elena continued service to others, especially those who came to her home pleading for assistance. Nor was it unusual for her to cook and serve meals herself, generally for the household servants with whom, contrary to the custom of her social class, she would often dine.

The examination for the degree was scheduled for June 25, 1678. The day before the exam Elena was informed of the two topics on which she was to give an hour's discourse. Because so many learned professors and students from universities as far away as England, as well as men of rank, flocked to Padua for the event, the exam's venue had to be changed from the university to the Cathedral of the Virgin. There, to the admiration of all present, Elena discoursed in classical Latin on some of the most difficult passages from Aristotle. After she responded brilliantly to even more complex questions, the applause was unrestrained. A decision by acclamation

---

[15] See Pynsent, *The Life of Helen Lucretia Cornaro Piscopia,* 58–62; Ann Kessler, *Benedictine Men and Women of Courage: Roots and History* (Yankton, S.D.: Sacred Heart Monastery, 1986) 229–30.

was rendered in public by the judges. Most of them would have been more than willing to award her a degree in theology, declaring that the philosophy doctorate was hardly an adequate honor for such a towering intellect.[16] Professor Rinaldini then garbed the thirty-two-year-old Elena with the doctoral insignia—the scholar's ermine shoulder cape, a ring, and a laurel wreath, which she received without any arrogance whatsoever. Honors and congratulations, as well as requests for her appearance at academies throughout Italy, poured in immediately. The prestigious societies also included her in their Role of Honor and all literary Europe sang her praises.

Death and Eulogies

Although Elena returned to Venice shortly after the exam, due to deteriorating health she was back in Padua within the year. Always fragile physically, the doctors treated her for infection, anemia, scurvy, and malnutrition. The latter was caused apparently by her secret and often imprudent penitential fasting. Elena also had pulmonary problems, later succumbing to tuberculosis, probably hastened by her ascetic lifestyle. After the last rites, with her mother and other dear ones present, she died on July 26, 1684. It is said that people in Venice and Padua ran through the streets with the news that "the saint is dead, the saint is dead."[17] In the coffin, according to her wishes, she was gowned in a Benedictine habit to which was added the doctoral shoulder cape. On her head was a double garland of lilies and laurels symbolizing her purity of life and her learning.[18]

Over 30,000 paid their respects as her body lay in state. More lined the streets as the horse-drawn hearse carried her coffined remains from her home to the abbey. Her funeral took place in the great monastery church of St. Justina. The entire university faculty attended in their academic regalia. The monks, many religious, as well as laymen and women of all classes were present. Padua's businesses and service agencies closed for the day. Elena's body was interred in the mortuary chapel of St. Luke (now known as the Cornaro Chapel) at the abbey. Her remains are presently in the first row in front of the altar among several abbots and disinterred collected bones of monks long dead.

---

[16] A copy of the document certifying her doctorate with the names of the sixty-four signatories is in Maschietto, *Elena Lucrezia Cornaro Piscopia,* 241. Only Fusco mentions a "scholarly dissertation."

[17] Gabrielle Forbush, who has written scholarly articles about Elena, consented to do one for *MS* magazine (January 1975): "Lost Women" (p. 56).

[18] Internet: http://iberia.vassar.edu/vcl/information/libstaingl.html, includes a brief life of Elena, as well as a description and illustration of the Vassar window.

A life-size carrara marble statue of Elena, originally part of the mausoleum her father had commissioned in the famous Basilica of St. Anthony, now commands a niche off the assembly hall of the old university building. Other remnants of the mausoleum went to collectors, but a head and shoulders sculptured memorial was placed in the nave of the Basilica by her younger brother, Girolamo, in 1727.[19]

Eulogies abounded throughout Europe as Italian, French, and German academies and towns scheduled memorials.[20] Praise accompanied condolences from the renowned of Europe, including the Duke of Lorraine, King John III Sobieski of Poland, and Pope Innocent II. A prominent Venetian eulogist described her as a "hydra of learning and virtue" who "professed seven sciences." He compared her theological knowledge to Hildegard's, her poetry to that of Sappho, and her other talents to those of some of the most renowned men in astronomy, philosophy, and languages.[21]

Six months after Elena's death, the faculty of the Sacred College of Philosophers and Physicians of the university, naming her a heroine, commissioned a large medal in her honor, a mark of distinction never before shown to any graduate.[22] American recognition was delayed. It was only in 1906 that a huge stained-glass window in Vassar's Thompson Library portraying the famous examination was installed.[23] In 1947, a fresco mural of Elena, promoted by Vassar alumna Ruth Crawford Mitchell, was painted by Giovanni Romagnoli of Bologna in the Italian Room at the University of Pittsburgh. It was the same Vassar alumna who also, in 1978, spearheaded the worldwide recognition of the three-hundredth anniversary of Elena's triumph. The Italian celebrations included one at St. Justina attended by Benedictine oblates from all over the world, guests of the abbot primate from Rome and the monks' community.[24]

---

[19] Fusco, *Elena Lucrezia Cornaro Piscopia, 1645–1684*, 40.

[20] An original program copy of the 1686 Roman memorial ritual, the *Pompe Funèbre*, is in Vassar's Thompson Memorial Library. Dean Rogers, director of special collections, in spite of construction obstacles (August 2000), not only made it available to me but also made it possible for me to view the window off limits during the renovation.

[21] Pynsent, *The Life of Helen Lucretia Cornaro Piscopia*, 73.

[22] Fusco, *Elena Lucrezia Cornaro Piscopia, 1645–1684*, 95. The medal is now in Padua's Civic Museum.

[23] It was appropriate that the first woman's college in the United States honor the first woman college graduate. Matthew Vassar, speaking to the trustees in 1861, claimed that "there is not, in the world, so far as is known, a single fully endowed institution for the education of women" (handwritten manuscript, Box 1, Folder 204, 2–3, Vassar Library). See also letters dated September 21, 1904, to July 21, 1905, from the Church Glass and Decoration Company of New York to John Hardman & Company, Birmingham, England, concerning the great window.

[24] Gabrielle E. Forbush, "The Triumph of the Inquiring Mind," *Vassar Quarterly* (Winter 1978) 8; Maria I. Tonzig, "Elena Cornaro: 1678–1978," *Benedictines* 31:1 (1977) 40.

Legacy to Oblates

Contemporary oblates can justly take pride in this outstanding woman. She leaves to the twenty-first century a true Benedictine legacy, having exemplified the Rule's maxims of lifelong learning, devotion to holy reading and reflection *(lectio)*, prayerful liturgy of the Hours, and ministry to those in need. In her last delirium, she often uttered Benedict's call to prayer which begins the liturgical day hours, "O God, come to my assistance, O Lord, make haste to help me." She followed her conscience in all her actions and showed the world that women could be both saintly and scholarly. I hope this essay will prompt contemporary oblates to become better acquainted with Elena, their oblate ancestor. She is to be claimed, admired, and, in some aspects, imitated.

Although her unusual contribution was almost entirely forgotten for two centuries, the devoted work of a Benedictine abbess and the enthusiasm generated by women academics in the United States has brought about a renewed interest in this outstanding, brilliant young oblate, a true heroine. She remains a noteworthy forerunner for the Benedictine Dom Jean LeClerq's ideal expressed in his classic work, *The Love of Learning and the Desire for God.*

See also Tonzig's Italian biography, *Elena Lucrezia Cornaro Piscopia: Prima Donna Laureata nel Mundo* (Venice: n.p., 1980), which lists the numerous articles published worldwide noting the three hundredth anniversary of Elena's reception of the degree.

4

Patrick Crowley: Oblate of St. Benedict

Patty Crowley

Patrick F. Crowley was born in Chicago, Illinois, on September 23, 1911. He, with his older brother, Jerry, grew up on Junior Terrace near the lakefront on the city's north side. After attending St. Mary of the Lake Grade School and Loyola Academy for high school, he continued on to the University of Notre Dame and received his law degree from Loyola University Law School. Upon completing his schooling he joined his father's law office, where he practiced corporate law until his death in 1974.

I got my first glimpse of Pat Crowley in 1934. I was a sophomore at Trinity College in Washington, D.C., spending the Easter vacation at home in Chicago. On Good Friday, my mother and I went to *Tre Ore* Services at Holy Name Cathedral. After the liturgy had commenced, I noticed two handsome young men, late arrivals, standing in front of the confessionals. As the service progressed, the two men managed to become even more noticeable as they took turns disappearing into the center door of the confessional to rest on the only available chair. In and out, in and out, for three hours. On Easter Sunday a friend invited me to dinner where, lo and behold, I ran into one of the young men, Pat Crowley. The following summer I met him again in Wisconsin at the home of mutual friends, the Brennans. We dated a little that summer, but I left in the fall for a year at the Sorbonne in Paris. Throughout my junior and senior years of college he wrote diligently. He made several trips to Washington to see me and even flew in for my senior prom. Air travel was uncommon in 1936 and considered pretty risky. A year after graduation we were married, a marriage that proved to be surprising and wonderful. Our family consists of four biological children, one adopted child, and one foster child.

In 1945, Pat's Catholic Action Group decided to join one of the "third orders" of lay people associated with religious communities such as the Dominicans and Franciscans. They chose the Benedictines and were also attracted to St. John's Abbey in Collegeville, Minnesota, because it was a forerunner of liturgical reform in the Church. One weekend the members of the group and their wives drove to Collegeville and were received into the abbey as oblates of St. Benedict.

Pat loved the Benedictine Rule. It was family-oriented and democratic (though it clearly stated that the abbot or father was head of the family). It was humorous and, well, not very specific. "You didn't have to do anything," he would say. Besides, as Pat was fond of pointing out, the Rule of St. Benedict allowed the monks to drink wine. He often referenced that passage by saying you could "drink into satiety." In the Crowley household Pat often referred to himself as the abbot and frequently referred to beloved passages from Benedict's fifteen-hundred-year-old rule. The abbot was "to make no distinction of persons"—everyone, that is, was to be treated fairly and as an individual. The abbot was to "remember who he is." Mindful of this role, Pat would pause just before midnight every New Year's Eve to pray and reflect upon the past year with his family and their guests. He would remind them to "remember who they were" by not taking themselves too seriously. His favorite advice from the Rule, however, was to take counsel "even from the youngest," and so at night after dinner meetings in which plans and problems were discussed, he always made it a point to hear the wisdom of the smallest present. The most important time, though, was Sunday dinner. The abbot, dressed in suit and tie, would lead a discussion of that morning's Scripture or talk about the doctrine of the Mystical Body, which captured for him the wondrous unity of all humanity in Christ. There was a rule at the Crowley table: you never had a private conversation with anyone else, no matter how many were present. All talk was directed through Daddy to those with whom you shared your meal.

Pat's deep commitment to the spirit of the Benedictine Rule led us to seek out a Benedictine education for our children. This was not an easy task as the closest Benedictine school was St. Scholastica Academy on the north side of Chicago. At the time this school was over-subscribed and not accepting students from beyond the city limits. We were determined. Through selling diocesan newspaper subscriptions, we secured a scholarship for our eldest daughter, Patsy. It worked! She became a Benedictine Sister in 1958 and has lived well her parents' much admired Rule of St. Benedict as a member of St. Scholastica Monastery in Chicago. Presently she is the director of Deborah's Place, a shelter for women who are homeless (with four different locations in Chicago) providing a total of 129 apartments for women.

Another of Pat's favorite things from the Holy Rule was the injunction "Let all guests be received as Christ." In the following years when the Christian Family Movement (CFM) was so central to Pat's life, he took very seriously this clear injunction regarding reception of guests. People from all over the world visited the Crowley household, some famous, some not. I recall we got into the habit of always setting an extra place at the dinner table for the guest that had not yet arrived. Somehow or other it was always filled. Pat delighted in including everyone in the dinner conversation so he would start the ball rolling by asking everyone around the table to take turns in telling about themselves and how they got there. On one particular night, about halfway through second helpings, a gentleman introduced himself, told us he had been graciously met at the door when he rang the bell and was having a wonderful time, but he was here to sell encyclopedias. We all had a great laugh, but we didn't buy the books.

Pat's understanding of receiving each guest as Christ did not stop at the hospitality of his table, but extended to his pocketbook as well. Many a person received financial help. Of course, he never talked about that. His service and dedication to the Little Brothers of the Poor showed his compassion.

The Benedictine Rule also instructs the abbot to "teach by example." Pat did this by working for the things he believed in, following his conscience. As a participant in the Exchange Student Program of the American Bishops' National Catholic Welfare Conference and the subsequent arrival of students from all over the world, Pat became "Daddy" to all of them. CFMers throughout the United States were encouraged to become involved in the political world. He believed that a good citizen had to be active in his civic world to effect change where change was needed. Then came our participation in the Papal Birth Control Commission. We shared the conviction that married couples had a role to play in this critical issue which affected us so profoundly. However, the subsequent promulgation of the papal document, *Humanae Vitae,* again forbidding the use of contraception, was disappointing and deeply affected our spirits.

Pat Crowley was a communicator. His overwhelming belief in the goodness of human beings, his clear rational thinking, and his easy manner were very effective tools when speaking to others. Those traits, combined with his infectious good humor and genuine love of life, are what attracted me to him and brought so many others into his orbit. Pat's life was an example for all those who find the Rule of St. Benedict an attraction. It is timeless in its application to both families and religious communities, for it speaks of the Gospel message which translates to all across the centuries.

5

Faith in Action: The Lives of
Patrick and Patricia Crowley

Margaret Colleton

The character of the American Catholic laity changed radically during the second half of the twentieth century. Beginning in the late 1940s, laypersons became more involved in the life of the Church. As individuals and as groups, they improved their own lives and reformed their communities by participating more actively in the liturgy, taking on important social issues, and integrating their faith more fully into their daily lives. Pope Pius XII said in 1957:

> The relations between the Church and the world demand the presence of lay apostles. The *consecratio mundi* [consecration of the world] is in its essence the task of laymen, of men who are intimately involved in economic and social life, who take part in government and in legislative assemblies.[1]

A more active laity did not emerge merely as the result of a Vatican decree, however. Rather, it came from the laity itself, catching on in homes and parishes, and spreading throughout the United States and all over the world. One of the greatest forces behind this change was the enthusiasm and hard work of two Benedictine oblates, Patrick and Patricia Crowley. As leaders of the Christian Family Movement, as delegates to the Papal Birth Control Commission, and as political and social activists, the Crowleys exerted an influence on the Church and its members that was at the time unprecedented for laypersons. In his account of the history of the Christian Family Movement, *Disturbing the Peace,* author Jeffrey M. Burns says of

---

[1] John N. Kotre, *Simple Gifts: The Lives of Pat and Patty Crowley* (New York: Andrews and McMeel, 1979) 3.

Pat and Patty: "Together they formed one of the most significant, if not the most significant, lay couple in the history of the U.S. Catholic Church. Former University of Notre Dame president, Theodore Hesburgh, C.S.C., is fond of saying that 'if they ever canonize a married couple, it should be the Crowleys.'"[2]

Their story is certainly remarkable. Both Pat and Patty came from affluent backgrounds. Pat's father, Jerome, was a well-known attorney in Chicago, and his mother, Henrietta, was the daughter of the O'Briens, who owned the flourishing paint and varnish company based in South Bend, Indiana. Patty, born in 1913, was the eldest of O. J. and Marietta Caron's family. O.J., originally French Canadian, had founded a successful textile company near Chicago. The Higmans, Marietta's parents, were a wealthy and prominent family from St. Joseph, Michigan. Patty gives a charming account of how they came together in Chapter 4 of this book.

As a couple, Pat and Patty complemented each other extraordinarily well. As Patty says of her husband in Chapter 4:

> Pat was a communicator. His overwhelming belief in the goodness of human beings, his clear rational thinking, and his easy manner were very effective tools when speaking to others. Those traits, combined with his infectious good humor and genuine love of life, are what attracted me to him and brought so many others into his orbit.

Patty, in turn, is an exceptionally competent woman. She is highly intelligent, efficient, and organized. As Pat used to say, "She could run General Motors."[3] John Kotre says of the couple, "Hers was the animus, his the anima." He gives this example: "'Oh boy, let's have a convention,' [Pat] would say with glee, and Patty would coordinate the incredible detail that made the convention happen."[4] It was a powerful combination, resulting in a number of great accomplishments. Perhaps the most notable was the Christian Family Movement.

The Christian Family Movement

American Catholics in the first half of the twentieth century concerned themselves with following the rules. They attended Mass on Sundays, fasted on Fridays, said the rosary occasionally, and did their best to avoid sin as it was defined by the Church. The role of lay Church mem-

[2] Jeffrey M. Burns, *Disturbing the Peace: A History of the Christian Family Movement, 1949–1974* (Notre Dame, Ind.: University of Notre Dame Press, 1999) 11.

[3] Kotre, *Simple Gifts,* 81.

[4] Ibid., 54–5.

bers, as they had been taught to understand it, did not include reflection, analysis, or activism where their faith was concerned. Accordingly, they worked at their jobs and raised their families. They socialized with each other, but were beginning to be troubled by a lack of meaning in their lives. As Pat later reflected, "The hunger to do something positive and permanent gnawed deeper inside—though perhaps it didn't show much outside."[5] In the 1940s the Christian Family Movement provided Pat and Patty and thousands like them the opportunity to act on this desire.

The Christian Family Movement was based on the Observe-Judge-Act method for Catholic Action developed by Canon Joseph Cardijn in Belgium. When the movement spread to America, one of its proponents, Father Reynold Hillenbrand, expanded its application, forming a businessmen's cell in Chicago in 1943. Because they worked in different professions, the men's group did not share the vocational specialization that characterized its European predecessors. They soon identified a common interest, however: all were young fathers. They agreed it was a good starting point but, according to Pat Crowley, one of the original members of this Catholic Action group, they planned to "straighten out marriage and then move on to something serious."[6] And yet, as they began to focus on marriage and family life they quickly realized that their subject *was* serious. Moreover, it was both worthy and in need of their attention. Burns writes, "The movement could not focus on the family as an isolated unit; rather, it had to address all the institutions affecting family life—parish, city, nation, world."[7] The Crowleys would later recognize that the Church fell into this category as well. It was during this initial period in the movement that Pat and Patty became Benedictine oblates of St. John's Abbey in Collegeville, Minnesota. (See Chapter 4 for details.)

This concept of family life appealed to many Catholic couples who were ready for an opportunity to devote their energies to activities more meaningful than bridge games and parties. The movement began to expand: men formed more cells, and their wives followed suit and formed their own. It wasn't long before the members realized that segregating family-focused groups by gender made little sense and formed couples groups. Soon, these couples groups were springing up throughout the country, and membership was increasing almost exponentially. As Burns notes, the Crowleys played the lead role in the success of the movement. "Though there is some debate as to who should be designated founder of CFM, there is no doubt that the driving force behind the success and

---

[5] Ibid., 35.
[6] Burns, *Disturbing the Peace,* 19.
[7] Ibid., 55.

spread of CFM was the Crowleys. Rightly, they are called Mr. and Mrs. CFM."[8] Pat and Patty used their extensive personal contacts throughout the country to increase CFM's membership and promote its activities. In 1957, Pius XII recognized their accomplishments and the value of the movement by bestowing upon them the Church's *Pro Ecclesia et Pontifice* medal. For more than twenty years the Crowleys led CFM with dedication and enthusiasm, and their efforts benefited the Church as a whole and countless families throughout the world.

The Papal Birth Control Commission

In 1964, Pope Paul VI summoned the Crowleys to Rome to participate in the fourth meeting of the Papal Birth Control Commission. The commission had originated in 1962 when Pope John XXIII, at the suggestion of Cardinal Leo Joseph Suenens, selected a group of six men to reevaluate the Church's ban on contraception. The group met for two days of discussion on the subject in October 1963. Their unanimous conclusion was that further study was necessary. The second and third meetings of the commission took place in 1964. The original members were joined by nine new ones. Again, they agreed that more information was needed. They wished to consult more experts in relevant fields of study. Most notably lacking, they found, was the input of those most directly affected by the issue, the married laity.

At the fourth meeting, membership jumped to fifty-eight. Though they were a small minority, women and married couples were included at last. Unexpectedly, viewpoints began to shift. While most members brought to the commission the assumption that the pope neither could nor should repeal the ban on contraception, many began to find, upon closer examination, that the Church's position was not well founded. A few members remained rigidly opposed to change, but the majority found compelling arguments for reform. It seemed that the Church's ban on contraception did not have a defensible foundation in Scripture, history, reason, or science. Garry Wills writes in *Papal Sin: Structures of Deceit:*

> As soon as people began to think independently about the matter, the whole structure of deceit crumbled at a touch. The past position could not be sustained, even among these people picked by the Vatican itself, much less among Catholics not as committed as these were. And it was absurd to speak of the non-Catholic world as ever recognizing this "natural law of natural reason."[9]

[8] Ibid., 11.
[9] Garry Wills, *Papal Sin: Structures of Deceit* (New York: Doubleday, 2000) 93.

By the end of the fourth session, opponents of change had become a very small minority.

The final meeting was the longest of the five, lasting nearly three months from the beginning of April to the end of June 1966. It was during this last session that Patty gave a candid and moving presentation. In the years since the rhythm method had been approved, couples using it as a form of birth control had discovered that it had some serious flaws. With the help of Notre Dame sociology professor and fellow commissioner Donald Barrett, the Crowleys had conducted a survey to analyze these concerns in detail. They sent questionnaires to CFM couples throughout the world and received three thousand replies from eighteen countries.[10] While some couples did find it an effective method of birth control, most were dissatisfied with it for two reasons. Because most women do not have regular menstrual cycles, the method did not prevent pregnancies as successfully in practice as it should have in theory. In addition, couples found that it placed undue strain on their marriages by requiring them to abstain from intercourse during the time when their bodies led them to desire it most strongly.

Patty's address was aimed at providing the other members with a true "sense of the faithful." She recounted "awful stories" of frustrated couples who had responded to the survey and shared with her the most intimate details of their lives. They were all faithful and committed Catholics, but they questioned the wisdom of the Church on this issue. Because of rhythm, they felt needlessly estranged from each other and they struggled under the burden of excessively large families.

In the end the fifteen voting members of the commission decided by a margin of nine to three (three members abstained) that the Church's teaching could and should be changed. To the surprise of nearly everyone involved, however, this was not the end of the issue. Wills reports, "An agreement had been reached before the vote was taken to submit only one report for the Commission, but Cardinal Ottaviani and Father Ford, seeing how things were going, had prepared a document of their own, which would later be misrepresented as an official minority report."[11] The two stayed in Rome after the end of the last session and secretly lobbied to discredit the commission's report and to "reconvert" the pope, who had reportedly been favorably impressed upon first reading it. They were successful: Paul disregarded his own delegation's conclusions and issued *Humanae Vitae* in 1968.

---

[10] Robert McClory, *Turning Point: The Inside Story of the Papal Birth Control Commission, and How* Humanae Vitae *Changed the Life of Patty Crowley and the Future of the Church* (New York: Crossroad, 1995) 88.

[11] Wills, *Papal Sin,* 93.

Life After *Humanae Vitae*

At one point in the commission's proceedings Pat had urged his fellow participants, "Let us help the Holy Father to scuttle this question so we can get on to the work of being Christ to the world."[12] After leaving the final meeting, he and Patty did just that. They left assuming that Pope Paul VI would follow the recommendations of the commission, and were shocked and disillusioned by the news that he had instead issued *Humanae Vitae*. Like hundreds of theologians, they publicly dissented. "To Patty, [the encyclical] was a sudden, unprovoked blow, coming when years of work, absolutely voluntary and carried out with the sincerest intentions, seemed on the verge of success," wrote Kotre.[13] According to Patty, they were never even thanked for participating. "The disappointing result of the promulgation of *Humanae Vitae* deeply affected our spirits," she said.

And yet, their disappointment did not prevent them from doing God's work in the world as they had always done. In addition to the numerous new projects they took on, the Crowleys continued their work with CFM, broadening its focus even further to focus on civil rights, ecumenism, and international issues, expanding its constituency, and establishing the International Confederation of Christian Family Movements (of which they were elected president couple). As mentioned in Chapter 4, they were active in housing foreign exchange students and refugees. They also encouraged other families nationwide to do the same.

Pat and Patty also became more directly involved in the political arena. They were enlisted by Democratic peace candidate Eugene McCarthy to help run his 1968 presidential campaign. That year's Democratic National Convention in Chicago was the scene of the infamous rioting, and the Crowleys took on the responsibility of getting many of the demonstrators, young people who had come in support of McCarthy, out of jail. The nomination went to Hubert Humphrey. McCarthy ran again in 1972, still with no success, but as Kotre noted, Pat never lost faith in him: "Though Patty and everyone around him disagreed, he always felt McCarthy could attract a large following, implement his ideas, and even win the presidency . . . . McCarthy struck Pat as a man of integrity who was not afraid to introduce moral questions into the political arena."[14]

---

[12] McClory, *Turning Point,* 126.
[13] Kotre, *Simple Gifts,* 103.
[14] Ibid., 117.

The Legacy Lives On

In 1971, a lump was discovered in Pat's chest and diagnosed as breast cancer, a disease rare in men. He had surgery to remove much of his left breast and underarm, but neither this nor his chemotherapy prevented him from remaining active. He traveled with Patty to plan the 1974 World Family Congress in Africa, a three-week trip that included visits to cities and to remote villages in several countries and even a safari. A second surgery in 1974 revealed that his cancer had spread. Pat remained full of hope and enthusiasm for life. He attended the congress (called La Familia '74), spent four days in London alone with Patty, and then returned home to spend his final months with his family and friends. He died peacefully at home on the evening of November 20, after having spent the day entertaining visitors and praying with his family.

Needless to say, Patty was devastated by Pat's death. She described her response to the news that his diagnosis was terminal: "It hit me in the bottom of my heart. We had always been like one person."[15] Learning to live without him was terribly hard. Nevertheless, "Patty declined a quiet widowhood," as Kotre said. With determination that would have made Pat proud she remained faithful to their mission, "the work of being Christ's hands in the world." As she put it, "[Pat] would have me do it and he's helping me do it."[16]

Since then she has taken on new projects of her own (such as Call to Action and various women's issues), served on numerous boards, accepted awards both for herself and in Pat's honor, and written and delivered talks on their favorite subjects. Today she still lives in their Chicago apartment and devotes much of her time to direct service. Most of her energy goes to Deborah's Place, a shelter providing housing and programs for women who are homeless. This is an organization she helped found and which her daughter (now Sister Patricia, O.S.B.) directs. She is also involved in prison ministry at the Metropolitan Correctional Center. Even in her late eighties Patty continues to put her faith into action.

One need look no further than the Crowleys for proof that individuals can make a difference in the world. As leaders of CFM, they helped hundreds of thousands of people around the world to become more involved in the life of the Church. Even now, generations later, the American Catholic laity continues to follow the example they set. As delegates to the Papal Birth Control Commission, the Crowleys showed that lay people did have a voice in the Church. Perhaps of equal importance was their dissent from

[15] McClory, *Turning Point,* 164.
[16] Kotre, *Simple Gifts,* 184.

Humanae Vitae, by which they showed that it was possible to love the Church without agreeing with it on everything, and that personal conscience should sometimes take precedence over Church doctrine. As political and social activists, Pat and Patty advocated moral values in the public and secular arenas, again exemplifying a commitment to serve God in all aspects of their lives.

Just as Pat and Patty were models of CFM and its ideals, and also of Gospel values in general, so too were their lives a tribute to the Rule of St. Benedict. It is hard to imagine a family more dedicated to the virtue of hospitality. Not only did they open their home to dozens of foster children, exchange students, and refugees, but they also encouraged others to do the same. There was always room for one more at the Crowley table, and each guest was truly received as Christ. Pat and Patty were deeply committed to a balance between work and prayer in their lives, and true to their vocation as Benedictine oblates they lived the Gospel values and the spirit of the Rule in the secular world. As a young lay woman, I am particularly inspired by the Crowleys. Moreover, I am profoundly grateful to them, for as a result of their life's work the Catholic Church is now one in which I am able to participate actively. Father Hesburgh was correct in his estimation of their importance in Catholic history, and while Pat and Patty Crowley may never be canonized, they led lives of holiness and faith that seem worthy of such an honor.

6

Evelyn Davie's Dream Deferred

Mary Ruth Coffman, O.S.B.

In the sesquimillennium of St. Benedict's birth (1980), the Benedictine Sisters of Cullman, Alabama, established an oblate chapter, a gift to their community and to the Church in Alabama. Named to direct the chapter was S. Maurus Allen, O.S.B., a vibrant and charismatic religious, known widely for her retreats and spiritual direction. In August 1980 she submitted to Catholic papers throughout the southeast news stories inviting interest in affiliating with Sacred Heart Monastery as oblates. To her surprise, she heard from more than forty people and completed plans for the initial retreat and induction of charter members on October 5, 1980.

Among the potential members who arrived on the announced weekend was a dignified, soft-spoken African American lady named Mrs. Evelyn J. Davie. She arrived after a three-hour bus trip from St. Jude Parish, Montgomery, Alabama. It took courage as well as endurance for an African American to come to Cullman, reputed throughout the state to exclude blacks from its city limits. The only African Americans in the county lived in a small enclave in the southwest corner, called simply "The Colony." Residents there had been granted land following the Civil War and had held on to it tenaciously, despite many offers to buy lots.

The monastery to which Evelyn traveled, one of very few in the Deep South, is the only Benedictine women's monastery in the nation created by a union of members from two communities, rather than being founded by a single priory. Its pioneers came from St. Walburg's in Covington, Kentucky, in 1881, and, in 1898, from Holy Name Priory in San Antonio, Florida, via St. Mary's in Pittsburgh, Pennsylvania. Eight sisters from each community united in 1902 and were directed by the Bishop of Mobile to build a motherhouse in Cullman, near St. Bernard Abbey, founded nine years earlier. Concerned that in an area of sometimes virulent anti-Catholicism the sisters would not be able to attract vocations or to sustain themselves financially, the bishop had given his permission for an independent foundation very reluctantly. Despite its poverty, the community survived, attracted sufficient vocations for its ministries, and contributed significantly to Catholic education in the diocese. It was a charter member of the Congregation (now Federation) of St. Scholastica, approved by Rome in 1922. One of its prioresses, Mother Mary Susan Sevier, was president of that federation during the crucial renewal chapters from 1968 to 1971. Today, the major ministries at Sacred Heart Monastery are the Benedictine Spirituality and Conference Center, which serves as many as four thousand people per year, and Benedictine Manor, a retirement home for independent living serving up to forty residents.

A Seeker Responds

Of all these things Mrs. Evelyn Jackson Davie knew very little when she arrived in Cullman in October 1980. Nor was she concerned about any political implications of her presence. Hers was a profound search for prayer and spiritual growth, and Sister Maurus's invitation in Catholic papers seemed directed specifically to her:

> What are Oblates? They are men and women who associate themselves spiritually with a monastery or convent in order to share in the prayers and good works of the monks or nuns. These persons see that in many ways they can live according to the Rule of St. Benedict . . . as far as their lifestyle allows. They do not leave their homes, their families, their place of work, or their occupations. . . .
>
> Today there are thousands of oblates in all parts of the world, praying and working in spiritual union with the community with which they are affiliated, and receiving spiritual strength and inspiration from the Benedictine way of life.[1]

For Evelyn Davie this was a call to belong to a religious community, something she had dreamed about in her youth, a dream given up in deference to her parents' wishes. In the meantime, she had married happily, devoted herself lovingly to her four children, and pursued a teaching career—but she never forgot the dream entirely. Now she realized that she might be able to affiliate with a religious community, sharing their prayer and spiritual life without having to leave her fulfilling life in Montgomery.

---

[1] *One Voice* (August 18, 1980).

She was one of the first to respond to Sister Maurus's invitation, and she became a charter member of Sacred Heart Monastery's oblate chapter. Until her death sixteen years later, Evelyn lived her oblate life fervently and joyfully.

Evelyn Jackson was born in New Orleans on October 12, 1908, the daughter of James Nathaniel and Florence Beard Jackson. She had an older brother, Vernon, always sickly, who died at the age of twelve, leaving Evelyn as an only child. Her parents were industrious, and they were ambitious for Evelyn. Her father was a skilled carpenter much in demand in the surrounding neighborhoods. A fine seamstress, her mother needed only a picture to be able to make a beautiful creation for her many clients. All her life Evelyn remembered how beautifully her mother had dressed her, making even her coats. Her father was quiet and mild-mannered, but her mother was fiery, determined, fully conscious of her worth. Evelyn remembered how her mother resisted the prejudice against blacks. In those days in the segregated South, white people did not usually address African Americans with a title, but only by their first names. When a white client asked Evelyn's mother whether she could call her by a "shorter name" (read "first name"), she replied with dignity, "Mrs. Jackson is my name."[2]

Her parents were dissatisfied with the education Evelyn was receiving in the segregated school system and decided to send her to a Catholic school, though friends and relatives warned them that it would be like "throwing their daughter to the wolves." Her Baptist father and Methodist mother decided to take that chance. They enrolled her in Xavier Prep School in 1923, established seven years earlier by Mother Katherine Drexel of Philadelphia. Thus it happened that Evelyn became one of many young African Americans who benefited from the work of that renowned foundress, canonized as a saint of the Catholic Church on October 1, 2000.

By the time Evelyn graduated from Xavier Prep in 1927, the normal school for training teachers had been added, and Evelyn received her bachelor of science degree in education from that college on June 5, 1930.[3] Two years later, the school achieved university status, and Evelyn began to study for a master's degree in education at the new Xavier University, which even today is the only institution of higher learning for African

---

[2] Throughout this essay, information about Evelyn's personal life is based on telephone and personal interviews with (1) Evelyn's children: Florence Lemon, Joanne Davie, Benjamin Davie, and Margaret Davie; (2) some of her friends: Roberta Short, Essie Smith, Carolyn Tillage-Colvin, Regina Nelson, and Mary Anzulovic; (3) a cousin, Maxine Johnson; (4) oblates Harris Hand and Martha Madrid; and (5) Sister Maurus Allen, O.S.B., director of the oblate chapter at Sacred Heart Monastery.

[3] Registrar, Xavier University, New Orleans, Louisiana.

Americans in the United States. It was providential that Xavier was available just at the time that Evelyn needed a good education. Her life illustrated admirably that for which Mother Katherine had hoped: a college where black students could receive a quality education, preparing them to teach or to enter other professional fields which had formerly been closed to all but a very few of their race.

In the fall after her graduation from the normal school, Evelyn joined the faculty of Holy Ghost Elementary School in New Orleans, one of the schools founded by Mother Katherine and staffed by her sisters and lay teachers. By that time, the twenty-two-year-old young woman felt that she could follow her religious convictions, in spite of the pain it might cause her parents. She was baptized at Holy Ghost Catholic Church on September 23, 1930.[4] At first her mother told her that she need not come home any more, but her father quietly assured his daughter: "You know your mother; she'll change her mind. You always have a home with us." As he predicted, Evelyn's mother soon relented and welcomed her beloved daughter home, despite being disappointed with her conversion.

A more difficult moment arrived in the summer of 1937, when Evelyn told her parents that she had been accepted to enter the Sisters of the Holy Family, the second religious community in the United States founded specifically for African American women. The date for her entrance (along with some of her friends from Xavier University) had been set, she had bought the various items she needed for the convent, and she had resigned her teaching position at Holy Ghost School.

Evelyn's cousin and godchild, Mrs. Maxine Johnson, who spent all her summers with the Jackson family, described the scene when Evelyn told her mother of her plans. Mrs. Johnson said there was "a great sadness in the house." Mrs. Jackson suggested that perhaps Maxine should return to her own home; only later did the young girl learn the reason for the sadness. Evelyn's mother was devastated; having descendants was extremely important in black families, and Mrs. Jackson looked forward to Evelyn marrying and providing her with grandchildren. In the end, Evelyn could not bear to cause her mother so much pain; she gave up her plan to enter the convent. But it was a difficult decision, and Evelyn worried for years that she had pleased her parents rather than God.

A Life-Changing Decision

She had a more immediate problem: she had resigned from Holy Ghost School, and it was too late to find another position in a Catholic

---

[4] Church Secretary, Holy Ghost Parish, New Orleans, Louisiana.

school in New Orleans. She went to her friends, the Blessed Sacrament Sisters at Xavier University, to ask for help. As it happened, that very day the sisters had received a call from their sisters staffing St. John's Elementary School in Montgomery, Alabama. School had already started, and they were missing a teacher for the fourth and fifth grades. Would Evelyn come to Montgomery, they wondered? She responded promptly: she would go. Since the Great Depression was still a painful reality in 1937, she was glad for any opportunity for a teaching position. Years later, one of her own daughters asked Evelyn how her mother felt about her going so far from home. "It was all right," said Evelyn, "because I would still be her child. She thought that if I entered the convent, I would be lost to the family forever." Besides, she would be returning to New Orleans each summer to pursue her master's degree. But that decision in 1937 was more life changing than Evelyn could have guessed. As it happened, she would spend the rest of her life in Montgomery, that "Cradle of the Confederacy" that would become world-famous for its part in the Civil Rights Movement of the 1960s.

During her first year in Montgomery a friend said to Evelyn, "I know a young man you should meet," and to that man, "I know a young woman you should meet." The eligible bachelor was Benjamin Davie, who had been a teacher and principal in a county school in the small town of Brundidge, southeast of Montgomery. He liked teaching, but he needed to make a better salary. Urged by his older brother, Epreval, who was later to become one of the first black railroad conductors in the South, Ben took a job on the railroad, working as a dining car waiter. Since he had practically raised Benjamin, Epreval was important in the Davie family, and Evelyn's children all had vivid memories of their "Uncle E." Compared to most work that was available to African American men in the South, on-train railroad jobs provided a good living. Waiters belonged to one of the first unions open to black men; some of the men who would later play important roles in the Civil Rights Movement in Montgomery learned leadership skills and developed important connections in that union.

Evelyn and Ben dated for five years, with intermissions while Evelyn returned to New Orleans each summer to study at Xavier University. Finally, in 1942, Ben said, "Either you marry me this summer, or you can look for someone else." She was only nine hours from her master's, but she realized that Ben was serious. The two were married at Holy Ghost Parish in New Orleans on July 20, 1942. Evelyn never had the opportunity to finish her graduate degree.

In March 1943, Evelyn resigned from St. John's School to prepare for her firstborn, a little girl born in May. Evelyn was a devoted mother, but she needed an outside job to help with family finances. Nearer to her house than St. John the Baptist was a new elementary school located on the ground floor of an impressive five-year-old Catholic church. This was the first structure in "The City of St. Jude," founded nine years earlier by Rev. Harold Purcell, nationally known Passionist missionary and then founder/editor of *Sign,* one of the best of the Catholic magazines in the country. Father Purcell left his Passionist community in order to found a center for desperately poor black people in Montgomery, where they lacked adequate medical care as well as schooling. In the midst of the crippling Depression and despite poor health, this dynamic priest managed to raise money to construct his magnificent church-school combination only four years after he arrived in the area. At the time of his death in 1952, he had constructed a new building for the schools, a social service center providing direct help for the poor, and a general hospital that was the first integrated facility in Montgomery—three years before *Brown v. Board of Education* in 1954. Evelyn transferred her family to St. Jude Parish and joined the faculty of the elementary school as a third grade teacher. Thus she was affiliated once again with a pioneering effort on behalf of African Americans in the South. Evelyn became well acquainted with Father Purcell, the irascible founder with the gruff manner and the deeply compassionate heart.

Evelyn and Ben had four children: Florence, born May 22, 1943; Benjamin, August 20, 1944; Joanne, March 10, 1949; and Margaret, April 2, 1951. During her years at St. Jude Elementary School, Evelyn taught each of her children at some point. They learned to expect no favoritism from their mother; instead, she often made them an example when they misbehaved or failed to do their homework—circumstances they still remember with good-humored chuckles. Despite their "special" treatment, none of them ever doubted her love for them. During these years, Evelyn's mother died, and her father came to live with the Davie family in Montgomery. He enjoyed five years with them before his death and burial in Montgomery.

Tension increased significantly in the Cradle of the Confederacy and throughout Alabama with the 1954 *Brown v. Board of Education* decision of the U.S. Supreme Court outlawing segregation in public schools. When Mrs. Rosa Parks was arrested on December 1, 1955, for refusing to give her bus seat to a white man, black leaders organized the famous Montgomery Bus Boycott, which ignited the Civil Rights Movement. Chosen as the spokesperson for the group was the new pastor of Dexter Avenue Baptist Church, Dr. Martin Luther King Jr. Evelyn's husband Benjamin, a member of Dr. King's church on Dexter Avenue, was well acquainted with the dynamic young minister. As a member of the union of dining car waiters, Benjamin was, like the other members, militant on the subject of equal rights. He must have worked with Mr. E. D. Nixon, a union member who led the organization of the bus boycott and who recruited Dr. King to be the spokesman for the movement. As it became apparent that blacks were not going to ride the city buses, white extremists became violent, bombing leaders' houses and shooting at the blacks walking to work. When Ben Davie could not find a ride, he was forced to walk the five or six miles to and from the railroad station for his job. The youngest of the Davie children were too young to understand the full import of events, but they do remember their father leaving for work on foot. Whether Ben's trudging to and from work during the bus boycott contributed to his early death is not known, but he died at age fifty-five on April 15, 1958, not quite sixteen years after his marriage. Friends were surprised that the death in the Davie family was not Evelyn, since she had been quite ill in the preceding year. The family was honored when Ben's pastor, Dr. Martin Luther King Jr., who was becoming nationally known, came to their home to offer his condolences.

From Loss New Strength

At forty-nine, Evelyn found herself a widow with four children aged seven to fourteen, for whom she was now totally responsible, despite her own poor health. In addition, she was caring for her aged father, who was living with the family. Using the seamstress skills she had learned from her mother, Evelyn saved money by making many of her children's clothes, as well as the costumes they needed for various school productions. More than ever, Evelyn was grateful for her education from Xavier, since now her teaching had to be the main support for her family. Later on, Evelyn and her cousin Mamie reached an agreement about a lovely house on Cleveland Avenue (now Rosa Parks Avenue). Mamie bought the house, and Evelyn paid all the operating and living expenses, including food. It was a good arrangement for all concerned.

Though Evelyn loved teaching at St. Jude, she found it difficult to provide for her family on a Catholic school salary. Since she was an excellent teacher, it was not long before she found a position at a public school, George Washington Carver Elementary School, just across the street from St. Jude. In the new setting, she still excelled as a teacher, vouched for by one of her students who recalled that "she had only to walk into the classroom and clear her throat to make the whole place grow quiet." Her effectiveness as a teacher was further evidenced when, a few years later, she became one of the first African American teachers to be transferred to an integrated public school, Flowers Elementary. Though her students loved her, Evelyn did not have an easy time of it. She confided to a friend years later the pain she felt when some of the white teachers left the table when she approached to eat her lunch. But her gentleness and innate dignity, as well as her good teaching, eventually won over her colleagues.

The Davie family experienced another famous Civil Rights event in 1965—the march from Selma to Montgomery. Since Evelyn was a full-time teacher, she did not join the long trek from Selma, nor could she join the crowd of women of the parish who made hundreds of sandwiches and gallons of coffee and tea for the marchers who stayed at St. Jude the last night of the march. However, she did give in to her two youngest children, Joanne and Margaret, when they begged to be allowed to join the marchers on their final lap. On the last day of the march, people reassembled at St. Jude's and headed toward their goal, the Alabama state capitol. There, not far from the spot where Jefferson Davis took the oath as President of the Confederacy in 1861, Dr. Martin Luther King Jr. spoke to a cheering, integrated crowd from all over the country: ministers, priests, actors, musicians, political leaders, nuns, and hundreds of citizens. Margaret, Evelyn's youngest, remembers that some people along the march route threw things at them, but the girls savored the historic experience, which they shared with their mother that night.

After more than forty years of teaching, Evelyn retired in 1974. By that time, all four of her children were well launched into their own lives. Evelyn's good influence is manifest in their lives. As her son Ben says, "We are all God-seekers; we learned that from our mother." Florence graduated from Evelyn's alma mater, Xavier University, with a bachelor's degree in psychology, and from Atlanta University with an M.A. in social work. She is now a psychiatric social worker in Atlanta. Ben attended Tuskegee Institute, served in a communications unit of the Air Force in Alaska and in Germany, then finished in accounting at Alabama State University in Montgomery. Currently, he is a senior contract administrator with MARTA, the transportation system in Atlanta, and, as an aside, edits a newsletter for Montclair Estates, where he and his family live. Joanne earned a degree in psychology from Morris Brown in Atlanta and is now a teacher of special education in that city. Margaret, the youngest, calls herself the rebel in the family: she attended Xavier University for two years, but dropped out in the seventies to travel throughout the country with various groups demonstrating against the Vietnam War, apartheid in South Africa, and racism in this country. Later she had her own business, preparing and marketing health foods. Currently she is finishing a degree in psychology from Troy State University, preparing to earn a master's in physical therapy. Margaret chuckles as she says that since she had given her mother the most grief, it was only right that she should take care of her in her last years.

Evelyn's influence extends to her grandchildren. One of them, Florence's daughter Eve, volunteers as a "big sister" for underprivileged children. Malcolm, Ben's son, has been involved in various kinds of volunteer social services. As a result, he was one selected to carry the Olympic torch in Atlanta in 1996—an event which Evelyn watched on television with great pride shortly before she died on July 29, 1996.

With her children grown and educated, Evelyn entered a new phase of her experience. She volunteered for a multitude of activities at the City of St. Jude: making beautiful doll clothes for Christmas gifts for poor children, working with some of the children in the Father Purcell Memorial Hospital for Exceptional Children, and reading to patients at St. Jude Hospital. A daily communicant, she regularly took Communion to the sick, sometimes bringing them fruit and fresh vegetables at her own expense. Outstanding in organizing skills and in her concern for people, she was often elected to office: the parish council at St. Jude, the Archdiocesan Council of Catholic Women, the Ladies of Charity, the Ladies Auxiliary of the Knights of Peter Claver, the St. Jude Pastoral team, and the Phyllis Wheatley Federated Club. She organized the "2048 Club" for elderly parishioners at St. Jude (2048 is the street address) and participated faithfully in a prayer group. One of the St. Jude pastors, Msgr. William James, often called her the "pillar of the parish" when he introduced her to new people.

Though she never drew attention to herself, Evelyn's good works did not go unnoticed. Some of her friends and admirers at St. Jude Parish nominated her for the 1991 Humanitarian of the Year Award, given by the *Montgomery Advertiser* and the *Alabama Journal* to one who exemplified "the highest ideals of Judeo-Christian compassion."[5] To the delight of all who knew her, Evelyn was selected for that honor, which was presented in an impressive ceremony on January 19, 1991, by Mr. Richard Amberg Jr., publisher of the two papers sponsoring the award. Archbishop Oscar Lipscomb of the Mobile Diocese honored the occasion with his presence. There were testimonials from many friends and co-workers and from her four children and grandchildren. One testimonial summed up Evelyn's contributions:

> Literally hundreds of persons, perhaps thousands, through the city have experienced her generous, thoughtful, and prayerful stability and compassion; her sense of both hope and independence are marked by wisdom and responsiveness. As a teacher of small children in segregated, then integrated, public schools, she is eminent. . . . By honoring her the city honors its intelligent and brave citizens—however unknown—who serve both justice and peace.[6]

[5] *The Montgomery Advertiser* (January 1991), in the papers of Mrs. Essie Smith, oblate.
[6] S. Eleanor Harrison, o.s.b., "Testimonial," submitted to *The Montgomery Advertiser* in support of the nomination of Evelyn as "Humanitarian of the Year, 1991."

In 1980, Evelyn was happy with her life. Her beloved children were living good lives. She had more than fulfilled the hope that Mother Katherine Drexel had for the institutions she founded in New Orleans to train teachers to provide a better education for black children. Her volunteer work gave joy and meaning to her days, and she loved her activities at St. Jude Church. She was rich in friends, and daily Mass and frequent prayer experiences gladdened her soul. But when she saw in the diocesan newspaper the invitation to become a Benedictine oblate, she realized immediately that this experience could bring a new and more profound dimension to her spiritual life, one that would fulfill her early dream of dedication in the religious life. That initial oblate retreat at Sacred Heart Monastery in 1980 confirmed her hopes, and she became an oblate novice then and made her final oblation a year later.

A Dream Shared

Not content simply to rejoice in this new spiritual relationship, Evelyn immediately began to call other ladies from St. Jude Parish to share her oblate dedication. Within several years, she created an oblate "cell" in Montgomery, composed of women who made the yearly retreat at Sacred Heart and who gathered frequently at her house for shared prayer, Scripture study, and occasional retreat days. Members included Essie Smith, Carolyn Tillage-Colvin, Queenie Richardson, Thelma Cheeks, Ruth Craig, Jean Gadson, Dorothy Thomas, Mary Sauer, and Mary Anzulovic. Sister Maurus, oblate director, called the Montgomery cell the most successful of the various groups which grew out of the oblate chapter at Sacred Heart Monastery. Nor did it cease with Evelyn's death in 1996. Members still attend the yearly retreat, and they meet at St. Jude for prayer and outreach activities, under the leadership of the new "abbess," Mrs. Essie Smith.

Evelyn was a rich leaven among the oblates at Sacred Heart Monastery. Reverend Harris Hand, a Methodist minister in the group, called her a profound "spiritual presence," a kind of "unofficial prioress" in the group. When the Montgomery group arrived, he said, it seemed that the annual retreat really began. Mrs. Martha Madrid, a Hispanic American, noted that having Evelyn in the group added a unique diversity, a sense of universality. The St. Jude "cell" led a memorial service for her at the October retreat following her death, and the oblates still share remembrances of Evelyn at their annual meeting at Sacred Heart Monastery in the fall of each year.

And what of Evelyn's own response to her oblate commitment? Mrs. Mary Anzulovic, a Montgomery oblate who enlisted Evelyn as godmother for two of her children, sensed that being an oblate gave Evelyn "peace and rest," because it fulfilled her early desire to give her life totally to God. Sister Maurus perceived in Evelyn a lifelong yearning for some kind of mystical union with God. Living by the Rule of St. Benedict as an oblate in her own way of life, Sister said, took her "into the reality of her wisdom age and deepened it." Hers was a genuine, lifelong journey of seeking God, one that found a perfect response in Benedict's promise: "As we progress in this way of life and in faith, we shall run on the path of God's commandments, our hearts overflowing with the inexpressible delight of love."[7]

---

[7] *Rule of St. Benedict,* Prologue, 49.

7

Prayer and Work in the Light of
Dorothy Day

Rita McClain Tybor

The handwriting was shaky and the draft was written on an envelope but an aging Dorothy Day answered with her customary directness. She declined the invitation to affiliate with another religious order with a simple fact: "I'm a Benedictine oblate."[1]

Oblates are lay men and women who share a spiritual kinship with a monastic community as they apply the wisdom of the Rule of St. Benedict to their own unique circumstances. They have an ardent desire to seek God and to imitate Christ more perfectly.[2] In this summons oblates are very much in step with the universal call to holiness set forth by Vatican II.

Dorothy Day (1897–1980) was an oblate of St. Procopius Abbey, Lisle, Illinois. She was also a convert to Catholicism, a suffragette, an activist, and a prolific writer. Along with French-born peasant Peter Maurin, she co-founded the Catholic Worker Movement. Day was an advocate for the homeless and the American worker. She championed many social justice causes and held fast to an unqualified position of pacifism. At times the life of Dorothy Day was mired in controversy as she challenged the Church and became a catalyst for social change. Even so, a group of Church historians and theologians have hailed Dorothy Day as the twentieth-century's

---

[1] Brigid O'Shea Merriman, *Searching for Christ: The Spirituality of Dorothy Day* (Notre Dame, Ind.: University of Notre Dame Press, 1994) 262 (#100).

[2] Alcuin Deutsch, *Manual for Oblates of St. Benedict* (Collegeville: The Liturgical Press, 1948) 16–19.

most outstanding lay Catholic[3] and the Vatican has approved the opening of her cause for canonization.[4]

While many claim her patronage, Dorothy Day's trust in God seems to offer a special witness for those who follow the Rule of St. Benedict with its direction "to place your hope in God alone."[5]

Early Life

Some would like to see Dorothy Day canonized because her conversion—after serious moral transgression—offers hope to others. As a young adult she cavorted with a bohemian group in Greenwich Village and was pregnant at the age of twenty-one. She had an abortion in the hopes of holding on to the relationship, but the affair ended. Another romance led to a brief marriage and a subsequent divorce. She settled into a common-law marriage with Forster Batterham and their child, Tamar Therese, was born out of wedlock.

How, then, did Day undergo such a dramatic transformation? Her own writing, especially her autobiography, *The Long Loneliness,* sheds some light on this question.

The book describes her early religious fervor that included—among other things—a love of the psalms,[6] a sentiment that is central to the Benedictine tradition of prayer. The rebellion of young adulthood may have cooled this early ardor, but when Day entered the Catholic faith at the age of thirty she began a personal pilgrimage that included five decades of activism and compassion. She did not deviate from this call as she interpreted the Gospel in a most literal manner and held fast to her convictions even when they led to jail time for acts of civil disobedience.

Day's faith may have been dormant during the years of her youthful defiance, but when this period came to its close, she was profoundly faithful to the Roman Catholic Church even when she decried its actions. She often said, "The Church is the cross on which Christ is crucified."[7]

Dorothy Day was born in 1897, the third of five children to John and Grace Day. While her life began in Brooklyn, she spent her formative years crossing the continent—from East, to West, to Midwest, and back

---

[3] *America* (December 18–25, 1999) 5.

[4] Tracy Early, "Sainthood Cause for Dorothy Day Opened," *The Catholic Post* (March 26, 2000) 3.

[5] *RB 1980: The Rule of St. Benedict in Latin and English,* ed. Timothy Fry (Collegeville: The Liturgical Press, 1996) RB 4.41; 183.

[6] Dorothy Day, *The Long Loneliness,* illustrated by Fritz Eichenberg, introduction by Robert Coles (San Francisco: Harper & Row, 1952, 1980, 1997) 28–9.

[7] Ibid., 150.

East—as her family followed the sportswriting career of her father. She was six when they moved to California and eight when she arrived in Chicago. Her somewhat ordinary childhood included unusual intellectual preoccupation. Entries in *The Long Loneliness* describe her idealism, her native inquisitiveness, and her reflections on the hidden injustices of the city. She pondered these things as she took her baby brother for long carriage strolls in the Chicago neighborhoods.[8] As a teenager she was delving into political thought, influenced at times by an older brother's writing for a newspaper that focused on labor issues.[9]

These impressionable years may have influenced Day's social consciousness and later ideology, but these early concerns were not tied to religion. Her father and mother, raised Congregationalist and Episcopalian respectively, did not promote any religious training for their children. At the age of twelve, when Dorothy expressed an interest in joining the Catholic Church, she was directed toward the Episcopal community where she attended services for at least a year, though apparently not encouraged by her parents. She was baptized and confirmed an Episcopalian.[10] In college, when the lectures of her professors denigrated religion, Day turned to political solutions for the human dilemmas of the world. Consequently, when she followed her family's move to New York City in 1916, she eagerly joined the controversial political arena of the era.

Supporting herself with the meager earning of a freelance writer, Day aligned herself with communists and socialists as she sought a way to care for the masses. It was during this youthful energetic ebullience that she enjoyed the friendship of people like Eugene O'Neill, John Dos Passos, and Malcolm Crowley. This was also the phase of her life that included the love affairs and the abortion. Day later called those years "a time of searching."[11] The resolution came with her conversion to Catholicism, a painful decision that ended the sometimes-idyllic love that she shared with Forster Batterham. When he responded to the baptism of four-month-old Tamar Therese with intense bitterness, Dorothy began to see the heavy price she would pay for her own conversion. Nonetheless, she chose her faith over the relationship and later wrote, "I can truthfully say that I gave up human love when it was its strongest and tenderest because I had experienced the overwhelming conviction that I could not live longer without God."[12]

[8] Ibid., 36–7.

[9] Ibid.

[10] Ibid., 28–9.

[11] Ibid., 93–109.

[12] Mel Piehl, *Breaking Bread: The Catholic Worker and the Origin of Catholic Radicalism in America* (Philadelphia: Temple University Press, 1982) 18.

Her conversion may have settled her spiritual longings but joining the Church increased her personal suffering. She lost her lover, the father of her child, and was now set apart from former radical friends. Her employment was also uncertain. She continued writing, now for Catholics rather than Communists, but she yearned for something more in her life. In 1932, while writing about a hunger march in Washington, she visited a shrine and offered, "a special prayer, a prayer which came with tears and anguish, that some way would open up for me to use what talents I possessed for my fellow workers, for the poor."[13]

Peter Maurin and the Catholic Worker Movement

On her return to New York, Dorothy met Peter Maurin (1877–1949), an itinerant French peasant and social agitator who urged her to start up a Catholic newspaper for the unemployed. Together they launched the Catholic Worker Movement, "historically significant as the first major expression of radical social criticism in American Catholicism."[14] In Day's later recollections, she was convinced that the Catholic Worker Movement would not have been realized without Maurin: "From the start I had all these ideas, but I didn't know how to put them in action."[15] Peter Maurin was the key. In a discussion of Day's leadership, Robert Coles suggested that Maurin served as a much needed lay confessor or spiritual guide for Day.[16] Coles explained, "I had eventually realized that she had, indeed, learned how to be a convincing moral leader with the help of someone [Maurin] with whom she worked in tandem, and whom she regarded as a master teacher—or rather, an emissary of the Master of all of us."[17]

The work of Day and Maurin continues to bear fruit. The Catholic Worker newspaper—still published today—has been a steady vehicle to draw attention to the poor and the oppressed. The movement also included houses of hospitality—others might call them homeless shelters—and Catholic Worker farms. Day and Maurin focused on the works of mercy and the outcome of their work cascaded into many areas.

The Catholic Worker's original House of Hospitality on New York's Lower East Side eventually spawned other houses. Today it is estimated that there are over 130 Houses of Hospitality, most in the United States

[13] Day, *The Long Loneliness,* 166.

[14] Piehl, *Breaking Bread,* 25.

[15] Robert Coles, "On Moral Leadership: Dorothy Day and Peter Maurin in Tandem," *America* (June 6–13, 1998) 13.

[16] Ibid.

[17] Ibid., 14.

and Canada, but there are others in England, Germany, Australia, Mexico, and New Zealand.[18] There is no official organization for the movement. Those who want to start such a house (or farm) are free to study Day's words and adapt them as desired. Some of these houses of hospitality are now established for troubled teens or battered women.[19]

The Catholic Worker movement also includes rural agricultural communities. One Benedictine oblate who puts this idea into practice with his family (they have a garden, a little herd of goats, and earn cash by weaving and other crafts) notes that the Catholic Worker farms have been regarded as sources of produce for urban souplines and as places of retreat for harried city folk. He explains that this movement back to the land was sought "not to the end of self-sufficiency or for rugged individualism, but towards a gentler interdependence, towards ways of earning a living that do no violence to oneself, to others, or to the earth."[20]

When Dorothy Day died in 1980 (Maurin had predeceased her by more than thirty years), some friends wondered if the Catholic Worker would survive. While most movements are perpetuated with detailed governance structures, Day's legacy is loosely organized, sustained more on dedication than on data. One Catholic Worker described this characteristic, "It was an organism, after all, not an organization: no bylaws, no dues, no trustees, no annual convention, no central kitty flush with foundation or government lucre."[21] The prevailing view at Day's funeral was the faith-based one Dorothy had offered in her final years about the Catholic Worker: If God wants it to survive, it will.[22]

Benedictine Influence

Benedictines, both the religious communities and lay oblates, follow the lead of their founder, St. Benedict of Nursia (ca. 480–ca. 550), who is known as the father of Western monasticism. The Rule of St. Benedict is a remarkably adaptable document that has endured for more than 1500 years.

While Dorothy Day read *The Desert Fathers* by Helen Waddell and *The Oblate* by Joris Huysmans, Peter Maurin is credited with introducing her to the tradition of St. Benedict. In *Searching for Christ: The Spirituality*

[18] T. Wright Townsend, "The Reluctant Saint," *Chicago Tribune Magazine* (December 26, 1999) 15.

[19] Ibid.

[20] Brian Terrell, "Monastic Roots of the Catholic Worker Movement," *The Catholic Worker* (December 1999) 8.

[21] Colman McCarthy, "Houses Keep Dorothy Day's Spirit Alive," Minneapolis *Star Tribune* (November 11, 1997) 13A.

[22] Ibid.

of Dorothy Day, Brigid O'Shea Merriman, O.S.F., expertly traces the impact of monasticism in Day's life. She explains that Peter Maurin brought Benedictine spirituality to the Catholic Worker Movement and that it was not until Dorothy met him in 1932 that "she became more fully aware of the heritage of St. Benedict. Peter represented for Dorothy a Catholicism deeply rooted in the tradition of which monasticism in its Benedictine expression played an important part."[23] Merriman explains, "Though not limited to this group alone, the Benedictine charism places great value upon identification with Christ, on community, on hospitality and a harmony between prayer and work. Dorothy was drawn to these aspects of the Benedictine charism, and thus they were abundantly expressed in her own spirituality."[24]

The Benedictine roots of the Catholic Worker were apparent in every area of the movement. Stanley Vishnewski, one of Day's co-workers, described this Benedictine influence in a letter to a friend:

> The Benedictine Tradition has had a great influence on the Catholic Worker.
> Peter Maurin used to tell us in his conferences how the Benedictine Monks swept over Europe after the fall of the Roman Empire and established "Farming Communes" which helped keep learning alive during the so-called Dark Ages.
> I am sure that without the influence of the Benedictines that there would be very little in the Catholic Worker Movement—For from the Benedictines we got the ideal of Hospitality—Guest Houses—Farming Communes—Liturgical Prayer. Take these away and there is very little in the Catholic Worker Program.[25]

Benedictine Oblate

While Dorothy Day's work was affected by the Benedictine values espoused by Maurin, it was not until 1955 (twenty-three years after the start of the Catholic Worker, five years after Maurin's death) that she officially affiliated with the order as an oblate.

Dorothy Day knew many people in the Church. Since Day and Maurin lived by voluntary poverty, the Catholic Worker movement depended on the financial support of others. Many of Day's earliest affiliations with religious organizations—and monastic communities—began with monetary donations to the Catholic Worker movement. Dorothy also met others during her cross-country speaking tours—which, by the way, were quite

---

[23] Merriman, *Searching for Christ,* 74.
[24] Ibid., 81.
[25] Ibid., 107.

unusual in her day, especially as she traveled by bus. The Catholic Worker newspaper, too, provided a format for an exchange of ideas and publications with influential writers and academics. Finally, Day met clergy and religious leaders as she engaged speakers and retreat masters for the Catholic Worker programs.

Thus, in 1955 when Day became an oblate of St. Procopius Abbey, twenty-five miles southwest of Chicago, she had already established several ties to this community. Day had visited the school to speak to students. She had also enjoyed the friendship of some of the monks, particularly Chrysostom Tarasevitch, O.S.B., who was known for his efforts toward rapprochement between the Roman Catholic and Russian Orthodox churches. When Day was in Chicago on speaking tours she often called or visited Chrysostom at St. Procopius as they shared an interest in Russian spirituality and literature.[26] She was also a friend of Rembert Sorg, O.S.B., a monk of St. Procopius Abbey and the author of *Towards a Benedictine Theology of Manual Labor.*[27]

Day knew the mission of St. Procopius Abbey and she was also aware of the strength and prominence of other Benedictine monasteries. She chose an affiliation with St. Procopius Abbey and explained this predilection:

> My special love for St. Procopius is because its special function is to pray for the reunion of Rome and the Eastern Church. The monks can offer Mass in the Eastern or Roman rite and when Fr. Chrysostom [Tarasevitch] came to give us retreats at Maryfarm, we sang the liturgy of St. John Chrysostom.[28]

A copy of her oblation papers indicates that Dorothy Day professed her oblation to St. Procopius Abbey in Lisle, Illinois, on April 26, 1955.[29] Her investiture took place in Holy Innocents Parish Church in New York City.[30] According to Christian Ceplecha, O.S.B., current oblate director at St. Procopius Abbey, the monks of the Lisle abbey periodically conducted retreats and days of recollection for a group of their New York oblates.

This long distance affiliation may seem unusual by today's standards but Ceplecha recalls that the role of the oblates in the 1950s was basically a tie to receive spiritual nourishment. There were days of recollection and some meetings but the goal of oblation was simply to enrich a devotional life. "To go beyond that," cautions Ceplecha, "I think we are reading what happened later into the past."[31] In order to promote this devotional life,

[26] Christian Ceplecha, O.S.B., personal interview, 24 February 2000.
[27] Merriman, *Searching for Christ,* 105.
[28] Ibid., 107–8.
[29] Lisle, Ill. St. Procopius Abbey Archives, Benedictine Oblate Papers.
[30] Ibid.
[31] Ceplecha-Tybor Interview.

oblates followed a manual published by The Liturgical Press, Collegeville, Minnesota. Ceplecha describes this book which oblates often kept close at hand. "It included one or two weeks of the Liturgy of the Hours—the Breviary as we said in those days—in English, of course."[32] It also included other prayers, litanies, and a Benedictine calendar of saints. The 1948 edition of this oblate manual has four sections: Secular Oblates of St. Benedict; Spiritual Life of the Oblates; Prayers and Devotions; and Ceremonial.[33]

The November 22, 1940, issue of the St. Procopius school newspaper leads with a front-page headline: "Dorothy Day Speaks About Her Work Among the Poor—Lay Catholic Worker Talks to Big Turnout."[34] But it was five years later, when Ceplecha was a young monk studying for the priesthood, that he had the opportunity to hear Day speak. "Her dress was plain, she wore no make-up, but she spoke as somebody who knows what she is doing and is very dedicated in doing it. [She was] totally dedicated to Christ and to the poor."[35] It was often Dorothy Day's lone presence that seared the memory of those who met her. Dorothy herself eventually realized—with the gentle prompting of Peter Maurin—that her message was more than the spoken words. She said, "Sometimes I'd try hard to get it right. . . . Peter would remind me, later, that it's not only what you say, but how you say it."[36]

Dorothy saw her oblation as a tie to all Benedictines. She wrote of this, "Now I am a professed oblate of the St. Procopius family, and have been for the last two years, which means I am a part of the Benedictine family all over the world, and a member of the Benedictine community at Lisle and every month a newsletter comes from St. Procopius."[37]

Other Monastic Affiliations

Day's affiliations with other monasteries began with a tie to the English Benedictine congregation at Portsmouth, Rhode Island, which is traced to her friendship with Ade Bethune, a staff artist for the Catholic Worker.[38] Some of Day's other Benedictine friendships included Mother Benedict Duss, O.S.B., of Regina Laudis Abbey, and Brother David Steindl-Rast, O.S.B.,

[32] Ibid.

[33] Deutsch, *Manual for Oblates*.

[34] "Dorothy Day Speaks about Her Work among the Poor," *The Procopian News* (22 November 1940) 1.

[35] Ceplecha-Tybor Interview.

[36] Coles, "On Moral Leadership," 9.

[37] Merriman, *Searching for Christ*, 106.

[38] Ibid., 101.

of Mount Savior Monastery.[39] Of particular note is her connection with St. John's Abbey in Collegeville, Minnesota, through her friendship with Virgil Michel, O.S.B., renowned as a prime mover in the American liturgical movement.[40] Merriman's book explains that Day affiliated herself with the Benedictines precisely because of the personal contacts with such noteworthy Benedictines as Virgil Michel of St. John's.[41] (Incidentally, in 1926 Michel founded The Liturgical Press, the publishers of this volume.) Day also shared a close friendship with Thomas Merton, a Trappist of Gethsemani Abbey. Merriman summarized some of the similarities of these kindred spirits:

> They had been influenced by some of the same thinkers; both were converts who loved the church; . . . both employed writing skills to raise the consciousness of others, yet felt that what they did was so little; both anguished over a world situation in which there was no peace; both relied on the monastic tradition as a framework for their lives, while moving beyond a rigidly archaic interpretation of its meaning for the contemporary world.[42]

Prayer: Work of God

While Dorothy Day is often remembered for her apostolic works, she was also deeply committed to prayer, which is the heart of the monastic tradition. As her work broadened and became more demanding, she remained faithful to a spiritual life that included prayer, sacrament, and Scripture. There are many lures to turn one away from prayer. The *Catechism of the Catholic Church* notes "lack of faith" as the "most common yet most hidden temptation" as "a thousand labors or cares thought to be urgent vie for our priority" when we begin to pray.[43] Day's fidelity to prayer did not diminish during her very active life. Consider, for instance, her 1965 penitential offering in Rome for the last session of the Second Vatican Council. It included a ten-day fast at a convent with nineteen other women. They began the day with Mass and prayer and followed with a morning of silence, reading, writing, and praying.[44]

Prayer, though, was not reserved for special events. In fact, when Jim Forest, former managing editor of the Catholic Worker and friend of

[39] Ibid., 108.

[40] Ibid., 76.

[41] Ibid., 144.

[42] Ibid., 119.

[43] *Catechism of the Catholic Church* (New York: Image Book, Doubleday, 1995) #2732, 719.

[44] William D. Miller, *Dorothy Day: A Biography* (San Francisco: Harper & Row, 1982) 480.

Dorothy Day, summarized all that he had learned from her about social justice, prayer was at the top of his list.

> First of all, Dorothy Day taught me that justice begins on our knees. I have never known anyone, not even in monasteries, who was more of a praying person than Dorothy Day. . . . If you find the life of Dorothy Day inspiring, if you want to understand what gave her direction and courage and strength to persevere, her deep attentiveness to others, consider her spiritual and sacramental life.[45]

This life of prayer gave direction to Day. Once when she was asked about her goals, she disappointed her interviewer by suggesting that there was no clever plan, that "we were throwing ourselves at the mercy of Jesus!" She said, "I told him I'd never thought about it; I told him we never really thought too far into the future—we weren't planners. We just went with our hearts, and we prayed and prayed for direction from God and his Son."[46]

Her prayers were not abandoned in times of doubt. In fact, she wrote of her reception of baptism, penance, and Holy Eucharist (received soon after her loss of Forster Batterham), "I proceeded . . . grimly, coldly, making acts of faith, and certainly with no consolation whatever. One part of my mind stood at one side and kept saying, 'What are you doing?' . . . I felt like a hypocrite when I got down on my knees."[47] Yet, Day was also blessed with joy in prayer. In her "Letter to an Agnostic" she admonished: "You have not felt the ecstasy, the thankfulness, the joy, which caused the Psalmist to cry out, 'My heart and my flesh rejoice for the living God.'"[48]

She would steal the early morning hours for her spiritual exercises and she did this almost daily, year in and year out, explaining: "My strength . . . returns to me with my cup of coffee and the reading of the psalms."[49] In her seventies Dorothy Day reflected on the importance of prayer. "More and more I see [that] prayer is the answer," she wrote. "It is the clasp of the hand, the joy and keen delight in the consciousness of that Other. Indeed, it is like falling in love."[50]

---

[45] Jim Forest, "What I Learned about Justice from Dorothy Day," *Salt of the Earth* (July/August 1995) 22. (Reprinted with permission from Salt of the Earth, Claretian Publications.)

[46] Coles, "On Moral Leadership," 10.

[47] Day, *The Long Loneliness,* 148–9.

[48] Dorothy Day, "Letter to an Agnostic," *America* (4 August 1934; reprint with foreword by George M. Anderson, 17 April 1999) 8.

[49] Patrick Jordan, "An Appetite for God; Dorothy Day at 100," *Commonweal* (24 October 1997) 12.

[50] Ibid., 13.

Witness to Oblates

As an oblate I am moved by Day's commitment to prayer. Eileen Egan writes of Dorothy Day: "Her fidelity to prayer was her path to the transformation called for by the witness of peace, voluntary poverty, and mercy to the needy."[51] As a Christian, I have pursued various apostolic works but it took an affiliation with the Benedictines to lead me to a greater fidelity to prayer. While Benedictine communities frame their days around a rhythm of prayer—with an ancient tradition to safeguard solitude and silence—as an oblate it is a challenge to forge a prayer life that is both practical and persistent. Dorothy Day's example follows the gracious lead of St. Benedict without becoming unduly regimented.

The following anecdote continues to impress me. A donor came into the Catholic Worker House and gave Dorothy a diamond ring. Dorothy thanked her for it and put it in her pocket. Later, a rather demented lady came in, a somewhat irritating regular at the house. Dorothy took the diamond ring out of her pocket and gave it to the woman. When a staff member questioned Dorothy about this, suggesting it would have been better to sell the ring and pay the woman's rent for a year, Dorothy replied that the woman had her dignity and could do what she liked with the ring. She could sell it for rent money or a trip to the Bahamas, or she could enjoy wearing it, like the woman who originally gave it to Dorothy.[52]

This incident suggests to me that Day was able to run a movement without being run by the movement. She related to others in unnerving freedom and stunning freshness that speak of God's presence. For Day, love was the measure of all things, and that love did not get lost in the shuffle. I believe that it was Day's life of prayer that gave her the ability to remain charitable in the midst of human difficulties. She wrote, "It is hard to love. It is the hardest thing in the world, naturally speaking. . . . It is never the brother right next to us, but the brothers in the abstract that are easy to love."[53]

Dorothy Day's absolute reliance on God continues to inspire me. So often, the elements of her life seemed very disordered by the world's standards as she gave up many human comforts to follow her faith. But her own writing shows that her love for God ordered her life in a most holy and profound manner. Her vision gives me great hope. In a world that is often overcome with despair and futility, her fidelity sets a straight path that seems to say, "Persevere. God will provide."

---

[51] Eileen Egan, *Peace Be with You* (Maryknoll, N.Y.: Orbis Books, 1999) 303.

[52] Forest, "What I Learned about Justice," 23.

[53] Dorothy Day, *Meditations* (Springfield, Ill.: Templegate Publishers, 1997) 131.

Perhaps Dorothy Day will be canonized in the future. In faith we already know that her love endures. We also know that she was influenced by the monastic tradition and shared her own gifts to raise the social consciousness of the Church. Dorothy Day clearly identified herself as a Benedictine oblate. She acknowledged that her oblation joined her to the Benedictine family all over the world. As followers of St. Benedict, it is our certain honor to share the work, the prayer, and the kinship of Dorothy Day. May God be glorified.

8

Eric Dean: Presbyterian Pilgrim

Phyllis K. Thompson

Eric Dean is known to numerous oblates of St. Benedict and to oblate directors in North America for his book *St. Benedict for the Laity.*[1] It was published posthumously and continues to be staple fare for individuals who sense they are being called to live as non-monastic Benedictines. Dean was a husband and father, a college professor, a Presbyterian minister, and an ecumenical oblate. It is important for a reader to see how those various strands of his life were influenced and enhanced by his ongoing awareness of the Benedictine charism and spirituality.

The promise Eric Dean wrote and uttered when he became an oblate in March 1983 gives some insights into this Benedictine spirituality:

> In gratitude to God for all the blessings of my life, and with special thanks for his providence which led me to this place, I—Eric Dean—offer my life to God to live according to the Gospel and the Rule of Holy Father Benedict as an oblate of Mt. Saviour Monastery.
>
> Making this promise in your [the monks'] presence, I ask your prayers on my behalf—as I assure you of mine on yours, that, under God's protection, we may meet at the last in our heavenly home together with all whom we have loved.[2]

Providence brought Dean to this moment after a nearly twenty-five-year journey; that journey is as much a part of Dean's oblational and Benedictine-inspired life as the six years he bore the official label "oblate."

---

[1] Eric Dean, *St. Benedict for the Laity* (Collegeville: The Liturgical Press, 1989).

[2] Eric Dean's handwritten diary from 1982–83, with his oblate promise on 9 March 1983.

A journey usually has a goal, but often the journey is as significant as the intended goal. Dean engaged wholeheartedly in his particular journey; yet his pilgrimage did not end the day he became an oblate. Nor did his oblational life begin only on that date.

Essential Biographical Data

Eric Dean was born in London, England, in October 1924. His elementary and secondary education occurred there; he then joined the military, serving in the Royal Air Force from 1942 into 1947. Part of his training as a flight navigator took place in Quebec, Canada; he also served in England and India in those years. In April 1947 Dean emigrated to the United States, earning his B.A. at the University of Chicago in 1950. Graduate studies took him to the Divinity School at the same university, where by 1959 he had earned his B.D. in systematic theology and his Ph.D. in historical theology. He was ordained in 1955 as a minister in the United Presbyterian Church of the USA.[3] During his studies at the University of Chicago he met his future wife, Betty Jane Garrett, of Racine, Wisconsin. They married in July 1948 and had three children: Daphne, Eric Jr., and Jonathan.

Dean taught at Wabash College in Crawfordsville, Indiana, from 1957 until his death in May 1989. As a Presbyterian minister, Dean not only preached regularly at Wabash College's chapel services, but also did supply work for numerous local Presbyterian congregations. He also served on various local, state, and national boards of the Presbyterian Church.

In 1988, Dean was stricken with a malignant brain tumor. Dean died at home in May 1989, after living without complaint through the six months during which he lost his ability to speak, read, and remember.[4]

The Benedictine Factors

One component of Eric Dean's life, thus far left out of the above biographical sketch, is the rationale for this chapter: the Benedictine element, which drew Dean not only to become an oblate, but also to strive to witness to the Benedictine charism in his life. Somewhere during the early 1960s—the beginning of that twenty-five-year journey mentioned earlier—Eric Dean began to number among his acquaintances several of the

---

[3] Now the 1983 Reformed Presbyterian Church of the USA. Source: "Where Did the Presbyterian Church Originate?" PC (USA) Information Website: www.pcusa.org/pcusa/info/pcorigin.htm. 3 October 2000.

[4] Betty Dean, widow, personal interview, 16 May 2000.

monks from the Archabbey of St. Meinrad. Some became very close friends, as recalled by Dean's widow and some of the monks from St. Meinrad.[5] That began an entirely new aspect of Dean's life, one which lasted until his death in 1989.

This was the era of Vatican II, when the Catholic Church began to open doors and windows to new ways of acknowledging and interacting with non–Roman Catholic Christians. Dean's contact with the monks engendered and encouraged much lively discussion in the areas of philosophy, theology, and ecumenism. Two of Dean's closest monastic friends "were in the forefront of the revised theology program at St. Meinrad in the early and mid-60s . . . and Dean himself was very *avant garde* in those days."[6] Dean too was "very much a part of the post–Vatican II move toward ecumenism."[7]

Dean was the first non–Roman Catholic to be invited to give the commencement address at St. Meinrad in May 1965; he was asked again in May 1970. In the intervening period, Dean spent a number of years there as a visiting professor of ecumenical theology. Later, he was invited to join the board of overseers of St. Meinrad's undergraduate liberal arts college and its graduate school of theology; he served on that board from 1969 until his death in 1989. Much of the correspondence available in St. Meinrad's archives makes its clear that Eric Dean had a particular concern that courses and degree options would allow for interested Protestant students at the graduate level.

The Puzzle

At this point a reader might ask, "With all this contact with St. Meinrad, how is it this man became an oblate of Mount Saviour, a good distance away?" That question was behind some of the research for this chapter; the results, I hope, will present the reader with the picture of a man whom we all recognize: a person of faith who challenged his faith and let it be challenged, ultimately a seeker after God whose search was enhanced and deepened because of his strong connection to two Benedictine communities.

---

[5] May 2000 interviews with various monks from St. Meinrad Archabbey: Timothy Sweeney, O.S.B., former archabbot (10 May); Hilary Ottensmeyer, O.S.B., one of the former president-rectors of St. Meinrad's School of Theology and a very close friend of Dean (11 May), and Eugene Hensell, O.S.B. (14 May). It should be noted that Fr. Hilary died a few days after our interview.

[6] Eugene Hensell, O.S.B., president-rector at St. Meinrad at time of Dean's death, personal interview, 14 May 2000.

[7] Harry Hagan, O.S.B., former vice-rector/provost at St. Meinrad, personal interview, 18 May 2000.

Between 1957 and 1989, Eric Dean had three sabbatical leaves from Wabash College. Sabbaticals typically are times when an academic gets a set amount of time off from all regular work—teaching, office hours, committees. Sabbaticals allow a person to spend time and expend energy differently. The length of a sabbatical depends on the particular institution, but it is a period when a person does research on a topic of interest, usually related to one's academic specialty. But sabbaticals also allow a person time to refocus and reenergize, to rethink one's relationships, i.e., to look reflectively at one's place in various communities—family, church, work, volunteer organizations. Sabbaticals can be journeys, pilgrimages.

During two of his three sabbatical years from Wabash College (1967–68 and 1981–82), Dean spent four months each visiting numerous Benedictine and some Trappist communities in North America. His initial intention in 1967–68 was to study "the twentieth-century monastic Office."[8] This proved problematic because the Church was caught in the tidal wave of changes immediately after Vatican II. Dean's diaries from the four-month period in 1967–68 make it obvious he found most of the Benedictine communities struggling to make decisions about revisions in language, chant, the structure of the *opus Dei,* and liturgical practices at Mass. He wrote:

> Things were changing so quickly, that after having visited one monastery and taking voluminous notes of the content and style of its Office, I would leave for a few weeks to visit another monastery and, upon my return, would find the whole Office re-structured and my notes useless. A few experiences like this and I just gave up my original plan and decided to see just what I could learn from the monastic experience.[9]

Although he found it difficult to complete the study he had intended, when he shifted his focus, he found one place where stability in the *opus Dei* and liturgy existed, even in those tumultuous years: Mount Saviour Monastery in Elmira, New York, a place where the monastic experience encouraged him to admit that the "monastic form of life and its influence may be truly reforming elements in this period of ferment."[10] This is supported further by the oblate director at Mount Saviour who indicated that, "given the flux in the immediate post–Vatican II era, Eric Dean may well have appreciated the stability of prayer and liturgy here, since many forward-thinking changes had occurred *before* Vatican II, thanks to Fr. Damasus."[11]

---

[8] Fred L. Hofheinz, "A Presbyterian Minister in a Benedictine Monastery," *U.S. Catholic* (October 1968) 24.

[9] Ibid.

[10] Ibid.

[11] James Cronen, O.S.B., current oblate director at Mount Saviour Monastery, but also when Dean became a candidate and oblate, personal interview, 26 September 2000.

Background on Mount Saviour

The existence of Mount Saviour Monastery is due in large measure to the work of one man: Damasus Winzen, O.S.B. (1901–71), a monk originally from the Beuronese Benedictine congregation at the Abbey of Maria Laach in Rhineland, Germany. Its original founders were heavily influenced by the Solesmes congregation in Normandy, France.[12]

The foundation at Mount Saviour, and its becoming an independent monastery in 1950, was greatly influenced by the character of Damasus Winzen. His "insights [were] *avant garde* to say the least in 1923."[13] Winzen was sent to the United States in 1938; his new acquaintances and friends there were ecumenical. In this, Winzen "differed from his Catholic colleagues" by displaying "a leaning toward ecumenism that was as rare at that time in America as it had been in Germany."[14] One person wrote of him: "Damasus was already living, thirty years before it took place, the spirit of John XXIII and Vatican II."[15]

In the intervening years between 1938 and 1950 and through lectures and retreats he gave, Winzen acquired a group of followers who wished to become oblates before there was even a specific monastery to which they could become affiliated. The history of this is quite fascinating, and Madeleva Rourke's book is the most authoritative study of this; but that group of individuals sprang up unplanned and never lost hope that a monastery would come into existence. Since that momentous day in 1950, over "three hundred oblates from every walk of life, Catholic and non-Catholic, clergy and laity, have been received as members of Mt. Saviour."[16] This group was, and still is, very ecumenical in makeup. Damasus Winzen never forgot the advice he received from Cardinal Montini before the latter became Pope Paul VI: "Open the doors, Dammaso, spread the tent," a paraphrase of Isaiah 54:2.[17] Winzen's ecumenical interests and exchanges continued until his death in 1971: the background of guest speakers and other visitors to Mount Saviour was inclusive, although he never forgot "his roots were in the Latin Rite."[18]

Eric Dean's diaries indicate that he encountered this openness and diversity firsthand. But he would have experienced something else. Ahead of other institutions within the Church, Mount Saviour Monastery "had

[12] J. Madeleva Roarke, *Father Damasus and the Founding of Mount Saviour* (Pine City: Madroar Press, 1998) 35.

[13] Ibid., 65–6.

[14] Ibid., 100.

[15] Ibid.

[16] Ibid., 126.

[17] Ibid., 193.

[18] Ibid., 201.

been given permission to experiment with . . . both the Divine Office and the rituals of the Eucharist."[19] So by 1967, when Dean would have first visited Mount Saviour, there was already a stable use of the vernacular in both the Office and at Mass, of concelebrated liturgies, and of the laity receiving Communion under both species.[20]

Finally, at Mount Saviour Dean would have experienced the ambiance of a Benedictine community whose size and monastic lifestyle, to Dean's mind as he contemplated the Rule, truly honored Benedict's guidelines. The *Opus Dei,* chanted six times a day, took priority; then there was Mass, then the community's ministry to guests and the maintenance of a dairy herd.[21] Mount Saviour was a small enough community that the members could attend to all the daily chores themselves (although guests could help if they wished), and male guests ate with the monks and helped in the monastic kitchen. Meals were simple because the monks cooked for themselves. Guest quarters were simple, but not so austere as to be uninviting.

Whereas Dean's sabbatical in 1967–68 involved visits to nine Benedictine and Trappist houses over four months, his sabbatical in 1981–82 involved visits to only three monastic communities over four months; this time he chose to spend more time at each, with the ultimate intent of writing a book related to his monastic experiences.[22] The book never came to pass; but that trip resulted in Dean becoming an oblate candidate at Mount Saviour in February 1982, after he had been there a month.[23]

More of the Journey, Some Answers to the Puzzle

With this background, a reader may still wonder how, while living close to the Archabbey at St. Meinrad where he spent twenty years doing volunteer work, Eric Dean could have become an oblate of another community. Some of the reasons are fairly straightforward.

First, despite his ties to St. Meinrad, Dean faced the reality that non–Roman Catholics were not permitted to become oblates of that com-

[19] Ibid., 227.

[20] Ibid., 228.

[21] Eric Dean's handwritten diary from 1967–68 sabbatical trip. On an undated page of comments, Dean notes his sense that, after visits to various monastic houses, the "Office is inversely related to the size of the community and the nature of its apostolates." Dean also discussed this and related perceptions in a summer 1970 article in *Encounter.*

[22] Alberta White, "Dean Spends Month in Monastery," *Crawfordsville (Indiana) Journal-Review* (6 March 1982) 4.

[23] Eric Dean's handwritten diary from the 1981–82 sabbatical trip where he notes that he became an oblate candidate after Vespers on 18 February 1982. It should be noted that the book referred to is not the one published by The Liturgical Press in 1989, but a separate one he intended to have published.

munity. By 1985, however, the manual of the national organization of oblate directors encouraged Benedictine communities to accept non–Roman Catholics; by then Dean was affiliated with Mount Saviour.[24] Clearly, with ecumenical oblates dating back to the 1950s, Mount Saviour was ahead of its time. Mount Saviour's openness in this area and its major focus on hospitality were some things Dean clearly appreciated.[25] Yet, Dean, even as he experienced the ecumenical openness at Mount Saviour, never took Communion at that monastery's liturgies. He did this out of respect for his Presbyterian commitment, "out of respect for the non-openness of our [the Roman Catholic] altar, and to honor the pain he felt over this, that is, that he could not receive."[26]

Second, the demands of Eric Dean's family life, his full-time position at Wabash College, and pastoral duties meant that the time he spent at St. Meinrad, of necessity, was spent on board of overseers' business. The constraints of schedules and administrative responsibilities prevented Dean from spending the kind of time there he would have liked. Further, a St. Meinrad monk noted that "Mount Saviour had a purer, clearer monastic presence; externally, Mount Saviour was more contemplative."[27] Clearly, Dean "was strongly influenced by, and responsive to, the spiritual dimension" at Mount Saviour.[28] This atmosphere would allow Dean—a busy man wherever he was in Indiana—to accept Christ's invitation in Mark 6:31, and see Mount Saviour as that quiet place.

Third, the size of the monastic community at St. Meinrad, and the nature of its enclosure, almost by default prevented the kind of intimate contact with the day-in, day-out community life that Dean was able to experience at Mount Saviour. Dean, no matter how close some of his friendships were, or how much contact he had with St. Meinrad's monks, would not have been able to have the same kind of "up close, first-hand" lived monastic experience as he could at Mount Saviour. In addition to this, as one St. Meinrad monk remarked, "Mount Saviour would appeal to someone who is highly intellectual, and then the group at Mount Saviour was very much so. And topics would have been discussed differently there than they were here."[29] Finally, St. Meinrad's Archabbot Lambert noted that

[24] 12 October 2000 e-mail from Meinrad Brune, O.S.B., oblate director at St. Meinrad Archabbey.

[25] James Cronen, O.S.B., oblate director at Mount Saviour Monastery, personal interview, 26 May 2000.

[26] Martin Boler, O.S.B., prior of Mount Saviour Monastery, personal interview, 26 September 2000.

[27] Timothy Sweeney, O.S.B., personal interview, 10 May 2000.

[28] Martin Boler, O.S.B., personal interview, 26 September 2000.

[29] Eugene Hensell, O.S.B., personal interview, 14 May 2000.

"Eric visited a number of monasteries, but at some point something else kicked in. As Pascal said, 'The heart has reasons reason does not know.'"[30]

In the face of these realities, it is obvious that Eric Dean was fed by two major streams of lived Benedictinism, and he opted to savor every drop. His interest in one monastic community or the other never waned. He honored his board commitment to St. Meinrad right until his final illness, and he visited Mount Saviour annually after he became an oblate, again, until the year of his final illness.

Dean's Benedictinism Lived Out

Dean was first and foremost a family man, then a Presbyterian minister and college faculty member. It is in these roles that his twenty-five-year journey into the Benedictine charism and spirituality bore fruit. In the introduction to his book Dean writes about his son's responsiveness to the various monks who were welcomed into their home. But the hospitality was mutual: Dean's wife and children occasionally accompanied Dean to St. Meinrad.[31] He took his students on occasional excursions or weekend junkets to some monasteries. Dean was also instrumental in reciprocal weekend exchanges between philosophy students at both Wabash and St. Meinrad, so that Vatican II's approved constitution on ecumenism could "be put into practice at a practical level," thus allowing these young scholars to better "understand and respect the individual consciences of others."[32]

Son Jonathan recalls the many backpacking trips he shared with his father, when Dean often compared backpacking "to the simplicity of life as one experienced it in a monastery" where

> that simplicity led one to an acute awareness of the one thing which led a person to that endeavor. In backpacking, everything fades into obscurity save the intense relationship one experiences with Nature; . . . in the monastery one is completely immersed in the presence of God. This is the lesson I took from that comparison.[33]

For years Dean was faculty advisor to a camping/hiking club at Wabash; one can surmise that he shared some of these same thoughts with students.

In the many sermons—some published,[34] some not—one also sees strands of the Benedictine charism weaving in and out; and, in numerous

[30] Lambert Reilly, O.S.B., archabbot of St. Meinrad, personal interview, 11 May 2000.

[31] Dean, *St. Benedict for the Laity,* 7–8.

[32] Editorial, *Lafayette (Indiana) Sunday Visitor,* 23 May 1965.

[33] Jonathan Dean, Eric Dean's son, e-mail, 19 August 2000.

[34] Eric Dean, *The Good News about Sin: Sermons Preached in the Wabash College Chapel* (Crawfordsville, Ind.: A Sesquicentennial Publication of Wabash College, 1982).

lectures and published articles, Dean's growing appreciation for the Rule of St. Benedict and the way it can be applied to a typical non-monastic life is also visible. Dean gave a Benedictine witness to colleagues and students at Wabash College, to people in local Presbyterian congregations, and to readers of various Presbyterian publications.

Certain themes recurred in those public utterances and writings. The concept of "community" was one, and it was central to Dean. It is no wonder that he quotes from Alistair MacIntyre's 1984 book, *After Virtue,* at the beginning of his own book. Drawing on MacIntyre's discussion of the people of imperial Rome, Dean saw a contemporary parallel when it came to

> the construction of new forms of community within which the moral life could be sustained so that both morality and civility might survive the coming ages of babarism and darkness. . . . What matters at this stage [now] is the construction of local forms of community within which civility and the intellectual and moral life can be sustained through the new dark ages which are already upon us.[35]

There are references to both the necessity and value of community in his 1989 book, but he returned to this important concept frequently in talks and sermons he gave at Wabash College.

Dean often spoke to students about the parallels he saw between monastic life and college life, noting the interplay of freedom with order, the uniqueness of individuals and their gifts as they relate to the interdependence of work.[36] But the love and mutual respect that are central to monasteries, the challenge of openness, vulnerability, and simplicity—these too have their parallels on a college campus.[37]

It was important for students—at this Presbyterian-founded college—to learn that, historically, monasteries and colleges were founded by the same people.[38] They heard that "to be a college is to be standing in a long tradition that is Christian," and thus the term "college" has more than a mere legal, corporate, or commercial significance.[39] Dean saw it as necessary for the Wabash community to hear that "all Christian [persons] have a vocation, a calling."[40] How Benedictine for that same community to hear that at Wabash "we should feel more comfortable with saying that

---

[35] Dean, *St. Benedict for the Laity,* 5.

[36] Eric Dean's Wabash College Chapel sermon "Wabash and Other Monasteries" (n.d.).

[37] Dean's untitled, unpublished manuscript submitted December 1967 to *Presbyterian Life,* 2.

[38] Dean, "Wabash and Other Monasteries," 3.

[39] Dean, *The Good News about Sin,* 164.

[40] Ibid., 33.

our work here is the pursuit of God."[41] "Liberal learning is the intellectual worship of God."[42]

Dean, writing openly as a Protestant in a broader setting, believed that monasteries "can serve us well as exemplary communities,"[43] as examples of places where individuals can "manifest authentic personality."[44] Monasteries are where individuals are accepted for who they are, where persons "live an embodied life unselfconsciously ordered to nature . . . an existence which does not prey upon itself."[45] Thus, monasteries are where people can live in groups while dealing with the kind of aggression that is necessary for survival[46] at the same time they serve one another and are "responsive to the needs of" others.[47] "Monasteries . . . go beyond the biological family and witness to the possibility of a communion worthy to be called the body of Christ."[48]

As such, Dean applauded the strides being taken on various fronts to advance ecumenical study and dialogue, and it is obvious he engaged in some of these: attendance and a lecture given at the Institute for Ecumenical and Cultural Research at St. John's Abbey in Collegeville, Minnesota, for example.[49] The kinds of endeavors of which he spoke and in which he engaged, and his own thinking, predated the more well-known work of writers like Kathleen Norris and Esther de Waal,[50] but, given his solid sense of history, theology, and philosophy, he certainly would have understood de Waal's perception that one of the beauties of Benedictinism is that it looks back to an undivided past and looks forward to an undivided future.[51]

[41] Ibid., 166.

[42] Ibid., 168.

[43] Eric Dean, "St. Benedict's Way: A Protestant Appraisal of Monasticism," *Encounter* 31:4 (Summer 1970) 335.

[44] Ibid., 330.

[45] Ibid., 332.

[46] Ibid., 335.

[47] Ibid., 330.

[48] Ibid., 335.

[49] Dean's handwritten diary from 1967–68 sabbatical trip, entry about 23–24 September 1967 visit to St. John's Abbey, Collegeville, Minnesota.

[50] The principal text of *St. Benedict and the Laity,* the book The Liturgical Press published in 1989, existed in a previous version: in a different format, with no editing and no apparent copyright, and privately printed, for sole use of the oblates at the archabbey. It was printed and available in May 1983, two months after Dean became an oblate at Mount Saviour. By the time Dean decided to submit it as a new manuscript to The Liturgical Press, Esther de Waal had come upon the scene with *Seeking God: The Way of St. Benedict,* a book The Liturgical Press published in 1984. So these two authors were likely composing their texts simultaneously, unaware of each other.

[51] Spoken by de Waal at a retreat given in Nanaimo, British Columbia, October 1995; here she further noted that the Benedictine tradition "takes us away, back, and beyond—to a time

Conclusion

Eric Dean's knowledge of Benedictine principles and spirituality involved much academic research; that was the nature of the man and his profession, his "calling." But it did not remain on paper or in books; it permeated the person himself. Dean's writings are one facet of his witness to a lived spirituality, of his sharing what he knew with the communities which mattered to him, communities where, like St. Paul, Dean assumed we are "united in the same mind and purpose" (1 Cor 1:10), and where the values of Benedictinism, incorporated into the secular world, would allow all of us "to achieve interior peace and . . . seek the good of [our] communities without sacrificing individual value."[52]

This brings one back to Eric Dean's handwritten promise as an oblate, his desire to offer his life to God. This was in 1983, and six years followed where he fulfilled this promise. But there are actually twenty-five years that precede that promise where he did the same—for Benedictines and others—in the spirit of Benedict. He took his personal interest in monastic life and spirituality and shared it publicly. "He thoroughly grasped the Benedictine vision and translated it for the ordinary person."[53] Eric Dean "let his light shine forth and, as such, brought forth his gifts to the community and accepted others' . . . [he] realized that what is shared is gift, and must be given back."[54]

Herein is a lesson for all oblates: to witness to a lived spirituality by being light, by being gift and accepting others as gift. Not all oblates are college professors, but all oblates have a calling, and that is to seek God from within their own places in the world. Not all oblates get extended periods of time off from work, but all need to find ways to answer Christ's invitation in Mark 6:31, and see the monasteries with which they are affiliated as "quiet places away" and sources of spiritual sustenance. Every oblate lives within various communities. To understand and grow from the paradoxes and benefits of those communities, especially when they are ecumenical, is a worthy facet of any oblate's pilgrimage as a Christian. So, too, are the challenges of living a life of openness and simplicity, and of striving to be a peace-filled and peace-engendering individual.

The Rule of St. Benedict asks all Benedictines, professed or oblate, if they are "hastening toward their heavenly home" (*RB* 73:8). For nearly

---

before all the splits, the politics, the divisions of the Reformation, before the schism between eastern and western churches, before the great universities of the twelfth century encouraged the split between the intellect and the imagination" (source: author's verbatim notes).

[52] Hofheinz, "A Presbyterian Minister in a Benedictine Monastery," 24.

[53] Eugene Hensell, O.S.B., personal interview, 14 May 2000.

[54] Lambert Reilly, O.S.B., personal interview, 11 May 2000.

thirty years Eric Dean's answer was a resounding "Yes," and for thirty years Dean was a "true pilgrim," seeking not "any territorial possession [but] a spiritual inheritance."[55] In those thirty years, with the Gospel, the Rule, and the sustenance and encouragement of two Benedictine communities, Dean honored his calling, his vocation by "establish[ing] a school for the Lord's service" within his own life (*RB* Prol. 45).

[55] Esther de Waal, *A World Made Whole* (London: Fount/HarperCollins, 1991) 55.

9

Frances of Rome:
Patron of Benedictine Oblates

Susan Anderson Kerr

The patron saint of Benedictine oblates is a fifteenth-century Italian mystic, so little known that when one mentions St. Frances of Rome, what is usually heard is a reference to St. Francis of Assisi. There has been no major scholarly biography of her in English.[1] She is ignored or mentioned only briefly in surveys of the religious experience of medieval women. Histories of the Order of St. Benedict similarly contain few references to her life and work.

There are three possible reasons for her obscurity. Unlike her near contemporaries Julian of Norwich and Margery Kempe, she was not a writer; she left no letters or autobiography. The accounts of her visions were recorded by her spiritual director in the biography he wrote. What we know of St. Frances derives mostly from the proceedings for her canonization.

The variety in the circumstances of her life also contributed to her invisibility. She did not fit into established categories. As a wife, mother, grandmother, widow, founder of a congregation, healer, and spiritual director, she spoke to people in a wide range of circumstances. Since Frances appealed to such a diverse range of people, those devoted to her did not have an organized channel for sponsoring her cult or for research into her spirituality.

Finally, St. Frances' mysticism raises questions about the relationship of seeing and belief which are difficult to address. She saw her guardian

---

[1] Devotional biographies of her life appeared in 1931, 1960, 1984, and 1992. I have relied on the seminal work of Irene Hernaman, *St. Frances of Rome and Her Times* (London: n.p., 1931), for most of the details in the synthesis of her life which follows.

angel, the Blessed Mother, the Holy Child, the Crucified Lord, and Saints Peter, Paul, Magdalene, and Benedict. These visions are so characteristic of the way she was described in medieval times that paintings of St. Frances can be identified by two attributes: the habit of her community of oblates, a black gown with white veil, and by a guardian angel accompanying her.

Background of Her Life

Let us begin to understand St. Frances by looking at the connection between her and Rome, the place where she was born and lived. The reverence the Romans have for her includes their regard for her as the patron of drivers. They claim her in this manner because she was guided by her guardian angel. On her feast day, March 9, taxis[2] gather in the space between the Colosseum and the Forum near the church where her body is buried, Santa Maria Nuova. Each year the Olivetan Benedictine monks give the drivers a blessing before they process through the streets of Rome, and the Oblates of the Tor de Specchi convent open their doors to Romans who commemorate her feast with visits there.[3]

Early fifteenth-century Rome was not the Rome of the Renaissance; St. Frances lived just before the Rome of Michelangelo, before the fountains, St. Peter's, and Bernini. Hers was the Rome of plagues, feuds, warring vandals, a divided papacy; a Rome which had seen the rise of mendicant orders, Franciscan and Dominican, reformers who took the Catholic faith into the streets with works of charity, teaching and preaching, and fighting heresy. The monastic orders, both the Augustinians and the Benedictines, were in decline. Many lay people joined the confraternities which had formed to worship God, banding together for support during the civic unrest and famine, engaging in penitential practices, processions, meeting frequently to sing songs of praise.

Childhood and Marriage

Frances was born into a noble family in Rome in the year 1384. Her parents, Paolo de Bussi and Giacobella dei Roffredeschi, gave her the fem-

---

[2] Frances became the patron of drivers in much the same way that Clare of Assisi became patron of television: the Church extends the mystical gift of the saint into the protection offered to devotees. Clare could see events from afar, and Frances's guardian angel always guided her on the right route.

[3] Guy Boanas and Lyndal Roper, "Feminine Piety in Fifteenth-Century Rome: Santa Francesca Romana," *Disciplines of Faith: Studies in Religion, Politics, and Patriarchy,* ed. Jim Obelkevich, Lyndal Roper, and Raphael Samuel (New York: Routledge & Kegan Paul, 1987) 178.

inine version of the name of St. Francis of Assisi. Her parents were devout; her childhood, like that of many young girls, was shaped by her mother, who also chose an Olivetan monk of the church of Santa Maria Nuova as a confessor and spiritual director for her daughter. This priest, Don Antonio di Monte Savello, continued as her spiritual director for thirty-five years. When her parents overruled her request to enter religious life, and betrothed her at age twelve to Lorenzo Ponziana, a young nobleman, he counseled her to accept her parents' decision.

After her marriage, she continued an intense spiritual life of reading, prayer, and visiting churches. With her friend and sister-in-law, Vannuzza, she built a chapel in their palace, visited the sick, gave alms to the poor, and nursed the patients in the hospital of Santo Spirito. The tension she experienced in trying to combine intense devotions with the life of a wealthy Roman matron resulted in a breakdown. After a year of suffering, she was miraculously healed by a vision of St. Alexis.

From this crisis, Frances learned how to offer the three always interwoven threads of her life to God: first her family life, including her children, household duties, and role as wife; second her civic life of healer, spiritual director, organizer of almsgiving and charity for the poor of Rome; and third her spiritual life with its liturgical and mystical experiences. Interweaving these three threads is characteristic of Benedictine spirituality: just as the Rule counsels the monk to take his brothers into account in every aspect of his life in the monastery, so Frances continuously responded to her family and her city. Like a monk who finds in the enclosure of the monastery not a prison but a home, she created a sphere of inner freedom within the confines of this dense community.

Motherhood and Domestic Responsibility

In 1400, after five years of married life, Frances and Lorenzo had a son whom they named Battista. A year after his birth, Frances' father-in-law died, and the following year the household lost its mistress, her mother-in-law. The family unanimously chose Frances to run the household, acknowledging what must have been her superior gift for management. She was seventeen, younger than Vannuzza, who would have been the expected choice. She was thus in charge of a large, wealthy Roman estate, supervising servants and overseeing kitchens, food purchases and harvests. Because of their political sympathies, the family figured prominently as a center for papal support in Rome, and she was in charge of the entertaining associated with their role in the drama of the divided papacy.

This responsibility changed when plague and famine struck Rome a year after Frances had assumed responsibility for the household. Frances and Vannuzza were untiring in their efforts to relieve the suffering in the city, emptying the family's storehouses, to Lorenzo's dismay. Like the monks in Gregory's *Life of St. Benedict,* who begrudged St. Benedict's generosity when he gave away corn during a famine, Lorenzo was reproached for his skepticism as their own coffers were said to have been miraculously replenished. At this time Frances began to attract followers: other Roman matrons who gathered to help her with the needs of the city. Soon Frances found herself surrounded with a network of women who sought her for counsel with spiritual and family problems, and who emulated her example in acts of charity.

Three years after the birth of Battista, Frances and Lorenzo had another son, Evangelista, and three years following his birth, they had a daughter, Agnes. They named all of their children for saints, departing from the custom of Roman families of their class who named their children for family members.

Trials and Suffering

In 1405 Rome was plagued by a rival city. Ladislas, king of Naples, attacked the city, seeking to rule it. In the ensuing battle, Lorenzo, prominent in his support of the papacy and head of his legion, was wounded in a skirmish with Ladislas' soldiers. Frances nursed her husband to health, but the family's security was under threat. The troops of Ladislas now seized their eldest son, Battista, and sacked the Ponziani palace. Shortly afterward, Lorenzo was forced to go into exile for his safety. Frances and Vannuzza were left with Evangelista and Agnes, living in a corner of the ruined palace. As poverty and the plague again struck the city, the poor of Rome came once more to Frances' door seeking help.

At this time, her son Evangelista was struck down by the plague and died soon after. Within that same year, in the midst of widespread suffering and death, her only daughter, Agnes, also succumbed to the plague. This was a time of intense suffering for Frances. Two of her children were dead, the third held captive, and her husband still in exile. These tragedies, coupled with the suffering all around her, seemed to signal new depths in Frances' spiritual life. At this point she began to have the gift of supernatural healing. She traveled the streets of Rome with a salve she would apply, hoping those healed would attribute their cures to the ointment rather than to her.

At this time she also received a vision in which her recently deceased son appeared to her, announcing that from then on she would see her guardian angel who would accompany her as protector and guide. Just as Frances' experience mirrors that of the Desert Fathers in her vision of heaven, so she also was, like them, subject to demonic attacks. Her visions schooled her in the art of discernment of spirits.

Service to Family and City

In 1414, Ladislas of Naples died unexpectedly, freeing Rome from his menace, and the Church called the Council of Constance to address the need for reform. Now Lorenzo returned home to be reunited with Frances, and Battista was released from captivity. Lorenzo found that many in the city were turning to his wife for alms, healing, and reconciliation of quarrels. As a spiritual director, Frances had grown in authority, so that she now counseled some of the Olivetan monks of Santa Maria Nuova, notably one Don Ippolito who was later to support her during the vicissitudes of forming her young community of oblates.

Lorenzo and Battista returned to a ruined palace and to Rome's dismal economic situation. Gradually, however, the city was rebuilt, and their palace restored. The time had come for Frances and Lorenzo to choose a bride for their son, Battista. They decided on Mobilla, the daughter of another noble family. Mobilla adapted poorly to her new role. She dedicated herself to luxury and amusements, openly scorning her mother-in-law's path of service and contemplation. Her hostility melted after she suffered a breakdown from which Frances nursed her to health. Mobilla then changed her way of life and took over the management of their household in a responsible manner. Later she was to play a major role in the documentation of Frances's life which led to her canonization. Mobilla and Battista had children, and Frances was as devoted to her grandchildren as she had been to her own children.

In the midst of this intense family life, Frances' mystical life deepened. The effects of her prayer life were visible to others. To have a saint requires a community who perceives holiness, and Frances lived among people who observed her closeness to God.

Founder

Frances had long attracted the attention of women who wanted to give their time, wealth, and energy to the sick and the poor. Now they approached her asking her to give institutional expression to their way of life. They were attracted to the Benedictine order which they had come to know through the Olivetan monks at Santa Maria Nuova. The Olivetan monks began in the fourteenth century in Siena as a reform of the Benedictine life under Bernard Tolomei, and were later established in Rome. Frances had the support of two of their monks, Don Ippolito and Don

Antonio, in seeking permission of the general of the order to affiliate the small congregation of oblates with this Olivetan monastery. On the Feast of the Assumption 1425, Frances and her companions made their simple vows as oblates.

At first, the women remained each in her own household, but eventually they sought to have a house where they could live together in community. In 1426 Frances and several other oblates made a pilgrimage to Assisi. There the Blessed Virgin appeared to Frances, instructing her to have the oblates live together. It took them eight years to realize this dream, locating a house at the Tor de' Specchi which they purchased with their combined incomes. On the feast of the Annunciation in 1433, Frances and the other oblates went to Mass together at the church of Santa Maria in Trastevere and then entered their new home at the Tor de' Specchi.

Characteristic of their freedom, the oblates could live either in community or in their homes. Frances chose to remain with Lorenzo until 1440, the time of his death. By all accounts, theirs had been a happy marriage, with Lorenzo supporting his wife and feeling deeply blessed by her presence.

During those early years, the oblates elected Agnes de Lellis as their first superior. With monastic zeal for obedience, Frances deferred to her leadership, but was considered the spiritual mother of the community and bore their birth pains. The oblates lived under a rule of Frances' design. She gave them the Rule of St. Benedict and a set of constitutions drawn up under her direction. They wore a simple black and white habit as well as secular dress when in the streets of Rome.

In founding this group of oblates, Frances created a hybrid. She transformed the medieval practice of bringing child oblates to monasteries, by combining features of this practice with the new lay spiritual path of tertiaries which had arisen in the high Middle Ages. The oblates thus had advantages of both systems. Like the tertiaries, they participated in the charism and wisdom of an established religious order. This gave them the protection and stability which were not available to the beguines, associations of lay women which had arisen in northern Europe a century earlier, and to whom the oblates are often compared. The women who followed this path did so freely, unlike the medieval children entrusted as oblates who were unable to choose for themselves. However, like the child oblates, they brought with them monetary funds to build up the common good.

Death and Canonization

In 1440, four years after joining her sisters at Tor de' Specchi, Frances fell ill as she returned from visiting her sick son. She died surrounded by her oblate sisters and family during Lent on March 9, 1440.

Miraculous healings attended her death; her body was found to be incorrupt when moved to a new tomb in Santa Maria Nuova in July of 1440. Although her oblates initiated her canonization immediately, it was not until 1608 that Pope Paul V declared her a saint.

Like plant hybrids, the combination of elements responsible for the oblates of Tor de' Specchi proved difficult to replicate. Within a decade, the community faced lawsuits over property bequeathed them by members whose families wanted to reclaim it. While Frances' foundation was itself stable, it was not reproduced elsewhere. The institution was not destined to be a prototype for future growth of oblate communities; too many obstacles lay in the path of housing a lay Benedictine community.

What was innovative in Frances' new foundation was not that these women lived as uncloistered religious. In a survey[4] of women heads of households conducted in Florentine Tuscany in 1427, the second most common occupation, after that of servant, was *pinzochera,* the name for uncloistered religious. However, what Frances created was the union of lay with Benedictine spirituality, grafting lives of laity called to this vocation onto the Benedictine vine.

Pruned of specifically monastic attributes like communal property and the habit, the union of contemplative and active paths which St. Frances planted through the oblates of Tor de' Specchi flourishes among laity in the contemporary church. Because literacy is widespread, the sacramental nature of marriage more widely valued after Vatican II, and the Divine Office reformed for universal use, more people can identify with the story of St. Frances who, interrupted repeatedly from praying the office to attend to her husband's needs, returned to find the antiphon in her breviary written in gold. She continues to have companions who are inspired by her example.

[4] David Herlihy, *Opera Muliebria: Women and Work in Medieval Europe* (Philadelphia: Temple University Press, 1990) 159.

10

Rumer Godden: Oblate Novelist

Catherine Wybourne, o.s.b.

Rumer Godden was a prolific author who, like many authors aware of the impossibility of telling the whole truth, wrote and rewrote her own life story. Even to those closest to her she was something of an enigma;[1] to those who know her only from her books, she seems a distinctly Anglo-Indian enigma[2]—or, as she and Jon Godden described their childhood home, "English streaked with Indian or Indian streaked with English."[3]

The world in which Rumer lived almost exactly half her life, the world of British India, is already a fading memory. Few now understand the complexities of the society in which she lived or the codes by which she was expected to act. The ambiguity of her relationship with India, a mixture of love and something approaching fear, runs through her fiction and her life like the river image to which she was constantly drawn. In India all water is sacred, whether it be the mighty Ganges or the merest puddle; in the same way, all life is suffused with a sense of the spiritual. In the West that sense of living *always* in the presence of God is largely confined to those who are in some way especially committed to religious faith and practice, above all perhaps in the monasteries and hermitages which declare by their existence the primacy of God. For Rumer, religion

---

[1] Rumer Godden once called herself "the family enigma." See Anne Chisholm, *Rumer Godden* (London: Macmillan 1999) 42.

[2] Strictly speaking, Anglo-Indian refers to people of British origin born or living in India, Eurasian to people of mixed British and Indian parentage. Rumer's own use of "Anglo-Indian" was sometimes elastic.

[3] Jon Godden and Rumer Godden, *Two Under the Indian Sun* (London: Macmillan 1966) 46.

was all around, excluding nothing and no one. The little girl growing up in a household where God was worshipped in different ways by Buddhists, Christians, Hindus, and Muslims may not have known that Krishna was an incarnation of Vishnu, but she was as familiar with stories about him as she was with stories about Jesus, and stories were her way into the truth.[4]

Rumer's family was Anglican; she was sent to a number of Anglican schools, two of them convent schools; she even confessed to a fleeting desire to be a nun herself.[5] But as she grew older, and her life more turbulent, her attachment to the religion of her youth seems to have weakened, although Easter always retained significance for her. For a time she felt an attraction to Hinduism. Then, at the age of fifty, Rumer became a Roman Catholic and, a few years later, an oblate of Stanbrook Abbey, Worcester. Out of this experience came her novel *In This House of Brede*. Toward the end of her life she wrote that she saw herself as a house with four rooms: physical, mental, emotional, and spiritual: "With the spiritual, it was a long time before I would do more than peer in; now it is where I like best to be alone."[6]

Early Life

Margaret Rumer Godden was born in Sussex in 1907, the second child of Arthur and Katherine Godden (née Hingley). Until she became an adult she was always known as Peggie; her assumption of the name Rumer seems to have had something to do with consciousness of her identity as a writer. In 1908 she was taken back to India where her father worked as an agent for one of India's oldest shipping companies. As her elder sister Jon wrote, "Children in India are greatly loved and indulged, and we never felt that we were foreigners, not India's own; we felt at home, safely held in her large warm embrace, content as we were never to be content in our own country."[7] Part of that contentment stemmed from being part of a large and loving family. Of the four Godden girls—Jon (b. 1906), Rumer (b. 1907), Nancy (b. 1910), and Rose (b. 1913)—Jon and Rumer were especially close. Both were to become writers, but it was Jon who, in the family's estimation and Rumer's own, had the greater talent—a judgment today many might dispute. The sisters' joint account of the Bengali child-

---

[4] See the prefatory remark to Rumer Godden, *A Time to Dance, No Time to Weep* (London: Macmillan 1987).

[5] Ibid., 185.

[6] Rumer Godden, *A House with Four Rooms* (London/New York: Macmillan/William Morrow & Co., 1989) epilogue.

[7] Godden and Godden, *Two Under the Indian Sun*, 9.

hood reads like an idyll,[8] yet even paradise had its shadows and dark places where cruelty, disease, poverty, and death lurked. Privileged and protected though the Godden children were, they soon learned there were boundaries they might not cross. Arthur Godden's furious reaction to Rumer's having playfully taunted a Brahmin servant by uttering the sacred "Om" taught her an important lesson about respect for others and their religious beliefs.

Photographs of the family's large house beside the river at Narayangunj and the numerous servants suggest a secure, ordered world. In 1920, however, Jon and Rumer were sent back to England for their education, as was customary at the time. It felt like exile, and the girls went through English boarding schools at an alarming rate: five schools within two years. Eventually, but unusual for their time and class, they were allowed to attend a day school. At Moira House, Rumer encountered one of those rare teachers able to recognize and foster exceptional giftedness without spoiling or burdening the child. Mona Swamm gave Rumer an excellent training in the craft of writing, curbing her verbal excesses and setting exercises to develop her appreciation of literary technique. It was also while she was at Eastbourne that Rumer acquired Piers, the first of the Pekinese who were to be her canine companions throughout life, and had her first book brought out—by a vanity publisher.

Marriage and Writing

In the autumn of 1927, Rumer moved to London to train as a dancing teacher. She was musical and had always enjoyed ballet, but it was an odd career choice for someone with her background and a tendency to back trouble. When she returned to Calcutta in 1929 it was with the intention of setting up her own dancing school. She was later to regret the amount of time and energy she put into the venture, but the school was a success, even if the city was not to her liking. When Indians of the wealthier classes began to enroll, Rumer was forced to think about Independence and its consequences in a way she never had before. She began to see that freedom was necessary, that not all was as it should be. For a time, her social life was so active that there seemed little opportunity for thought. A radio interviewer once asked if it was true she had gone out sixty-seven nights running; she replied that it was, and not unusual for Calcutta.

It was in Calcutta that Rumer met Laurence Sinclair Foster, three years her senior. A stockbroker and accomplished sportsman, he possessed considerable charm. "His hazel eyes seemed always happy, as if there

---

[8] Ibid.

were no worries in the world."[9] After their marriage fell apart, friends would argue that their relationship was doomed from the start, but at the time things must have looked different, especially to the principals. Rumer was pregnant with their first child when they married in March 1934. They discussed the possibility of abortion, but Rumer rejected it out of hand— not for "religious" reasons as such, but because it was an easy way out at the expense of someone who had a claim on her love. She was determined to live with integrity, which meant being true to the values she held dear, the importance of family being one of them.

Rumer enjoyed setting up home in the ground floor of the old house they rented at Alipore; she enjoyed the companionship marriage brought. Although not well off, she and Laurence lived expensively with little to ruffle the calm of their existence—until the day she discovered the rent was in arrears. There was an awkward scene with Laurence, "Goddens have poisonous tongues," she recalled.[10] The quarrel was smoothed over while Rumer concentrated on making baby clothes in the oppressive heat. Their son, David, was born prematurely in August and lived only four days. Rumer's grief was lasting. Sixty years later, visiting Calcutta with a film crew making a documentary about her, she was terrified she might have to see his tiny grave again. Laurence did his best to comfort her and while on leave in England at the home of Laurence's parents, she gave birth to their daughter, Jane, in November 1935. Rumer's first novel, *Chinese Puzzle,* was published the same year. She discounted it as a false start: the book is certainly too mannered for today's taste but is an indication of her determination if not her talent.

Laurence returned to Calcutta, but it was almost a year before Rumer and Jane followed. At the time such separations were not unusual, and that year in Esher with Laurence's parents enabled Rumer to make contacts with the London publishing world which were to be important for her as a writer. Her second novel, *The Lady and the Unicorn,* published in 1936, shows her writing with sympathetic insight of the India she had known since childhood. Her story of a Eurasian family's dealings with Anglo-Indian society is not particularly well constructed, but the writing shows keen observation and a marked dislike of the less tolerant side of British India. Laurence was baffled by Rumer's choice of subject, as were most of their friends, and the book did not sell well. The couple's social life was becoming more difficult, too, because Rumer was flouting Calcutta's conventions.

---

[9] Godden, *A Time to Dance,* 97.

[10] Godden, *A House with Four Rooms,* 144, referring to an altercation with her second husband, James Haynes-Dixon.

In the summer of 1938 Rumer returned to England to await the birth of her second child at her parents' house in Cornwall. When she told her father she was writing a book about nuns, he advised her not to: no one would read it. On August 1, one month before the birth of her daughter Paula, she sent the manuscript to her agent. *Black Narcissus* was to prove an immediate best seller in both Britain and the United States. The story-line is simple: only with hindsight can the novel be read as a paradigm of the British experience in India. A group of British nuns start a convent, school, and clinic in Darjeeling, amid much skepticism from outsiders. Their idealism proves unequal to the realities of the situation, so they finally admit defeat and leave. Setting and character are deftly drawn; Sister Clodagh, apparently always in control but inwardly unsure of herself, may have more than a touch of Rumer in her. The only awkwardness comes from the handling of the Christian elements in the story, suggesting that the author was drawing more on memories from her schooldays than her own lived experience. The success of the book affected everything, including her marriage. She was, she says, "very happy."

War changed little at first. Rumer stayed in England with the children, writing and helping her parents, but Laurence, alone in Calcutta, urged her to return. In June 1940, with many misgivings, Rumer did return and settled down to a wartime routine which included writing on the veranda in the early morning and working as a volunteer in a hospital in the afternoon. Her life at this period could not be called happy, although she tried to make it so. The growing ambivalence of her feelings about Laurence and the sense of merely marking time as a writer colored everything. Then in 1941 came a crisis. Laurence had never been very successful as a stockbroker, but now his financial affairs became extremely involved. He left for military training without fully explaining the situation to Rumer, who found herself suddenly surrounded by exigent creditors. She paid them off, using the royalties from *Black Narcissus,* but relations between her and Laurence took a turn for the worse. There were to be happy times in the future, but they were to be increasingly interspersed with doubts and difficulties.

By January 1942 it was no longer wise to stay in Calcutta. Rumer and the children moved north to Kashmir, settling in Savitri Cottage, a small wooden chalet surrounded by orchards, an ideal refuge for a writer but not quite so ideal for a young mother with two children. It was here that Rumer's fourth pregnancy ended in a frightening miscarriage. She found solace in writing and in planning a move to an even more isolated spot, Dove House, where she intended to establish an herb farm. The beauty of Kashmir affected Rumer deeply, and some of her most powerful writing evokes the limpid clarity of the air and the almost menacing grandeur of the mountains. Here she hoped to find spiritual peace.

To help her straitened finances, Rumer decided to offer hospitality to a paying guest. Helen Arberry, a painter in need of rest among the cool Kashmiri hills, came to stay at Dove House in June 1944, but soon began to complain of pain and diarrhea. Rumer and the two children had also been having trouble, which Rumer put down to dysentery, common enough in India. But at lunch on June 23, Jane bit on a piece of glass. More glass was found in the food. Emergency treatment was given by the civil surgeon, which fortunately ensured that no one was killed, but the police became involved, and one of Rumer's servants was taken into police custody on suspicion of having tried to poison the family. Given the political situation, the possibility of reprisal by the local population was real; that seems to have worried Rumer as much as the suspected poisoning. In later years Rumer wrote and rewrote the episode in a way that makes it impossible to disentangle fact from fiction. What is indisputable is the fear the incident engendered, a fear that was to haunt Rumer for the rest of her life and possibly lies at the root of her ambivalence about India: fear of the treacherous servant. The decisions to leave Dove House and divorce Laurence coincided.

Return to England

Rumer went back to Calcutta and made a temporary home with Jon and her husband. The war was ending and it was clear once it was over that Independence would follow: the time had come to leave India. The return to England meant another temporary home with her parents. The Britain to which she returned was cold, everything was in short supply, there were no servants—and Rumer at this time was no cook. Fortunately, she had her writing. *The River,* a slightly fictionalized account of life at Narayangunj, was about to be published; a film version of *Black Narcissus* was under discussion; and London beckoned. In retrospect, she would say the year she spent in London was among the happiest in her life. The film version of *Black Narcissus* starred Deborah Kerr, David Farrar, and Jean Simmonds, and brought Rumer fame of a new kind; yet she was not completely happy with the film and remained moderate in its praise.

A New Course

The next few years saw Rumer's life taking new turns: in 1948 her divorce from Laurence was finalized and she moved to Buckinghamshire. Her output as a writer increased steadily. James Haynes-Dixon, a personable civil servant, who was also divorced and a good dancer, now began to play a major part in her life. Jean Renoir suggested turning *The River* into a film. For Rumer, the prospect of collaborating with another artist of the first rank was inviting, despite the practical difficulties posed by the fact that Renoir lived in Hollywood and she in Speen.

Autumn 1949 saw Rumer's marriage to James and her departure to Bengal for filming. James would wryly remark that Rumer had only accepted him because it solved the problem of what to do with Jane and Paula during the school holidays. But he was to provide Rumer with much affection and support, taking over the management of her financial affairs and generally doing his best to make life easier. After his death Rumer would exclaim how much he had loved her. About her feelings for him, she was always more reticent, yet the entry in her diary, "I do not want to be consoled—ever," is eloquent. Renoir and Rumer did not always see eye to eye over the way *The River* should be adapted for the screen, but the resultant film was critically acclaimed and hugely enjoyed by Renoir himself.

Back in England, Rumer struggled to adapt to a new routine which now involved James as a permanent addition to the household. She continued to write and write and write. She also continued to move frequently, an indulgence she was now better able to afford: White House Farm in Speen, with its small holding and dream of rural self-sufficiency, lasted a year; Pollards, not far away, where she tried to lay to rest the ghosts of Kashmir with her novel *Kingfishers Catch Fire,* was perhaps the happiest of all her homes. The next move was to Old Hall, Highgate, to be nearer to Jane while she trained at the Middlesex Hospital; then, when James retired in 1960, to Little Douce Grove in East Sussex. In 1956 Jane became a Roman Catholic; a year later her mother also converted. About this too, Rumer was reticent. Without access to her letters and diaries, it is dangerous to speculate on the reasons for her decision, but perhaps Catholicism's generous tolerance of preexisting religious forms and its happy acceptance of the material as a vehicle of the spiritual resonated with one brought up under Indian skies.[11]

In 1961, Rumer asked the Benedictine nuns of Stanbrook Abbey, Worcester, to pray for one of her family. Stanbrook is the oldest of the Benedictine houses for women in England, having been founded in 1623 by, among others, a direct descendant of St. Thomas More. Throughout its history the community has been characterized by a love of prayer, a love of learning, and an appreciation of human friendship. When Rumer and James asked to call at the monastery to give their thanks in person, they little realized the part Stanbrook was henceforth to play in Rumer's life.

---

[11] Gregory the Great warned Augustine, apostle of the English, not to tear down pagan shrines but to Christianize them. Similarly, Catholic ritual uses material things—candles, incense, water—as symbols of divine realities.

The then abbess, Dame Elizabeth Sumner, had the happy knack of suggesting just the right nun to meet a guest, in this case Dame Felicitas
Corrigan, herself a writer and musician of note. Rumer had admired the
Stanbrook Abbey Press's fine edition of Siegfried Sassoon's *The Path to
Peace,* which owed much to Dame Felicitas's friendship with the poet, and
thoroughly enjoyed the meeting. It was a chance remark of Dame Felicitas
that she wished someone would write a book about nuns as they really
were that led to one of Rumer's most popular books, *In This House of
Brede.* Before that came to pass, Rumer and James had the shock of seeing their lovely East Sussex home burn to the ground. The next move was
to Lamb House, Rye, where Henry James had once held court.

Rumer did her homework thoroughly for *In This House of Brede,*
spending five years on its writing. Brede is not Stanbrook, though much of
the book's detail is drawn from Stanbrook as it was in the early 1960s.
Rumer was at great pains to try to enter into the world of the enclosed nun,
a world which, as she had already discovered, did not imply a closed mind.
As an oblate, she tried to live according to the Benedictine Rule as far as
circumstances allowed, but this was largely a private matter of which there
are few records. In 1968 she sent the book to Dame Felicitas and on June
19 the abbess herself wrote, giving it her blessing: "[Dame Felicitas is]
happy about the book and thinks it first rate. This . . . does not surprise
me but it does please me very much." Of all the praise heaped upon the
book this, and Jon's unexpected but warm and generous tribute, "a stu-
pendous achievement . . . real, true, and authentic," probably pleased
Rumer most.

The novel works best on two levels: it can be read as pure entertain-
ment, or as an analysis of the spiritual growth of Philippa, the main protagonist, who has to come to terms with some very negative experiences
and emotions. Many have seen autobiographical touches in its pages. It
does indeed make surprisingly tough reading when one knows something
of Rumer's life, and perhaps the record of Philippa's gradual change of
heart echoes changes in Rumer's own. The novel achieved considerable
popular success, helped by a film version starring Diana Rigg, which came
out in 1975 (a film Rumer herself disliked intensely), but perhaps the most
telling measure of its impact was the flow of letters that continued long
after its publication.

Last Years

In the early 1970s Rumer became anxious about James's health. Another move occurred in an effort to provide him with more suitable accom-
modation, but in October 1973 he died. Rumer was stunned. For years he

had managed the business side of her life. As it became clear that for the last couple of years he had not been well enough to keep her affairs in order, her difficulties increased. She moved to Scotland, to be nearer her daughter Jane, but it was in no sense a retirement. No fewer than twenty-six books were still to come from her pen; there were to be two more visits to India, the second accompanied by a film crew making a documentary about her life. There was also to be tardy official acknowledgment of her achievement in the form of an O.B.E. (the Order of the British Empire, a middle-rank decoration awarded by Queen Elizabeth II), which many thought should have been a D.B.E. (Dame of the British Empire, a more distinguished honor).

Rumer's last visit to India drew together many currents in her life. Deeply painful memories were brought to the surface, and something of a healing seems to have taken place. She told Jane that if she died, her body was not to be brought home: an Indian cremation would suffice. In fact, she died in Dumfries on November 8, 1998, at the age of ninety-one. She left instructions for her funeral: a Requiem Mass, white flowers, good (emphasized) champagne afterward, and her ashes to be buried with those of James in Rye. Throughout those last years, Rumer's friendship with Stanbrook continued and deepened. She was generous to a fault, but after her death it was not only of her generosity that the nuns who knew her spoke, but of her spiritual quality, a quality so often hidden from view by her reticence and the outward circumstances of her life. Few, if any, can have known the details of her life as an oblate, yet it is not difficult to guess how attractive the honesty and tolerance of the Rule of St. Benedict was to one whose personal history had its share of mistakes and failures. Rumer was never conventionally "pious," but it was as a Benedictine oblate that she finally entered the room of the spirit and quietly closed the door behind her.

11

Edith Gurian, Oblate Peter

Mary Anthony Wagner, O.S.B.

Edith Gurian was an extraordinary woman, a Benedictine oblate—a woman ahead of her time. When I attended St. Mary's School of Theology at Notre Dame, Indiana, my oasis for sharing my Benedictine manner of life was at the home of an oblate of St. Benedict, who was intent and intensely adamant about being Benedictine. And that was before the now broad and scholarly degree programs in liturgical studies at the University of Notre Dame; it was still pre-Vatican time in the Church.

When I first met Edith Gurian on the campus of the University of Notre Dame, with warmth, congeniality, joyous and almost childlike openness, she approached me saying, "I'm Oblate Peter." It was clear that Edith found her identity and worth in being Benedictine. As the years went by during my graduate studies there, I found in her a friend, a kindred spirit with whom I shared similar interests and values, especially about prayer and the Church at that time.

Edith Schwarzer was born on December 19, 1897, in Breslau, Germany (now Poland), to Clara and Paul Schwarzer. She had one older brother, Gunther. After the usual education and Normal School, she taught the elementary grades in a country school. It was in Breslau that she met her future husband, Waldemar, at the Quickborn, which her daughter Joan described as a rather advanced youth organization.

Waldemar had been born in Russia in the then-capital city of St. Petersburg in 1902. They were married in 1926 and moved to Cologne, where Waldemar was completing a Ph.D. degree. Their daughter Joan (Johanna) was born that year. For a brief time, Waldemar supported his family as the Paris correspondent for a Cologne newspaper. Waldemar was a gifted Jewish convert who had lived in the czarist days in old Russia and then on the American home front on the Notre Dame campus. He authored many books, for which he was esteemed as an analyst and critic of literary and philosophic ability. His aim, in his own words, was "to understand Bolshevism as a historical phenomenon."[1] The conclusion he came to in his writings was that Marxism was burned out. Waldemar became internationally recognized.

After being warned by friends that he was not safe under the Nazi regime, Waldemar decided to move to Switzerland, telling Edith that they were going on a three-week vacation. When the train crossed the border, however, he told Edith that they would not be going back to Cologne. We, unfortunately, have no idea how Edith and their small daughter responded to this. While they lived quietly in the country outside Lucerne, Switzerland, Edith kept a vegetable garden and gathered kindling for winter fires. It was a hard life for her. Further, she was undoubtedly anxious about their safety.

In 1937 Waldemar was offered a position as associate professor of politics at the University of Notre Dame in South Bend, Indiana. Since his beginning offer assured him only of a one-year contract, Edith and Joan stayed behind until his position was more secure. They arrived in the United States on April 1, 1938, and settled in South Bend close to the university. Dr. Sylvester Theisen, who was also at Notre Dame at various times, remembered that Edith was very devoted to Waldemar, taking him wherever he needed to go, because he would not drive. Edith herself was a genuinely critical thinker. Surely she and Waldemar enjoyed each other's minds over the span of their thirty-year marriage.

After Waldemar died in 1954 (which I now realize was shortly before I became acquainted with Edith at Notre Dame), she sought employment at the university library. Because the faculty at Notre Dame at that time did not receive social security benefits, Edith worked to support herself. She worked there until her retirement around 1962. She loved the intellectual life, her association with scholars, and the regular contact she had with books. We do not know whether it was difficult for Edith to get along on what she earned at her position in the library, but it was very evident to me that she lived a simple, yet dignified lifestyle. She had coped most of her life, it appears, with what was needed for a livelihood.

When she took advantage of the summer school programs in liturgy which were just being initiated under the direction of Michael Mathis, C.S.C., she soon surrounded herself with a new circle of friends. These included Godfrey Diekmann, O.S.B., Emeric Lawrence, O.S.B., Henri

---

[1] Matthew Hoehn, *Catholic Authors, Contemporary Biographic Sketches, 1930–1947* (Newark, N.J.: St. Mary's Abbey, 1952) 299–300.

Nouwen, and others. In Benedictine fashion, her simple home was a place of hospitality where she welcomed her university friends and liturgists for informal gatherings.

It was chiefly through her contacts with Diekmann that she learned of St. John's Abbey, and came to yearn to participate in the Benedictine monastic life there in Collegeville, Minnesota. In August 1949, in the presence of Abbot Alcuin Deutsch, she committed herself to the monastic way of life "insofar as her way of life allowed,"[2] as an oblate of St. Benedict, assuming the name Oblate Peter.

She was the one thereafter who arranged the informal gatherings of all Benedictines at St. Mary's School of Theology or the University of Notre Dame on every July 11 to celebrate together the Solemnity of the feast of St. Benedict. I also recall sharing meetings with her and Diekmann—one time celebrating Eucharist in the firehouse on the Notre Dame campus. My favorite experience of sharing the rich liturgical life that Edith lived in her home was when she would arrive to separate me from my desk of books to celebrate Sunday Vespers and eat a simple evening meal with her. Surrounded by books, icons, and symbols that reflected her own spiritual, monastic way of life, it was the one place in South Bend where I felt at home. During these times her sense of playfulness was exhibited by her companionship with a cat which would at times interrupt our praying of the psalms by an obvious, audible stretch at our feet. I was intrigued by the manner in which this cat could move around on shelves, maneuvering between candles and icons without displacing or disturbing anything—except my thoughts at prayer. For me, those were relished experiences of my own monastic life, during a time when I was separated spatially from my monastic community in St. Joseph, Minnesota, for the purpose of graduate studies. Edith remained in South Bend until 1988, when she moved to Kensington, Maryland, a suburb of Washington, D.C., to be near her daughter. She died on July 19, 1989. She requested that her remains be given to the George Washington Medical School for use in their anatomy classes, in accord with her own common sense and generous spirit of giving. The ashes were returned to her daughter a year later. As she had wished, her remains were to be interred in the cemetery at St. John's Abbey.

My last contact with Edith was when her ashes arrived for burial at St. John's parish cemetery in Collegeville. Her daughter, Joan, had traveled with her mother's ashes, which had been placed in a box that was designed and arranged by her. I recall the box in which there was a plain gingham bag containing her ashes, her mother's wedding ring, and her

---

[2] The wording used in the ritual form for the Final Commitment of an oblate of St. Benedict.

treasured Benedictine medal which had identified her as Oblate Peter during her life. On the top of the box, Joan had put her mother's large enameled medallion of the medal of St. Benedict.

A group of monastics and other friends gathered around the grave near a tree, overlooking Lake Sagatagan, and celebrated a memorial burial service prepared by Michael Kwatera, o.s.b. Joan remembers that the prescribed narrow six-foot grave necessitated careful lowering of that small urn down that depth. She recalls how Abbot Jerome Theisen, o.s.b., then the abbot of St. John's Abbey, lay down flat on the earth, carefully guiding the urn as far as his arm could reach.

The stone marker at her grave was designed by Joseph O'Connell, the late local, renowned sculptor in Collegeville. This was only fitting, as it was Edith who had recommended to O'Connell that he move to St. John's Abbey/University in Collegeville at the time she met him in his Chicago art studio. Thus, in a very real sense, O'Connell's reputation as a renowned sculptor also reflects the love and interest that Edith had for beauty, for other people, and for St. John's Abbey in Collegeville.

Indicative of the inner spirit of Edith is the Prayer of St. Gertrude, which is on the reverse side of her memorial card:

> You loved me first, it is You who have chosen me, not I who have chosen You. You are the One who of His own accord runs toward His thirsting creature. Without You neither earth nor heaven could excite in me one hope, nor draw forth one desire; effect and perfect within me that union which You Yourself desire; may it be in the end, the crown and consummation of my being.

This prayer is representative of the genuine humility, faith, and total emptying out of the heart of Edith Gurian, Oblate Peter. Her ninety-two years of life were formed by her Christian living and her fidelity to the monastic way of life, learned from St. Benedict through his Rule and association with Benedictine monks and nuns.

Whenever I reflect on the life of Edith Gurian, I perceive her as a genuine icon of the Rule of St. Benedict. She was obviously a seeker of God, reflected in her life of prayer, in her humble dignity as a woman, in her gracious hospitality to others—especially to her Benedictine friends. Edith Gurian was truly a Benedictine oblate who learned to "run on the path of God's commandments, her heart overflowing with the inexpressible delight of love"[3] through patient sharing in the sufferings of Christ that she might also deserve to share in his kingdom.

---

[3] RB Prol 49-50.

I owe a debt of gratitude to Joan Gurian, who lovingly shared memories of her mother and her mother's life with me.[4]

[4] Joan Gurian lives in Garrett Park, Maryland. She is retired from her work at the Argonne National Laboratory in Chicago, Illinois, where she had been employed as the statistician. She is currently engaged in compiling and organizing the personal letters of her mother, to be given to the Alcuin Library at St. John's Abbey in Collegeville, where Waldemar's books are a part of the library collection.

12

Henry II: Monk-King[1]

Hugh Feiss, O.S.B.

Henry II, who with Frances of Rome is regarded as the patron of Benedictine oblates, was Duke of Bavaria, then King of Germany, King of Italy, and Roman Emperor. He was a devoutly religious man who felt great responsibility for the well being of both state and Church. To understand his significance as patron of oblates, it is necessary to understand his background and setting, his political program, his relations with bishops, his marriage to Kunigunda, and his lifelong ties with Benedictine monks.

The Historical Setting[2]

Carolingian Rule in the eastern part of the Empire ended with the succession of Conrad I (911–918). His successor, Henry I (919–936), the founder of the Saxon dynasty, worked to establish his control over the nobility; he sought the cooperation of the Church in his efforts. He established a palace chapel and gained the right to appoint bishops, except in

[1] Henry became Henry II when he assumed the royal crown in 1002. However, because so many of the persons who figure in his story were also named Henry, it seems best to refer to him as Henry II and to his father as Henry the Wrangler. The author wishes to thank Anna Minore for strenuous efforts to secure many of the sources upon which this study is based.

[2] For overviews of Germany and the papacy from Henry I to Otto III, see *The Church in the Age of Feudalism,* ed. Hubert Jedin and John Dolan (New York: Herder and Herder, 1969) 205–17; Eamon Duffy, *Saints and Sinners* (New Haven, Conn.: Yale University Press, 1997); Benjamin Arnold, *Medieval Germany, 500–1300* (Toronto: University of Toronto Press, 1997) 83–95, 133–40; Klaus Guth, *Die heiligen Heinrich und Kunigunde: Leben, Legende, Kult und Kunst* (Bamberg: St. Otto-Verlag, 1986) 11–18.

Bavaria. Henry acquired the Holy Lance in 935. Its supposed association with Constantine gave his rule an imperial aura.

The coronation of Otto I (936–973) at Aachen symbolized his relationship to Charlemagne. He carried the Holy Lance into battle with him when he defeated the Magyars at Lechfeld in 955. He continued his predecessors' policy of using the Church to strengthen his political control. He wished to conquer Italy and be crowned emperor. Otto's opportunity came when the youthful and unworthy Pope John XII appealed to him for military help. John XII crowned Otto emperor in Rome in 962. The next year Otto deposed him. To solidify his position, Otto had his son Otto II crowned emperor in 967.

Otto II died in 983 at the age of twenty-eight; he was succeeded by his three-year-old son and namesake, Otto III, who came of age in 994 and traveled to Rome in 996. Pope John XV died that year, and Otto had his own relative, Bruno of Carinthia, installed as Pope Gregory V (996–998). In 998 Otto III deposed a papal usurper, John XVI, John Philagathos, who was his godfather. Zealously religious, Otto III consulted with Odilo, Abbot of Cluny; the hermit St. Romuald; and Adalbert of Prague. Gerbert of Aurillac, Otto III's former teacher, became Pope Sylvester II in 999. Otto III sought to extend his imperial influence and that of the Roman church to Poland and Hungary. He sent emissaries to Kiev and appointed Bruno of Querfort archbishop in charge of missionary efforts to the East. Otto died suddenly at the age of twenty-two in 1102, after he and Pope Sylvester had been forced from Rome by an uprising of Roman nobility.

Henry II's Family and Upbringing

Henry I, known as "the Wrangler," had unsuccessfully challenged his cousin Otto II for the throne. When the attempt failed, Henry the Wrangler was deposed and imprisoned in Utrecht. Later he was reinstated as Duke of Bavaria.[3] Henry the Wrangler married Gisela of Burgundy around 972 and the future Henry II was probably born in 973. Whatever the year, the day was May 6. In later years, Henry II liked to celebrate his birthday. He arranged to have the new cathedral of Bamberg consecrated on May 6, 1012. Five years before to the day, he had made his first donations to the building of the church. Even in a necrology from Merseburg listing names of dead people to be prayed for, Henry is listed under his birthday.[4]

---

[3] Stefan Weinfurter, *Heinrich II (1002–1024): Herrscher am Ende der Zeiten* (Regensburg: Friedrich Pustet, 1999) 14–21; Karl Hausberger and Beno Hubensteiner, *Bayerische Kirchengeschichte* (Munich: Suddeutscher, 1985) 75–84.

[4] Gerald Beyreuth, "Heinrich II," *Deutsche Könige und Kaiser des Mittelalters,* ed. Engel, Evamaria, and Eberhard Holtz (Leipzig: Urania, 1989) 84–93.

Young Henry II's upbringing was entrusted first to Bishop Abraham of Freising, then to the Cathedral at Hildesheim (978–985). His parents may have intended for him to become a churchman, since at the time he had little hopes in the political world. At Hildesheim he received a good grounding in grammar and rhetoric, theology and Church law. When his father was restored to the Duchy of Bavaria in 985, Henry returned to Regensburg for further education. There he studied in an atmosphere permeated with the monastic reform movement connected with the monasteries of Gorze and St. Maximin of Trier. At Regensburg he came to know and love the celebration of the liturgy. He was there when Bishop Wolfgang (d. 994) appointed Ramwold (d. 1001) of St. Maximin as reform abbot of St. Emmeram and introduced reformed observance into several women's cloisters. The revitalization of monastic life in the tenth century sought to reverse the decline of monasteries which had occurred during the preceding century. Secularization by laylords, alienation of property, and the incursions of Normans, Saracens, and Huns had taken a heavy toll. The reforms emanating from Cluny, Gorze, Trier, and Regensburg esteemed a strict following of the Rule of St. Benedict, solemn celebration of the liturgy, and freedom for monastic communities to choose their own leaders without interference from local magnates.[5]

In a charter of 994, Henry II is designated as associate duke with his father. Henry the Wrangler had been consolidating his power over the nobility so that he had more effective control over his duchy than the king did over his kingdom. In August 995, Henry the Wrangler took sick and died suddenly at Gandersheim, where his sister was abbess. His son Henry II succeeded him as duke. According to an early source, young Henry II was in the bloom of manhood, energetic and intelligent like his father. The new duke immediately called a meeting at Regensburg. One of the main items of business was the reform of the monastery at Niederalteich. The duke summarily deposed the abbot and appointed the reformer Godehard, a close associate of Henry the Wrangler. At first Godehard opposed the move, saying that the dismissal and appointment were a high handed and arbitrary act by one who was supposed to uphold the law, but Henry went ahead with his plan.[6]

The Political Aims of Henry II

Henry II was on good terms with Emperor Otto III and seems to have traveled with him extensively in the period 998–1101. When Otto III died

---

[5] Hausberger and Hubensteiner, *Bayerische Kirchengeschichte,* 85–90.
[6] Weinfurter, *Heinrich II,* 22–35.

suddenly in January 1002, Henry II was not the most likely candidate to succeed him nor the one most favored by the close associates of Otto III. He did have the support of the Bavarian nobility with whom he shared ties of blood, political aims, and a desire for religious reform. Moreover, not long before that he had married Kunigunda, the daughter of Count Siegfried of Luxemburg, which brought him some additional support. Henry could also claim descent from King Henry I, who was his great-grandfather. He moved quickly to assume the imperial crown. Like a new Moses, he intended to bring God's laws to the people of the empire. After being crowned king on June 7, 1002, he immediately began a wide-ranging journey through his realm, seeking to solidify his position.[7]

Henry's kingdom embraced a vast area. It was ruled by dukes, under whom there were counts and other nobility. He had to act very astutely and subtly to maintain control over them. Ritual and stage management were among his most important tools in maintaining rank and order. Henry also sought to control and reform the Church. As the Lord's anointed, King Henry believed he was responsible for remedying the sins of both clergy and laity.[8]

The Rule of St. Benedict warns the abbot that he will be judged on how well he performed his duties and secured the well-being of the monks entrusted to him.[9] This sense of the ruler's responsibility weighed heavily on Henry II. He wished to be "powerful and clothed in authority, the guardian of church and realm, who enforced the divinely established order and fostered peace."[10] Henry's sense of responsibility for Church and realm was heightened by a vivid sense of the final judgment, which may have been fostered by the turn of the millennium.[11]

Henry II believed that he had a responsibility not only to enforce the law of the realm, but also to use his great power and wealth to help the poor. Thus, at the Synod of Dortmund (1005) he decreed that, when a bishop died, the cathedral chapter of the place was to provide food for three hundred poor people and a sum of money for alms. King Henry II

---

[7] Ibid., 36–58. For comparisons between Henry II's policies and those of his predecessor Otto III and his successor Konrad (1024–1039), see Bernd Schneidmüller and Stefan Weinfurter, eds., *Otto III.–Heinrich II. Eine Wende?* (Sigmaringen: Jan Thorbeke, 1999), and Hartmut Hoffmann, *Mönchskönig und rex idiota. Studien zur Kirchenpolitik Heinrichs II. und Konrads II.* MGH Studien und Texte, 8 (Hannover: Hahnsche, 1993).

[8] Weinfurter, *Heinrich II,* 59–75.

[9] *Rule of St. Benedict,* 2.6–9, 34, 37–40; 55.22; 63.3; 65.22. For these texts, see Timothy Fry, ed., *RB1980: The Rule of St. Benedict* (Collegeville: The Liturgical Press, 1981). See Weinfurter, *Heinrich II,* 82–5.

[10] Weinfurter, *Heinrich II,* 79.

[11] Ibid., 85–92.

and Queen Kunigunda pledged themselves to feed an equal number of poor people and to give fifty times as much in alms.[12]

The Emperor's Associates: Officials, Bishops, and Nobility

Henry II traveled frequently throughout his kingdom; his periodic presence in many different places made his rule immediate and personal. By visiting secular and religious magnates, he was able to attach them more closely to himself. At the same time he had a stable inner circle of officials and helpers, including chancellors, notaries, and chaplains led by the chief chaplain, Archbishop Willigis of Mainz. He selected as his chancellors trustworthy and well-connected clergymen, many of whom he later promoted to bishoprics. Of the sixty-four bishops Henry installed in office, at least twenty-four had been chaplains in the royal chapel.[13]

From the beginning of his kingship, Henry worked closely with his bishops, whom he saw as his colleagues in leading the Church. Although he was zealous to free religious institutions from the control of local nobility, he himself encroached on existing rights of clergy to elect their own bishops. The bishops he appointed were for the most part educated men of good judgment. He sought to regulate the lives of cathedral clergy according to the regulations passed at Aachen in 816. Henry II valued the prayers of monks and cathedral clergy living the common life ("canons") and often visited a cathedral or monastery before beginning a military campaign. Prayer confraternities knit the clergy of different churches together with each other and with the king. Henry met with some of his bishops frequently, and he celebrated the great feasts of the Church in their company.[14]

Henry II regarded revolt and disobedience to the king as an affront to God as well, and he could be harsh and unforgiving toward rebellious nobility. At the beginning of his reign, he was very severe toward those who opposed his becoming king. From the start he curtailed the powers of his successor in Bavaria; later he deposed him. Henry even dealt harshly with the relatives of Queen Kunigunda when they encroached on his prerogatives. He strictly enforced the laws against marriage within the permitted limits of consanguinity. Some of his advisors urged him to show more mercy. In 1008 Bishop Bruno of Querfort wrote him: "Oh that you were also merciful and would win your people to yourself and find their affection not always with greater force, but also with mercy."[15] Henry II's failure

---

[12] Guth, *Die heiligen Heinrich und Kunigunde,* 40.
[13] Weinfurter, *Heinrich II,* 110–26.
[14] Ibid., 127–67.
[15] Cited in ibid., 192.

to listen to such advice created tensions between him and his magnates, both secular and religious.[16]

The Politics of the Emperor: Poland, Burgundy, Italy

Whereas Otto III gave great emphasis to Italy, Henry II concentrated his attention on the German heartland of his empire. Nevertheless, he had to give a great deal of attention to Poland in the East, to Burgundy, and to Italy. In each area he was involved in conflicts which ended in compromises. Boleslav Chrobry (992–1025), a Christian who had concluded a treaty with Otto III at Gensen in 1000 A.D., had a more exalted sense of his own role and independence than Henry II allowed. When Boleslav had himself chosen Duke of Bohemia, Henry insisted that Boleslav recognize that he received the dukedom by the grace of the king and that he promise fealty. Boleslav refused, and war followed. Henry II allied himself with several pagan groups, while Boleslav had the support of some German nobility. At the final peace signed at Bautzen in 1018, Henry II was forced to compromise his claims of overlordship in Eastern Europe.[17]

Burgundy was ruled by the rather ineffective Rudolf III (993–1032). Henry II was Rudolf's nephew, and Robert II of France (996–1031) was for a time Rudolf's brother-in-law. The three leaders maneuvered for position and power, without greatly changing the political situation. Rudolf recognized Henry II's overlordship, and Henry II positioned himself to succeed Rudolf, should Rudolf die before he did. In a later meeting with Robert II, Henry II, discharging what he took to be his responsibility for the good order of Christendom, urged the French king to foster Church reform.[18]

When Otto III died, Arduin of Ivrea had himself crowned successor as king of Italy. After hearing appeals from Italy for help against Arduin, Henry II marched there early in 1004. At Pavia on May 14, Henry II was crowned king of Italy by the archbishop of Milan. The bishops were left to oppose Arduin on their own when Henry hurried back across the Alps. Some years later, in order to strengthen his claims against Arduin and to settle a contested papal election, Henry decided to return to Italy and be crowned emperor. He spent Christmastime 1013–1014 in Pavia, where he met with bishops and nobility, as well as with Abbots Odilo of Cluny and Hugh of Farfa. In Rome on February 14, 1014, Henry II and Kunigunda were crowned emperor and empress by Pope Benedict VIII. The pope gave him a golden globe symbolizing his universal rule. Afterward a synod was held in Rome, where Henry II

---

[16] Ibid., 186–205.

[17] Ibid., 206–20.

[18] Ibid., 220–6.

urged the Roman church to adopt the custom of singing the creed at Mass and to include the *filioque*. Henry II made a third journey to Italy in 1021–1022 to support Benedict VIII, who was hard pressed by opponents in Rome and by the Byzantines. In the course of this Italian campaign, Henry expelled the abbot of Monte Cassino who had Byzantine sympathies and replaced him with Theobald. Again Henry II returned abruptly to Germany; he was not much interested in actually ruling Italy.[19]

Henry and Kunigunda

Henry married Kunigunda between 995 and 1000, when they were both in their twenties. They remained devoted to each other ever afterward. She was crowned and anointed queen on August 10, 1002. Throughout her life she tried to be at her husband's side. When he was on campaign she looked after his interests; when he was with her they celebrated great feasts of the Church together.

The royal couple never had any children. Since Kunigunda bore no children, Henry, like other rulers of those times, might have tried to break his ties with her. He did not.[20] In 1007, on the occasion of the foundation of the diocese of Bamberg, Henry indicated that he had given up hope that he and Kunigunda would have children. Hence, he wished to give his goods to the new bishopric, and so return them to God.[21]

In one of eight charters (official documents) which he issued on behalf of the women's monastery of Kaufungen which Kunigunda founded in 1017, Henry wrote: "At the request of our beloved wife, the royal Empress Kunigunda, we who are two in one flesh. . . ." Another charter refers to Kunigunda as Henry's "tent-mate" *(contubernialis coniunx)*, a Latin phrase suggesting shared campaigns, shared dangers, and a shared bed. An illustration in a liturgical manuscript which Henry II had the monks of Reichenau prepare for the church of Bamberg portrays Kunigunda as Henry's equal. Some charters refer to her as co-reigning with Henry or sharing in ruling the kingdom.

[19] Ibid., 227–47. On Henry II's political aims see also Guth, *Die heiligen Heinrich und Kunigunde,* 22–7.

[20] Guth, *Die heiligen Heinrich und Kunigunde,* 52, quotes a comment from the Cluniac monk Ralph Glaber (ca. 1030 A.D.): "When he realized that he could not receive children from her, he did not therefore send her away, but instead bestowed on the church all the patrimony which had been destined for their children."

[21] The establishment of the diocese of Bamberg and the construction of the cathedral there were projects very dear to Henry II and Kunigunda. For detailed discussion see Ludwig Fischer, *Heinrich II. und der historische Ideenreichtum des Bamberger Doms* (Freiburg im Br.: Otto Kehrer, 1956); Weinfurter, *Heinrich II,* 150–68.

Wife, queen, and then empress, Kunigunda was the one closest to Henry II. The wording of many charters indicates that she had great influence over the king. Over 25 percent of Henry's surviving charters refer to her requests or intervention—almost always on behalf of religious institutions. When her husband was away, Kunigunda sometimes made important decisions on his behalf. She exercised special influence over affairs in Bavaria. After Henry's death, she retired to the monastery at Kaufungen, where she died on March 3, 1033. There she was buried, until her remains were moved to rest beside those of her husband in the church they founded at Bamberg.[22]

Henry II, Friend and Reformer of Monks[23]

Henry the Wrangler had urged the introduction of Benedict's Rule in the family monastery of Niedermünster in Regensburg. To further the cause of reform, Henry the Wrangler designated the monk Erchanbert from Einsiedeln to be abbot of Niederalteich. Henry II continued his father's efforts at monastic reform in Bavaria during the years he was duke (995–1002). As emperor, Henry II aimed to shape the monasteries of the realm, and of all Christendom, according to a comprehensive plan. Monasteries were pressured to abandon local customs and connections in favor of a more uniform internal discipline and to function as centers of economic, political, cultural, and religious stability in the realm.

A charter which he issued and perhaps composed in 1017 for the monastery of Abdinghof near Paderborn echoes a statement of Gregory the Great in praise of lives dedicated to contemplation. Another charter issued by Henry for Burtscheid in 1018 declares: "The discipline of cenobitic monks originated in the time of the apostolic preaching. The Acts of the Apostles says that 'the community of believers were of one heart and one soul.' Because we value their way of life so highly, we give them earthly goods, so that they may share heavenly goods with us."

Henry II's lifelong devotion to St. Benedict originated in his early childhood. Henry became acquainted with the Rule of St. Benedict at least by the time he studied with Bishop Wolfgang of Regensburg. Henry had great veneration for Abbot Ramwold of St. Emmeram's in Regensburg, a reform-minded abbot. When Ramwold was buried in June 1000, Henry II

---

[22] Weinfurter, *Heinrich II*, 93–109; Guth, *Die heiligen Heinrich und Kunigunde*, 19, 50–3.

[23] This section is based on Weinfurter, *Heinrich II*, 168–85; see also Hoffman, *Mönkskönig und rex idiota*, 27–38; Kassius Hallinger, *Gorze-Kluny*, Studia Anselmiana 22–3 (Rome: Herder, 1950) 153–4, 180–7, 217–25.

helped carry the bier.[24] In 1013 Henry asked Abbot Gerhard of Seeon (1004–1021) to produce a manuscript containing the Rule of St. Benedict and several other Latin rules. The manuscript went first to the cathedral in Bamberg, and from there to the monastery of Michelsberg in Bamberg. It is probable that in 1019 Henry II gave to the church of Basel an altar antependium which he had produced at and for a monastery. On it Christ stands in the middle. Henry II and Kunigunda appear as very small, humble figures at Christ's feet. At Christ's sides are the three archangels and St. Benedict.

Early in his reign as king, Henry II began altering the legal status of some monasteries. He decreed that a number of monasteries in Bavaria which had hitherto been subject to the duke were now subject directly to the crown (and in a vague way to the pope). This freed them from local magnates who might interfere in the inner life of the communities or impose superiors of their own choosing. Henry II also confirmed the rights, possessions, status, and immunities for many other monasteries. On numerous occasions, monasteries appealed for his help and protection in conflicts with nobility and bishops. With gifts and privileges Henry also sought to improve the economic stability of the monasteries. Smaller monasteries he put under the protection of bishops, in particular the bishop of the new diocese of Bamberg. In some cases, by putting these monasteries under bishops, Henry II was able to lessen the power of local nobility.

As head of the church in the kingdom, Henry II saw it his duty to see to it that the inner discipline of monasteries conformed to the Rule of St. Benedict. For this reason, he insisted on appointing many abbots. One such was Godehard, whom he named first as abbot of Niederalteich and then, in 1001, of Tegernsee. Godehard met fierce opposition there and returned to Niederalteich the next year. Later, when Godehard became bishop of Hildesheim (1022–1038), the abbey of Tegernsee was granted the right to free election, suggesting that by then it had assimilated the way of life desired by the king and so no longer needed to be so directly subject to royal control. Meanwhile, in 1005 Godehard was entrusted with the royal abbey of Hersfeld. The monks there were no longer living a common life. When Godehard tried to establish a more disciplined monastic life, the monks fled. Gradually, they came back and were joined by new members. Godehard also reestablished the monastery school. By 1012 the new order was solidly entrenched, and Godehard could return to Niederalteich and turn his reforming zeal elsewhere. He was succeeded at Hersfeld by his disciple Arnold. Another disciple, Sigimar, took on the direction of Kremsmünster. Other disciples spread the reform to Carinthia and Hungary.

[24] Hallinger, *Gorze-Kluny*, 88–9.

Godehard remained in close contact with Henry II. At Niederalteich he built a residence for the king to occupy during his visits there.

Henry II intervened in two other important monasteries: Stavelot-Malmédy and St. Maximin near Trier. He entrusted the restructuring of life in these two monasteries to Poppo, who had become a monk under Richard of St. Vanne (1004–1036), a confidante of Henry II. After successfully overcoming opposition in these two communities, Poppo went on to become the leading monastic reformer in the empire under Henry II's successor, Konrad II (1024–1039).

Henry II's far-reaching efforts at monastic reform brought him into contact with Abbot Odilo of Cluny. Already in 1003 Odilo received a charter from Henry II for the Cluniac monastery of Peterlingen. The abbot visited Henry II in 1004 and 1007 and personally attended Henry II's coronation in Rome in 1014. Henry II seems to have visited Cluny on his way home from his third campaign in Italy late in the summer of 1022. At that time Henry II gave Cluny many royal gifts. The monks of Cluny included Henry II in their prayer confraternity.

In June 1022, during the same campaign in Italy, Henry II visited Monte Cassino. He was very moved by this visit to the monastery founded by St. Benedict. He gave the monastery rich gifts and was included in their prayer confraternity. In a charter he issued for Monte Cassino, Henry II declared:

> Although we wish every day by our efforts to help promote all places where God is praised, we now seek in a singular or special way to support that place in which the body of our venerable father, the most holy St. Benedict, is venerated. For we have always had a special love for him from our earliest days. We have been strengthened in our reign by his devout intercession and mercifully relieved many times when we have been sick.[25]

Toward the end of his life, Henry II intensified his monastic connections. He was included in the prayers for the departed offered at Fruttuaria. The chronicle of Lorsch declared that Henry II had such a great love for religious life that he was called "The Father of Monks." That was certainly true. He could also be called "Brother of Monks" because of his esteem for monastic life and "Lord of Monks" for his efforts at monastic reform.

Henry and Kunigunda in Legend

Henry II's esteem for Benedictine monasticism led to several legends about his desire to be a monk. One says that when Henry II and Kunigunda

---

[25] Translated from the Latin text in Weinfurter, *Heinrich II,* 304, n. 6.

visited the renowned monastery of St. Vanne in Verdun, Henry, sensing that his death was near, pronounced monastic vows before the abbot. However, the abbot insisted the emperor must not abandon his secular responsibilities.

A group of legends tell of St. Benedict healing Henry II of an illness. Around 1075 Amatus of Monte Cassino elaborates on Henry's recovery from his illness at Monte Cassino in 1022. Amatus reports that St. Benedict appeared to Henry while he was asleep. The saint traced a cross with his abbot's crozier on the place where Henry's pain was concentrated. Benedict told him: "Wake up healthy and alert, because you will not be troubled by this weakness in the future." A few years later, the chronicler, Leo Marsicanus, altered the story somewhat. According to him, Benedict appeared to Henry when the latter was half-asleep and in great pain. He said: "I know that up to now you have had doubts as to whether I actually rest here. However, let this be a sign for you, so that you won't doubt any longer. As soon as you get up, you will pass three kidney stones. Then, you will not suffer from this illness any longer. I am Brother Benedict." Another version of the story appears in a life of Henry II written in 1145–1146. While the emperor was asleep, Benedict appeared to him with a dissecting knife in his hand. He made an incision on Henry's body, removed the stone, and closed the wound which immediately healed. Benedict put the stone in the emperor's hand, so he could tell the story to his followers in the morning.[26]

Although their private life is unknown to us, the tenor of some of Henry's charters suggests that theirs was a normal marriage.[27] Nevertheless, a powerful legend maintained that Henry and Kunigunda lived as brother and sister, voluntarily abstaining from sexual relationships. This legend helped explain their childlessness, which otherwise might have been regarded as a punishment from God. It also reflects and inculcates a high esteem for virginity. The first suggestion that Henry and Kunigunda's marriage did not involve sexual intercourse is a lament for the dead emperor which was probably written at the time of Henry II's death. It declares that "he renounced sensuality and lived continently." Another lament refers to Henry as a "virginal bridegroom." Leo Marsicanus said in the Montecassino chronicle (ca. 1100) that, among other virtues, Henry possessed that of chastity. Shortly before his death Henry II is said to have told Kunigunda's relatives: "Receive back your virgin, whom you gave to me." The chronicle of Prior Fruolf of Michelsberg, written about the same time in Bamberg, says that Henry II never cohabitated with Kunigunda,

---

[26] Ibid., 168–9.

[27] It is possible that after being married for some years they agreed to abstain from sexual relations.

but loved her like a sister.[28] A later legend maintained that Kunigunda's virginity had been proved in an ordeal in which she walked unharmed across red hot iron. A life of Kunigunda, written for her canonization about 1200, tells of her miracles and virtues. Later preachers emphasized Kunigunda's likeness to the Blessed Virgin Mary, primarily on the basis of her supposed virginal marriage. In the later Middle Ages, veneration of Kunigunda exceeded that of her husband.[29]

Canonization

In the canonization proceedings for the pious couple, legends were intermingled with evidence of their undoubted virtues. Henry and Kunigunda were a faithful and loving couple. They venerated the saints, in particular Peter, Stephen, Michael, George, and Maurice, saints whose names appear in the dedications in Bamberg. They lived in the company of many sainted individuals who helped them in their onerous tasks of ruling over a vast, diverse realm. Henry promoted a disciplined, culturally significant form of monastic life. He appointed many worthy men as bishops and abbots and insisted on piety, celibacy, and liturgical devotion among clergy and monks. In the last years of his life, Henry II and Kunigunda attended many dedications of churches. In 1021 alone they attended the dedications at Michelsberg in Bamberg, Quedlingburg, and Merseburg.

When Henry II died in Grona near Göttingen on July 13, 1024, his body was taken to be buried in the cathedral he had built in Bamberg. On the first anniversary of his death, Archbishop Aribo of Mainz consecrated the monastery church in Kaufungen. On that occasion, Kunigunda made profession as a Benedictine nun. Contemporaries attest to her life of prayer and service in the monastery. Henry II was canonized by Pope Eugene III (1145–1153) in 1146. By then relations between Church and state were vastly different from what they had been during Henry II's lifetime. In part because of him, a succession of able and saintly men had become bishops of Rome. They took the lead in seeking a more comprehensive freedom for the Church than was possible or conceivable in Henry's time. The role of the secular ruler in the Church had been restricted. Emperors could no longer appoint and depose bishops and abbots as Henry II had done.

Henry II was canonized nevertheless because he was remembered as a devout king who had benefited the Church. His generous gifts to churches, the miracles said to have occurred at his tomb, the urging of Konrad III (1138–1152), and the church of Bamberg promoted the process

[28] Weinfurter, *Heinrich II*, 93.
[29] Guth, *Die heiligen Heinrich und Kunigunde,* 74–80.

of canonization. Two legates from Rome investigated Henry's reputation and miracles. The bull of canonization emphasized Henry's simple, spiritually motivated life, his chastity, and his fidelity to his spouse.

Kunigunda's process took longer. Her canonization was supported by the German kings and by the church of Bamberg. Celestine III (1191–1198) appointed three bishops and three Cistercian abbots to investigate her life, holiness, and miracles. About 1200 a cleric in Bamberg wrote her life, and the church of Bamberg renewed its campaign with Innocent III (1198–1216). She was declared a saint on March 29, 1200. She was praised for her virtues and her posthumous miracles.

Henry II, Patron of Oblates

Henry II lived long before there were oblates like those which exist today. At his time, monasteries were religious, cultural, and economic centers, with large extended families which included not only monks, but employees, serfs, retirees, friends, patrons, and the dead for whom the monks had promised to pray. Henry II was associated with many monastic families for many different reasons. Some abbots he had appointed; others were his advisers. He was instrumental in reforming many monasteries; he gave generously to many more. He was student, lord, father, and brother to monks and nuns throughout the empire, but especially in Bavaria.

His childless marriage was something of a scandal to his contemporaries. Because he had no heir, the inheritance which he had struggled to obtain in 1002 would go to others. Faced with that prospect, Henry II gave much of it to the Church. After his death, legend depicted Henry II in monastic terms: his was a virginal marriage, he made profession at Stavelot-Malmédy, he was cured by St. Benedict at Monte Cassino. In fact, Henry's greatest significance for oblates at the beginning of the twenty-first century is that he was a married layman who tried to live in his busy secular life the Christian faith he shared with his monastic teachers, collaborators, and brothers. He declared that he and Kunigunda were two in one flesh. They were also two in one spirit, and to a large extent that spirit was shaped by the Rule of St. Benedict. Henry and Kunigunda remained true to each other in the midst of separation and disappointment. They were lovers, friends, and collaborators in an extremely arduous task. Kunigunda could rightly join her husband as patron of oblates.

Henry II had a very strong sense of vocation. As successor to Moses and Charlemagne, he felt responsible for the well-being of Christendom, both within and beyond the borders of his kingdom and empire. He also had a strong sense of order and discipline. When monks didn't live as he thought the Rule required, when people violated the rules of the Church regarding marriage, when churchmen or nobility disobeyed God's anointed king, he felt obliged to intervene on the side of order. In part, his wide ranging authority and control were required by the centrifugal forces at work in the multicultural empire; in part, they were required to maintain order, justice, and peace among quarreling factions or institutions;[30] in part, they were a manifestation of his own personality. In retrospect, one may fault him for being too interfering, too controlling, too quick to reject local custom and tradition. Even if in hindsight such criticisms are justified, one cannot fault Henry II's sincerity, his genuine love for his people, for the Church, and for God. He was not perfect; no saint is.

When Henry II was crowned emperor in Rome in 1014, Pope Benedict VIII presented him with a gold sphere, a symbol of his far-reaching imperial authority. Later, Henry II gave the sphere to the monastery of Cluny. The sphere was encrusted with jewels and surmounted by a cross. The jeweled sphere marked with a cross suggests the suffering which imperial responsibility brought to Henry II and Kunigunda. In his acceptance of sphere and cross and his virtuous exercise of secular responsibility Henry is a model for oblates.[31]

Henry II lived at a time of great change. Europe was taking the first steps toward the renaissance and reformation of the twelfth century. The Church was gaining new vigor. In his active involvement in this renewal process, Henry II is again a model for oblates at the turn of another new millennium when change is occurring rapidly in society and in the Church which Henry II and Kunigunda loved so dearly.

---

[30] Ibid., 48–50.
[31] Weinfurter, *Heinrich II,* 98 and 136.

13

On the Road to Emmaus: The Spiritual Journey of Joris-Karl Huysmans

George C. Tunstall

Joris-Karl Huysmans is generally acknowledged in French literary histories as the leading writer of the literature of Decadence. This is based primarily upon his most famous novel, *A Rebours,* which appeared in 1884 and brought him almost immediate international recognition and notoriety.[1] But this is actually only one side of Huysmans' significance as a writer. He also played an important role in what is called the Catholic Revival in France during the late nineteenth century.[2] In addition to his purely literary talent, Huysmans was a perceptive and talented art critic. He was, in fact, one of the first critics to recognize and defend the artistic merit of the Impressionists, who were just beginning to produce their atmospheric "open air" works during the 1880s. He was also one of the first to call attention to the symbolic paintings of Gustave Moreau and Odilon Redon. In the area of French letters he championed the cause of the upcoming symbolist writers: Verlaine, Rimbaud, and Mallarmé. In brief, Huysmans was a very perceptive and articulate observer of French, especially Parisian, life and culture, both in his literary and critical works themselves, as well as in his voluminous correspondence with personal friends and important figures of his time.

As the title indicates, the present essay will focus on Huysmans' search for deeper meaning in life, as reflected especially in his Catholic

[1] See, for example, Jefferson Humphries' contribution for the year 1884, "Joris-Karl Huysmans Publishes His Novel *A rebours: Decadence,*" *A New History of French Literature,* ed. Denis Hollier (Cambridge, Mass., and London: Harvard University Press, 1989) 785–8.

[2] In this regard see Richard Griffiths, *The Reactionary Revolution: The Catholic Revival in French Literature 1870–1914* (London: Constable, 1966). The references to Huysmans in the text take up an entire column of the index (384–5).

novels. It will focus first on the writer's inner struggle and change in the late 1880s, a time during which he began to consider and question in what direction his life was heading, and then on how the Catholic faith influenced and eventually reshaped his life. Of special interest will be the path Huysmans followed in becoming a Benedictine oblate and what exactly was entailed in being an oblate in France at the end of the nineteenth century. First, however, some biographical and literary information will be necessary in order to set the stage for this study.

Biographical and Literary History

Huysmans was born in Paris on February 5, 1848.[3] Whereas his mother was from the Paris area, his father was a first-generation immigrant from Flanders whose family derived from a long line of famous painters that dated back to at least the seventeenth century. During the summers of his childhood the family went back to Flanders to visit relatives. While in Flanders, Huysmans' grandmother occasionally took him on day-long outings to visit several relatives who were cloistered nuns; such trips left an indelible impression on the writer. When Huysmans' father died suddenly in June 1856, his mother was forced to take a job and to move back into her parents' apartment, which was originally part of a Premonstratensian monastery. This apartment later became Huysmans' own home, the one in which he wrote most of his works. In 1857 his mother remarried; her new husband was a Protestant who purchased the bookbinding firm that was located on the first floor of the house in which the Huysmans family lived. One of Huysmans' early novels is set in this business that he later inherited and kept going.

After passing the examination for the baccalaureate in 1866, Huysmans began a thirty-two-year career in the Ministry of the Interior, where his maternal grandfather had previously worked. A year after his retirement from government service in 1898, Huysmans moved to a house that he had had built for himself in Ligugé, near Saint-Martin Abbey, a Benedictine monastery. There he began his novitiate as a Benedictine oblate in March of

---

[3] For further information on Huysmans' life see Robert Baldick's detailed biography, *The Life of J.-K. Huysmans* (London: Clarendon Press, 1955); Brian Banks, *The Image of Huysmans,* AMS Studies in the Nineteenth Century 7 (New York: AMS Press, 1990); or George Ross Ridge, *Joris-Karl Huysmans,* Twayne's World Author Series 31 (New York: Twayne Publishers, 1968). Less reliable is James Laver, *The First Decadent: Being the Strange Life of J. K. Huysmans* (New York: Citadel Press, 1955). Indispensable for bibliographical work is G. A. Cevasco's *J.-K. Huysmans: A Reference Guide* (Boston: G. K. Hall & Co., 1980), which offers an annotated bibliography of Huysmans' works, their translations, and the secondary literature in English on the author from 1880 to 1978.

1900; a year later he took his final oblation. This period of his life ended abruptly, however, in October of that same year when the monks abandoned their abbey in Ligugé as a result of the Law on Associations. Huysmans returned to Paris where he lived in a Benedictine convent before being forced to move elsewhere because of his deteriorating health. He died on March 12, 1907, after horrendous suffering due to cancer of the jaw and mouth, probably precipitated by decades of smoking cigarettes.

Huysmans began his literary career as a disciple of Émile Zola, the major protagonist of naturalism in the latter half of the nineteenth century. This was the starkest form of realism that focused on minute details of pragmatic reality in the attempt to offer an almost photographic reproduction of the outside world. The world outlook of naturalism was informed by the two basic principles of positivism: biological heritage and social ambiance. The literature of this movement focused on what was considered new material for literary portrayal: the sordid, disgusting, sometimes revolting aspects of life, usually related to the social upheavals wrought by the rampant industrialization of the period. Such subjects as prostitution, venereal disease, various types of addiction, etc., which had previously been taboo in respectable literature, now became accepted topics of the day.

Huysmans' Early Novels

Huysmans' early novel, *Marthe*,[4] about the life of a prostitute, is characteristic of this phase in his writing. His outlook at this point is summed up in a statement from the foreword to the work: "I write what I see, what I feel, and what I have lived through, the best I can, and that is all there is to it. This explanation is not an excuse; it is, simply, a statement of the end which I pursue in art" (reprinted in *Down Stream*).[5] These words already point to the fact that Huysmans' novels are strongly autobiographical in character.

Huysmans soon became frustrated with the limitations of this form of realism and began to seek other means of literary expression. It was at this point that he wrote *A Rebours*.[6] The main character in the novel, Des Esseintes, retreats from Paris into his singularly equipped chateau in

[4] Originally published under the title *Marthe, histoire d'une fille* (Brussels: Gay, 1876). Trans. Robert Baldick (London: Fortune Press, 1958).

[5] Joris-Karl Huysmans, *Down Stream (A vau-l'eau) and Other Works*, trans. Samuel Putnam (New York: Howard Fertig, 1975) 4.

[6] Joris-Karl Huysmans, *A Rebours* (Paris: Charpentier, 1884). There are two English translations of this work: *Against the Grain (A Rebours)*, intro. by Havelock Ellis (New York: Illustrated Editions, 1931); and *Against Nature*, trans. Robert Baldick (Baltimore: Penguin Books, 1959).

Fontenay, where he seeks refuge from a reality that he despises and that makes him physically ill. In this chateau Des Esseintes indulges all of the over-developed senses that were so negatively stimulated in the real world in an attempt to overcome the profound ennui that has apparently always plagued him. The visual, acoustical, olfactory, and gustatory senses are investigated in great detail in separate chapters of the work, each with its own bizarre distortion of reality into an instrument of tortured delight. But this overindulgence leads to a worsening of his physical and psychological condition that eventually necessitates his leaving this haven and returning to the urban reality from which he had originally fled. European avant-garde writers recognized immediately in Huysmans' novel a poignant expression of the *fin-de-siècle* mood that was beginning to pervade these last two decades of the nineteenth century.

Huysmans' next work, entitled *Là-Bas*,[7] is a study of Satanism and sadism, which, according to Terry Hale in his introduction to *The Oblate of St. Benedict,* is "generally considered the definitive account of *fin-de-siècle* Satanism."[8] It is narrated from the viewpoint of the character Durtal, who is quite obviously a persona for Huysmans himself. The narrative is made up of three different strands that intertwine but never really become completely integrated into each other. The first deals with Durtal's research into the figure of Gilles de Rais, the fifteenth-century Bluebeard, whose incredible sexual perversion and sadism attracted the narrator's attention; the second portrays the Satanism that fascinated a certain element of French society at the time and that finds its culmination in the description of a Black Mass near the end of the novel; the third thread throughout the work has to do with a certain Madame Chantelouve, who exerts diabolical sexual control over Durtal.

What is especially significant about *Là-Bas* is that in the novel Durtal begins to sense a deep-seated need for faith in order to make his life worth living. This is in fact a theme that has recurred in almost all of Huysmans' works prior to this one: the feeling that something was missing in the lives of his characters (and indeed in his own) that would have given their existence (as well as his own) a deeper meaning and focus. In the last chapter of *Down Stream,* for example, the main character Folantin receives notification that his Aunt Ursule, a cloistered nun, has passed away. This transports him into a reverie, in which "He envied her calm and silent life, and he regretted the faith which he had lost";[9] he understands

---

[7] Joris-Karl Huysmans, *Là-Bas* (Paris: Tresse & Stock, 1895). English translation: *Là-Bas (Down There)* (Langford Lodge: Dedalus Ltd., 1992).

[8] Joris-Karl Huysmans, *The Oblate,* trans. Edward Perceval (Langford Lodge: Dedalus Ltd., 1996) v.

[9] Huysmans, *Down Stream,* 178–9.

that "religion alone might heal the wound that is dragging [him] down."[10]
But then in the next breath he rejects the idea again in these words: "Good
heavens! it was paying dearly for the improbable happiness of a future life,
he thought. The convent appeared to him a house of detention, a place of
desolation and of terror: 'Ah, well, none of that! I don't envy the fate of
Aunt Ursule, any more.'"[11]

Apparently for some time now Huysmans had nevertheless felt a call
to return to the Catholic Church, but he somehow did not feel that he was
ready for it; he also seemed to doubt that he might ever be able to take that
step. Durtal experiences this phenomenon of attraction to—but simultane-
ous rejection of—the Church through a good portion of the novel to follow.

The Catholic Trilogy

Curiously enough, it is this same—and yet a transformed—Durtal
who is the central figure in the next three novels, the so-called Catholic
trilogy. Between *Là-Bas* and the next novel, *En Route,* Durtal/Huysmans
has gone through what is generally referred to as his conversion. Something had occurred within him; his direction in life turned from the former
path of carnal lust and indulgence to a search for redemption for his sins
and the desire for purification of his being. The change that occurred in
Huysmans himself between the writing of *Là-Bas* and that of *En Route* is
what forms the content of the latter work.[12] *En Route*[13] is divided into two
parts. In the first part of the novel Durtal encounters someone with whom
he can discuss his concerns, a certain Abbé Gévresin, who becomes Durtal's spiritual mentor and eventually convinces him to make a retreat at a
Trappist monastery, at which the Abbé himself has spent some time.

---

[10] Ibid., 179.

[11] Ibid., 179–80.

[12] In his letters from the period between 1891 and 1895 Huysmans mentions on a number of occasions the contrast between these diametrically opposed works; for example, in a
letter to Jules Huret from January 1, 1895, Huysmans writes: "As for the book itself [*En
Route*], it is, in some sense, the counterpart of *Là-Bas*. Having done Satanism, black mysticism, I am now venturing into divine mysticism, white mysticism" (as translated in *The
Road from Decadence, From Brothel to Cloister: Selected Letters of J. K. Huysmans,* ed.
and trans. Barbara Beaumont [Columbus: Ohio University Press, 1989] 142). He goes on
to explain the nature of *En Route* in these terms: "The plot of the novel is of the simplest;
I have re-used the main character of *Là-Bas*, Durtal, whom I have undergo a conversion and
send off to a Trappist monastery; in him, I have tried to note the episodes of a soul startled
by grace" (ibid., 142–3).

[13] Joris-Karl Huysmans, *En Route* (Paris: Tresse & Stock, 1895). ET: trans. C. Kegan
Paul (New York: Howard Fertig, 1976).

The mere thought of spending a week in such a monastery frightens Durtal terribly; he immediately comes up with all kinds of excuses to avoid having to put himself to the test in this way. He begins by telling his spiritual mentor that he does not know whether his precarious health could stand such rigors. In addition to that consideration, the matters of confession and Holy Communion concern him deeply. The abbé does not relent, and Durtal knows in his heart that he must now take this step, whether he wants to or not. He finally consents, and Abbé Gévresin makes the necessary arrangements. On the evening before his departure Durtal muses to himself: "I should have considered anyone mad, who, a few years ago, had prophesied that I should take refuge in a Trappist monastery; yet now I am going there of my own accord, and yet no, I am going driven by an unknown power, I am going as a whipped cur."[14] The first part closes with Durtal preparing for his departure to the monastery.

The second part of *En Route* depicts Durtal's experiences among the Trappists and his eventual conversion. As this part of the novel opens, Durtal arrives at La Trappe de l'Atre monastery, where he is warmly received and discovers that many of his fears were unwarranted. From the very beginning he feels comfortable with the housemaster, Fr. Etienne, who explains the modified rules that he, as a retreatant, must follow. Fr. Etienne introduces him to a Mr. Bruno, whom the housemaster has described beforehand to Durtal in these terms: "M[r]. Bruno is a person who has renounced the world, and, without having taken the vows, lives enclosed. He is what our rule calls an oblate, he is a holy and learned man, whom you will certainly like; you can talk with him during the meal."[15] Over dinner Durtal inquires of Mr. Bruno what being a Trappist oblate entails. Mr. Bruno describes the life of a Trappist oblate in this way: "His life is less austere, and more contemplative than that of a monk; he may travel if he will, and though he is not bound by vows, he shares in all the spiritual advantages of the order."[16] Previously the order had admitted what were called "familiars" (from Latin *familiares,* which means belonging to the family or household); they were oblates who wore a distinctive habit and took the three greater vows. They led the mitigated life of a person who is half layman and half monk. Mr. Bruno explains further that these oblates are still accepted among the true Benedictines, but no longer among the Trappists.

After the pleasant dinner with Mr. Bruno, Durtal experiences his first compline in this monastic community. After a bit of difficulty in becom-

[14] Ibid., 146.
[15] Ibid., 159.
[16] Ibid., 161.

ing oriented in the service, it ends with the "Salve Regina," which literally overwhelms Durtal. In the expanse of the eleven lines of this magnificent Latin hymn, sung in the plainchant so beloved by Durtal, the realm of divine grace has opened fully to the character in all its glory and consolation. The text of this passage in the novel[17] moves quickly—and almost imperceptibly to the reader—from an objective portrayal of what Durtal actually saw and heard to the inner realm of the soul in which the words in their musical embodiment conjure up certain moods and impressions, shaped by even more deeply-seated emotions, before returning abruptly to the external reality from which they momentarily have offered escape. He has experienced what is called in mystical language an *unio mystica,* or mystical union with the Divine.

The two epithets with which this passage ends, "sick and dazzled," reveal the current state of Durtal's soul: he has been dazzled from the beginning by the beauty of the Church and the art, music, and architecture to which it has given rise. He understands it perhaps better than most Catholics themselves, but he is moved to tears because of the deplorable state of his soul that is so completely tainted with sin that he is driven almost to despair. In the later chapters of this second part he is again sought out by sensual desires, experiences anxiety attacks engendered by them, and learns gradually how to combat them through prayer. By the time his stay at the monastery is over, he is a new man. It is with deep regret and gratitude that he leaves Notre Dame de l'Atre to return home to Paris.

Second Novel in the Catholic Trilogy

In the second novel of the trilogy, *The Cathedral* (1898),[18] Abbé Gévresin is preparing to leave for Chartres, where he will become canon as a favor to the new bishop, who is one of his oldest friends. He suggests that Durtal follow him there, which, after some initial hesitation, the latter agrees to do. There is also a new character who plays an important role in this novel, Mme. Bavoil, the abbé's housekeeper. She too was instrumental in convincing Durtal that he ought to move to Chartres.

In Chartres Durtal falls in love with the cathedral and begins to look into its past. What appeals to him especially is the fact that this magnificent cathedral represents a blend of the Gothic and Romanesque types of medieval architecture. Durtal is convinced that the older form, the Romanesque, represents allegorically the Old Testament, whereas the newer,

[17] Ibid., 165–7.
[18] Joris-Karl Huysmans, *La Cathèdrale* (Paris: Stock, 1898). Trans. Clara Bell (Langford Lodge: Dedalus Ltd., 1989).

or Gothic, is an allegorical representation of the New Testament.[19] He begins detailed studies into the architecture, liturgy, music, art, and symbolism of the medieval Church and especially into the cathedral at Chartres that then form the major part of this novel. He is aided in his endeavor by one of the priests in Chartres, the Abbé Plomb, who fills Durtal in on many of the detailed symbolic forms manifest in the cathedral.

The next stage in Durtal's spiritual journey forms the framework within which the studies of symbolism are presented, and so it is not surprising to find such words as "journey," "road," "path," "way," and "track" occurring frequently in the text. Whereas in *En Route* Durtal's spiritual mentor maneuvered him into the retreat in La Trappe which finally brought the long-sought-after purification of the character's soul, in *The Cathedral* Abbé Gévresin suggests that Durtal may have a calling to monastic life. Although Durtal has himself felt this draw in the past, he finds it difficult to come to any decision. Upon weighing the possibility of such a step, a number of things bother him. Foremost among these is the fear that he might thereby lose his freedom as an artist. By taking vows he would in effect be putting his will at the control of his abbot, who would have the power to require him to serve the monastery through some other means, if he wished. Even if he were allowed to write, everything he wrote would have to pass the muster of the prior, who might have no understanding of art.

Viewed from this perspective, the cloister can easily appear to be a type of incarceration, as Durtal muses: "The cloister! He must reflect a long time before making up his mind to imprison himself"; and a bit later: "It is imprisonment for life, with no mitigation of the penalty, no pardon and release."[20] On the other hand, though, he can also see the bright side: "A convent! Why, it was the only logical existence, the only right life! All these fears he suggested to himself were imaginary."[21] Caught in a quandary, he can find no final resolution. He prays long and hard, asking God for some sign concerning the route that he should take, but without response.

During the course of the novel there was, however, another way mentioned, a *via media* or "middle way," so to speak: *becoming an oblate.* Durtal inquires of Abbé Plomb concerning this possibility and how much freedom—or lack of it—is entailed in the life of an oblate, to which the abbé replies: "I can tell you this much: that in some other Benedictine Houses [than Solesmes] that I have visited the general system is that the oblate shall follow as much of the rule [of St. Benedict] as he is able for."[22]

[19] Ibid., 43.
[20] Ibid., 238.
[21] Ibid., 240.
[22] Ibid., 188.

When Durtal asks further specifically concerning the freedom to come and go at will, Abbé Plomb answers: "When once he has taken the oath of obedience to his Superior, and, after his term of probation, has adopted the monastic habit, he is as much a monk as the rest, and consequently can do nothing without the Father Superior's leave," to which Durtal mutters: "The deuce! Of course, if the ridiculous metaphor so familiar to the world were accurate, if the cloister were rightly compared to a tomb, the condition of the oblate would also be tomb-like, only its walls would be less airtight, and the stone, a little tilted, would admit a ray of daylight."[23] No, he is not yet ready for this way either.

Close to the end of the novel Abbé Plomb mentions to Durtal during a conversation that takes place in the presence of Abbé Gévresin and Mme. Bavoil, "I am going to Solesmes again a week hence, and I told the Reverend Father Abbot that I should take you [Durtal] with me."[24] Realizing that in this way his hand is being forced, Durtal at first says no, but then "by a nod signified acquiescence in the wish of all his friends."[25] As Durtal prepares to depart Chartres, Mme. Bavoil kisses him "affectionately, maternally" and says: "We will pray with all our might, our friend, that God may enlighten you and show you your path, may lead you Himself into the way you ought to go."[26]

Third Novel in the Catholic Trilogy

At the beginning of the third novel, *The Oblate of St. Benedict* (1903),[27] Durtal has already been living for eighteen months in Val-des-Saintes, not far from Dijon (in Huysmans' actual life he settles at Ligugé near Poitiers), where he is about to make his first oblation. When Abbé Gévresin dies suddenly back in Chartres, Durtal invites Mme. Bavoil to move to Val-des-Saintes to become his housekeeper and friend, which she eventually does. This novel will be of special interest to any oblate, because it contains a wealth of information both on the Benedictine Order and on the history and customs of the oblate from the medieval period until the end of the nineteenth century. Chapter six, for example, is devoted almost exclusively to a summation of Durtal's research into the history of the oblates from the eighth century forward. Durtal's first and final oblations are described in great detail, even down to the Latin text used in

[23] Ibid. 188–9
[24] Ibid., 306.
[25] Ibid., 308.
[26] Ibid., 338.
[27] Joris-Karl Huysmans, *L'Oblat* (Paris: Stock, 1903).

both ceremonies. The novel also reflects the essence of monastic life and spirituality in general at the end of that century.

Perhaps one of the best descriptions of what being an oblate entails is found in Dom Felletin's explanation to Durtal before he takes his final oblation:

> First of all . . . we must resign ourselves to the conviction that the oblate-hood of St. Benedict will never become widely popular; it will never appeal save to a chosen few; indeed, it requires so much of candidates that is diffi-cult to fulfil [*sic*]. The sole reason for its existence is the Liturgy; the life of a monk is the praise of God; the life of an oblate will also be the praise of God, reduced, however, to as much as he can give; to be a true oblate it is not enough to perform one's duties faithfully and communicate more or less frequently; one must also have a taste for the Liturgy, a love of ritual and of the symbolical; an admiration for religious art and for beautiful Services.[28]

Dom Felletin goes on to point out further that oblatehood is different from the other so-called Third Orders, into which anyone may be taken, in that the standards for oblates are higher: "We, on the contrary, aim at quality, not at quantity; we want scholars, men of letters and artists; persons who are not exclusively devotees."[29] He finally concludes: "Hence, to sum up: oblates should receive from the monastery spiritual direction, and the helps incidental to monastic life, but as regards all the rest they should be entirely free."[30]

This declaration fits Durtal's outlook completely. He would like to see groups of oblates gathered around their respective monasteries, adding through their individual talents to the quality of the whole monastic unit, much as was the case during the Middle Ages. Because of the political situation at the time, however, this was, unfortunately, not possible. Dis-couraged by the turn of events that cause the Benedictines to flee France rather than subject themselves to the anti-clerical regime in power, Durtal leaves the site of his beloved monastery and returns to Paris. And so the Catholic trilogy concludes.

Conclusion

There are two concepts which are of paramount importance for Huysmans' career as a writer and for his personal life. The first of these is the idea of "spiritual naturalism," which he discusses in detail at the begin-

---

[28] Ibid., 168.
[29] Ibid., 169.
[30] Ibid., 170.

ning of the first Durtal novel, *Là-Bas,* and which indicates that he has left the fold of writers who flocked to Zola's naturalism because it signals that Huysmans is searching for something the existence of which that group strictly denied: the transcendent. Durtal/Huysmans finally realizes that there is only one thing on this earth that can satisfy the deep-seated need that he senses in his soul, and that is the divine as it is manifested in Roman Catholicism, the power of which unified and shaped the European Middle Ages that are so dear to this writer and his literary persona.

The second concept is that of mystical substitution which comes up in a number of important passages in the Catholic trilogy. Huysmans' abiding love and respect for the saints of the Church and the legends surrounding them gave rise in him to an unusually strong belief in martyrdom and the ability of the individual to suffer in expiation for the sins of others. His belief along these lines was focused on the figure of Christ and those early believers inspired by his sacrifice. When Huysmans' protracted period of suffering came, as the cancer in his mouth and throat developed and spread and he underwent multiple operations to try to alleviate the excruciating pain that accompanied this affliction, it meant for him an opportunity to atone through his suffering for the sins of his earlier life. And so, to the amazement of his close friends, he was able to suffer through this terrible ordeal with an inner peace and acceptance that they found difficult to comprehend. In his journey of faith Huysmans had traversed territories of life that stretched from the depravity of sexual indulgence and Satanism in his earlier years to the transfigured life of a true believer and oblate of St. Benedict.

14

Emerson Hynes: A Vocation to Conversation

Owen Lindblad, o.s.b.

"Is there anyone here who yearns for life and desires to see good days?" God called out to the multitude of people. Emerson Hynes, a student at St. John's University, Collegeville, Minnesota, raised his voice and answered joyfully, "I do!" God said, "Keep your tongue free from vicious talk and your lips from all deceit; turn away from evil and do good; let peace be your quest and aim" (*RB* Prol. 15–17).

With these words, the Rule of St. Benedict captured the enthusiasm and idealism of a young man destined to live out in written and spoken words of peace the precepts of the master in a modern-twentieth-century milieu of academia, family, church, and social institutions. His was "a vocation to conversation,"[1] but also a vocation to *conversatio* in the spirit of Benedict.

Early Life

Emerson Hynes was born June 7, 1915, in Winnebago, Minnesota, the youngest of Muerton and Mary (Perrizo) Hynes' ten children. When Emerson was a year and a half old, Muerton Hynes died. Eldest son Stanley assumed a "father image" for the growing children on the family farm—especially for the "beloved child," Emerson. In the early 1930s when Emerson was a teenager, the family moved from the farm into town. By this time, the bright and gregarious lad had his eyes turned toward St. John's University where Stanley had begun his education.

[1] Eugene J. McCarthy, *The Hard Years: A Look at Contemporary America and American Institutions* (New York: Viking Press, 1975) 189.

St. John's University

St. John's was reputed as an outstanding liberal arts institution. Its modest beginnings stretched from a small priory and seminary built near St. Cloud in 1856 by five Benedictines from St. Vincent's Abbey in Latrobe, Pennsylvania, to its present location on a 2,400-acre tract of forested land twelve miles northwest of St. Cloud. St. John's Abbey and University enjoys world renown as an educational and liturgical center.

However, when Hynes became interested in St. John's, America had begun its plunge into economic depression. There was little money left over in the family for school. Nevertheless, the young man went to look things over. Walter Reger, O.S.B., college dean, noted the young man's scholarly interest and offered him a job in the library in exchange for tuition, room, and board. Hynes leaped at the opportunity. In 1933 he entered wholeheartedly into student life at St. John's. His interests in nature, farming, and philosophy found eager avenues for growth and challenge as he studied scholastic philosophy and theology, history, languages, art, the natural sciences, economics, and social and political science.

Student Days

The reflective, interdisciplinary mood surrounding St. John's University and Abbey quickened Hynes' love for learning and desire for wisdom. He read, he wrote, he discussed. He held impromptu gatherings in the dorm where lively intellectual exchange replaced idle college chatter. As a result of his openness and natural ease with people, he drew to his side lifelong friends such as monastic scholars Emeric Lawrence, O.S.B., Godfrey Diekmann, O.S.B., Martin Schirber, O.S.B., and future colleagues Eugene J. McCarthy and Stephen B. Humphrey.

It was not long before Hynes' words began finding permanent places in articles he wrote regularly for *The Record,* St. John's student publication which he edited, and *St. Benedict's Quarterly* for nearby St. Benedict's College for women. Referring to the article "Whither Cooperation?" published by Hynes in *Free America* (December 1937), former student and longtime friend William (Bill) Cofell continues to be amazed today by the young man's "excellence of expression" and mature literary style already evident at age twenty-two.[2] Emerson Hynes, the person, the writer, the teacher and philosopher, drew on the age-old Benedictine program of *ora et labora* to root him in a sense of wholeness, dignity, and community.

---

[2] William Cofell, notes and letter on Emerson Hynes. June 2000, Collegeville, Minnesota.

These were balanced elements of the day. The Benedictine motto, "Moderation in all things," became his byword and guide.

Influence of Dom Virgil Michel, O.S.B.

Hynes' love for learning led to a natural flow of love for God which assumed societal proportions when he found himself at the side of Virgil Michel, O.S.B., dean of students and leader of the liturgical movement in America. The two men worked together as teacher and student on studies dealing with social reconstruction, the encyclicals of Popes Leo XIII and Pius XI, and the development of rural living on the land. Hynes was enthusiastic about the rural way of life. In an unpublished essay written at the time entitled "The Eternal Peasant," Emerson lauds the advantages of farming and simple living. His studies in liturgy and social and agrarian reform became the focus and thrust of his life and precipitated his fuller participation in Benedictinism a few years later as an oblate.

Virgil Michel's key concepts of "justice," "common good," "person," and "human rights" reawakened a vital Christian sociology in the Catholic world. He united social action with the liturgical movement and believed that celebrating the liturgy would have a transforming effect on people's lives making it possible to create a more just social order. He encouraged the recitation of the Divine Office even by lay people, thus bringing minds and hearts into harmony with the Church.

Through an Institute for Social Studies offered at St. John's in 1935 by the Catholic Central Verein, Virgil Michel hoped to explore "the cooperative order, distributist-agrarian movement, money, and Marxian theories."[3] His message was that of the Gospel and consonant with the Rule of St. Benedict: a new look at unjust structures, materialism, and consumerism. Hynes himself later stated, "The Rule is a primary source for social principles."[4] He could not have found a mentor whose philosophy and ideals matched his own more closely. He drew deeply from the well of Virgil Michel in expanding his own beliefs and lifestyle.

Notre Dame and Catholic Rural Life

Graduation 1937 was a proud moment for Hynes as he received the traditional "Johnnie" ruby ring—his treasure for a lifetime. With scholarship in hand (thanks to Virgil Michel) for post-graduate work at the University of

[3] Colman J. Barry, *Worship and Work* (Collegeville: The Liturgical Press, 1956) 275.

[4] Emerson Hynes, unpublished essay: "The Black Monks." File 2471:4, 1948 (St. John's University Archives, Collegeville, Minnesota).

Notre Dame, the young man determined to return to St. John's as a teacher. During his two years at Notre Dame, he continued his study of Christian social thought and agrarian reform, particularly the cooperative movements and the philosophy of distributism which in theory aimed at common cooperative work available for all with maximum distribution of goods.[5]

Hynes was writing thought-provoking articles for *Columbia, America, Catholic World,* and several other magazines applying Catholic agrarian thought and Christian social principles to contemporary society and its problems. His first publication in *Commonweal* in October 1938 was entitled, "Catholic Rural Life Conference: The Most Vital Movement." Catholic Rural Life had gained momentum in Central Minnesota under the leadership of several bishops, Monsignor Luigi Ligutti, and some Benedictines from St. John's, including Virgil Michel and Martin Schirber, o.s.b. Hynes was one of the movement's eager proponents. In 1938 he published "The Dignity and Joy of Work" for *The Catholic Rural Life Bulletin,* applauding the usefulness and creativity of work and lamenting the loss of the human connection with nature and rural living.

During his years of study at Notre Dame, Hynes was introduced to his future wife, Arleen McCarty of Iowa, who was working toward a degree in library science at St. Catherine's College in St. Paul. The two became fast friends sharing common interests and a common Irish ancestry.

Kilfenora

After receiving his master's degree in apologetics in 1939, Hynes visited Ireland. In County Clare he discovered a ninth-century cathedral which he associated with the Hynes family. It was called Kilfenora, meaning "church of the north." Hynes kept the name in mind for his own future home, "a little church," built in Collegeville. When he returned to Minnesota he found that his friend Walter Reger, o.s.b., had arranged for him to teach at St. John's—a position Hynes held for the next twenty years as professor of ethics and sociology.

At this time, St. John's agreed to sell part of their "Indianbush"[6] just north of the abbey near Collegeville. Emerson and Arleen bought ten acres of sandy, birch-covered woodland and set to work constructing a small

---

[5] Aloisius J. Muench, *Oratre Fratres* (Collegeville: The Liturgical Press, 1939) 131. Bishop Muench of Fargo was one of the developers of the Catholic Rural Life Movement in mid-America in the 1930s.

[6] "Indianbush" refers to the prairie and woodland surrounding the Watab river land west of St. Joseph which was originally used as hunting grounds for the Sioux and Chippewa Indians.

barn in which they lived while building Kilfenora with help from Hynes' young friends and monks from the abbey.

Oblate of St. Benedict

Hynes was so filled with the rich legacy of his Benedictine environment, of worship and work, and the realization that this legacy was meant to take him into the future, that he desired to do all he could to assist himself spiritually. He asked to become an oblate of the Order. At an Investure Ceremony in 1940, Hynes received the Rule of St. Benedict, the medal, a small black scapular, and a manual marking him as a novice. He continued praying the Divine Office, studying the Rule, cultivating virtue, and meeting monthly with his director at the abbey.

Perhaps Hynes had discovered, along with his study of Pope Leo XIII, the importance attributed this spiritual affiliation with the Benedictine Order by the Pope's approval in 1898 of the Statutes and Rule of the Secular Oblates of St. Benedict. In 1923, Abbot Alcuin Deutsch revised and re-edited St. Vincent's manual for St. John's. Another updated edition appeared in 1937. It was Abbot Alcuin himself who received Hynes in his final profession as an oblate of St. Benedict on April 21, 1941.[7] Hynes received the name of the Benedictine saint he wished as his patron: Denis, his grandfather's name.

Marriage and Family

Two months later, on June 26, Emerson and Arleen were married in the Abbey Church. Walter Reger, O.S.B., was celebrant of the Mass with Godfrey Diekmann, O.S.B., master of ceremonies, Emeric Lawrence, O.S.B., deacon, and Martin Schirber, O.S.B., sub-deacon. The couple began to build their life together with an austere budget and high ideals around the Benedictine ambience they both valued. They were able to move from the barn (or "little house") to Kilfenora on December 8, 1941, though the cinderblock house on the hill was far from finished. For an article written several years later, Hynes distinguished between mere house building and the more important task of home building: "A home should be designed for family living. It should be part of a community."[8] This community developed over the years from a cluster of families gathered at the Collegeville/ St. Joseph area

---

[7] Arleen became an Oblate of St. Benedict on July 16, 1943. After Emerson's untimely death in 1971, she completed the task of raising the children and, in 1980, became a professed Benedictine sister at St. Benedict's Monastery, St. Joseph, Minnesota.

[8] Emerson Hynes, "Building a Home," *The Marianist* (October 1948) 12.

sharing similar intellectual and artistic interests. It was humorously referred
to as the "Movement" and the families often met at the Hynes' for scholarly
and spiritual dialogue as well as mutual assistance.

The Hynes' ten children arrived over the next fifteen years, beginning
with Denis on July 24, 1942; then, Mary, Patrick, Brigid, Hilary, Peter,
Michael, Timothy, Thomas More, and Christopher. Despite the lack of
electricity and running water in Kilfenora, Hynes, the eternal "positive
presence,"[9] wrote to his friends in the summer of 1942 that in addition to
their first son and a nearly finished house, "Lucia," the Guernsey cow had
produced a calf which they fattened and turned into steaks. Now they had
their own milk and butter, thirty pounds of honeycomb, and fruits and
vegetables from their garden.[10]

Influence of the Rule of St. Benedict in Family Living

From the beginning, the couple set out to make Kilfenora a "little
church" modeled on the "family ideal" of the Rule of St. Benedict and en-
spirited by Virgil Michel's liturgical reform. In an inspiring talk entitled
"Sacramental Protection of the Family" at the St. Bede Rural Life Summer School in 1945, Hynes articulated the values of family and church
which he promoted in his own household. Emerson and Arleen prayed the
Divine Office in English daily using the short breviary. Their children
joined in the antiphonal recitation of one or more daily prayer hours. Sea-
sons and feastdays of the Church year were celebrated with solemnity in
the home with creative expressions of family faith including special
prayers and songs, rituals, and dramatizations.

The Prologue and first few chapters of Emerson's worn brown copy
of the Rule have small checked passages indicating tenets he wished to
stress in the family: speaking the truth, making peace before the sun sets,
obeying without grumbling, serving God with the good things one has
been given, helping in time of trouble. Work was highly respected and a
daily schedule was kept by all. Hynes believed that having useful work to
do developed the ideals of good stewardship, independence, and self-sufficiency. Family council meetings were held as the Rule suggests, for "the
Lord often reveals what is better to the younger" (*RB* 3.3). Each family
member had an equal voice in affirming one another, making family decisions, and solving problems.

---

[9] Letter from Abigail McCarthy about Emerson Hynes. May 2000, Washington, D.C.

[10] St. John's University Archives, Collegeville, Minnesota, Emerson Hynes Correspondence (C, 2470.8, 1938–1952).

As parents, Emerson and Arleen strongly validated the individuality of their children. The following intimate description supplied by daughter Mary illustrates the point:

> They gave each of us a color that was just ours and bought color-coded cups and bowls so that we would know we had a special place at the table. . . . Every night we finished family prayers with a litany—a personalized appeal to our very own saint. . . . As part of the bedtime ritual or at a tearful needy moment, he or she put down the baby or the book, hung up the phone, put aside all other pressing tasks, and reached out, held us, hugged us and counted: (to 30) . . . seconds of loving for . . . and they would finish with a kiss or extra squeeze, a term of endearment and our name, the special one, the one that was just for whoever we were.[11]

Father, Teacher, and Friend

Hynes was a good disciplinarian but never raised his voice. Books were important to the family and his study was lined with them from floor to ceiling. He loved to read or recite poetry to his children and always encouraged their intellectual curiosity and wonder.

Benedictine hospitality reached out and shone, Arleen says, as their Aladdin lamp burned late into the night for students, neighbors, and professors who gathered regularly at the Hynes' home for "conversation": philosophic, metaphysical inquiry, and debate—little of which students encountered in their homes at the time.[12] According to Chapter 53 of the Rule, "Guests should be received as Christ," and in this Hynes was meticulous. "One always felt at home at the Hynes', welcome, and insured of good discussions," recalls Diekmann.[13]

From 1939 to 1959 Hynes taught large classes of seventy and eighty students at St. John's University. It is believed he was the first lay person to teach ethics in a Catholic college. He did so enthusiastically. Wise yet witty, Hynes loved to play with paradoxes which he slipped humorously into conversations. He became the friend and advisor of hundreds of students.

Edward L. Henry, a student of Hynes in the early 1940s, says:

> In my mind, he was a twentieth-century Socrates who used his Socratic methods to induce students to think. All the students who had him respected

---

[11] Mary Hynes-Berry, work in progress: *Telling Stories*. Chicago, Illinois.

[12] In these early years, the Hynes family home had no electricity. The mantle of their Aladdin lamp burned white-hot and gave off light. In the case of the crowded room at the Hynes', it occasionally flared up and doors and windows had to be opened for more oxygen!

[13] Godfrey Diekmann, o.s.b., personal interview about Emerson Hynes. June 2000, St. John's Abbey, Collegeville, Minnesota.

his quiet and humble approach and his respect. . . . There is no doubt that his deep respect for learning was responsible for steering me in the direction of becoming a teacher. . . . His high ideals impressed me with the responsibility of helping others get insights into the lofty heights of the true philosopher . . . and it was not only his high attachment to ethical ideals . . . but his willingness to live a life that called for sacrifice.[14]

Bill Cofell reflects on his former teacher's persona at this time: "He maintained his idealism despite the injustice and despair that had swept the country. He was a fine philosopher and ethicist concerned about systemic justice and ethical economic behavior. . . . He was a calm, reflective teacher . . . a powerful influence on my life." In 1953 Cofell returned to St. John's as a professor of English and a colleague of Hynes. He recalls the great admiration he felt for "this remarkable person" who gave "rational, delightful responses to questions." He says, "Emerson made regular visits to the faculty room. Here, he and Father Martin [Schirber] engaged in debate or argument. Both held different points of view. . . . Martin's was economic . . . but any response of Emerson's was hard to refute."

Hynes taught with Stephen B. Humphrey, professor of English, and Eugene McCarthy, professor of education and economics. The image of Hynes retained by these and other colleagues was that of a tall, slim man with his ever-present pipe in hand tapped out thoughtfully now and then against his St. John's ring while listening with deep respect and awareness to others.

In the early 1950s, Hynes became a lay member of the American Benedictine Academy (ABA) which had been reorganized in 1947 by Abbot Alcuin Deutsch, o.s.b., from the earlier National Benedictine Educational Association. The purpose of the organization was to stimulate research as well as historical and literary pursuits among Benedictines. Hynes was part of the Social Science Section of the Academy.

Writer and Lecturer

During his tenure at St. John's, Hynes continued writing for leading liturgical and intellectual journals including *Commonweal, Worship, Today, Ave Maria, The American Catholic Sociological Review,* and *Land and Home,* the official periodical of National Catholic Rural Life (NCRL). His published articles and pamphlets from 1938 to 1958 number 110.

Membership in NCRL and in the Catholic Family Movement (CFM) promoted by the Hynes' parish church, St. John the Baptist at Collegeville,

---

[14] Edward L. Henry, letter and notes on Emerson Hynes. June 2000, St. Cloud, Minnesota. Henry was also a colleague of Emerson in the 1950s at St. John's University as professor of political science.

led both Emerson and Arleen on speaking tours around the country. Topics included family life and marriage, liturgy and land, the Christian social principles and Catholic Social Action, but it was the land and agriculture that captured Emerson's prophetic voice. With the Rule of St. Benedict as guide, he defined stewardship, reverence for life, and community in the light of social and cultural trends. He urged the preservation of natural resources on a national level, the protection of small family farms, and education in new farming techniques and marketing.

As a strong proponent and leader in rural life issues, the Most Reverend George H. Speltz, Bishop Emeritus of the Diocese of St. Cloud, Minnesota, remembers Hynes' strong presence at the podium: "We often spoke together during the days of the rural life movement."[15] Hynes was active on the Board of Directors for NCRL and the American Life Association throughout the 1950s.

Mindful of his ethical obligations on the home front, Hynes founded the Workman's Guild at St. John's in 1943 to help employees and faculty work together in applying the principles of the social encyclicals. Their resulting action spelled out policies regarding hours, wages, working conditions, and holidays which continue to give shape to the college operations today. Along with Martin Schirber, Hynes created a Credit Union for the benefit of both workers and farmers around the abbey. He served as president of this organization from 1942 to 1959. The Collegeville Credit Union personally touched the Hynes' family after Emerson's death when it helped pay off family debts.

Hynes' "moderating influence" at St. John's helped lay the foundation for a strong lay staff membership whose influence in the governing process of the college has grown over the years.

Hynes was an "icon," according to Edward Henry, who typified what the inner spirit of St. John's wished to perpetuate. "He was not self-consciously Benedictine. He had no aspirations to become an icon, but his ideals and character fitted him admirably for that role" (letter and notes).

NATO and FAO

In November 1957 Hynes was selected on the recommendation of Eugene McCarthy, newly elected Minnesota state senator, to represent the United States at the North Atlantic Treaty Organization (NATO) Parliamentary Conference in Paris. Hynes looked upon this appointment as a further opportunity in the quest of peace and the building of the common

---

[15] Most Reverend George H. Speltz, personal interview about Emerson Hynes. June 2000, St. Cloud, Minnesota.

good. While in Europe, he flew to Rome where Msgr. Luigi G. Ligutti, now papal representative for the Food and Agricultural Organization (FAO), was headquartered. He was also honored by a private audience with Pope Pius XII.

Legislative Assistant

Shortly after Hynes' return to Minnesota, he was asked by Senator Eugene McCarthy to come to Washington, D.C., to serve as his legislative assistant. Hynes was forty-four years old. He was well established at Collegeville and in his teaching career. But the awesome task was one he could not shirk. "The family, the church, and the state are the basic social institutions," he upheld. "To defend and support them is an obligation."[16]

As legislative assistant Hynes brought his skills in research and knowledge of history and philosophy illuminated by the Christian social principles to issues and problems. He was fully aware of the impact of this responsibility. Friend, former student, and journalist on Capitol Hill, Albert Eisele, says, "Clearly McCarthy relied on Emerson's judgment and wise counsel, and often remarked to me and others that he consulted Emerson on matters large and small. . . . He was a good man who brought a much-needed sense of perspective, both spiritual and historical, to the Senate."[17]

However, the move from Minnesota was difficult. Diekmann speaks of Hynes' parting from the St. John's/Collegeville community: "We all felt a great loss at his departure to Washington D.C. but we knew he could do more good there." The "good" that this remarkable man did was later recorded by Eugene McCarthy in *The Hard Years:*

> Emerson had a vocation to conversation. He was most appreciated by people with desperate causes. When persons in great distress, or with problems for which there was no political solution, came by the Senate office, he would never say, "Don't send them in to see me." Often the same persons would come to me later and say, "Thank you for letting us talk to that man."
> . . . One did not start from scratch in discussing a problem with him. Few other members of the Senate, if any, had aides such as he to whom they could turn and ask, expecting an answer, "What did Plato (or Thomas Aquinas or Jacques Maritain) have to say about this?"

---

[16] Harry W. Flannery, "Assistant Senator," *Ave Maria* (May 14, 1960) 21.

[17] Albert Eisele, letter about Emerson Hynes. June 2000, Washington, D.C. Eisele is editor of *The Hill,* the largest Capitol Hill weekly newspaper. Eisele first came to Washington, D.C., in 1965 as a correspondent for the St. Paul, Minnesota, newspapers.

Abigail McCarthy further attests to Hynes' unique presence: "He was the very epitome of the Benedictine virtues of hospitality and stability. He was always there for his friends and those in need of help" (McCarthy letter).

New Home

The Hynes family took up residence in a large house in Arlington, Virginia, across the Potomac River from Washington, D.C., in January 1959. It was a shocking adjustment for the children who were accustomed to a small, personal, faith-filled community. Mary Hynes-Berry writes: "As I turned 14, my family moved from our rural home, from the life rich with ritual that we took for granted in rural Minnesota, to the sterile formula-ridden suburbs of Washington D.C." (Hynes-Berry work in progress).

In 1967 Hynes completed a writing project for the *New Catholic Encyclopedia*. In the essay entitled "Rural Society," he hailed the subjects close to his Benedictine heart: the dignity of the human person, rural values of home and family, land ownership, religious practice, and work. "Only the monastic orders," he wrote, "particularly those following the rule outlined by St. Benedict in the 6th century, have shown a clear preference for rural location. For several centuries the Benedictine and particularly the Cistercian monasteries were, in fact, the centers for improved methods of farming."[18]

Conclusion

Hynes served on McCarthy's staff for twelve years. In 1968 he worked closely with the senator during the presidential campaign. Despite a stroke suffered in 1969, Hynes recovered sufficiently to continue serving through the completion of McCarthy's second term in January 1971. Six months later, however, on July 29, Emerson Hynes died after a second stroke. He was fifty-six years old.

A man of unique brilliance and intense love for life, he "couldn't quite go gentle into that good night," daughter Mary writes. Perhaps still pondering life's greatest question, he had, nonetheless, "Clothed . . . with faith and the performance of good works" (*RB* Prol. 21), discovered the way, pursued the quest, and attained "the loftier summits of . . . teaching and virtues" (*RB* 73.9) that Benedict offers all those called to life everlasting.

A funeral Mass was celebrated at Our Lady Queen of Peace in Arlington with burial nearby. Emeric Lawrence, homilist, paid enduring tribute to

---

[18] Emerson Hynes, "The Rural Society," *The New Catholic Encyclopedia* (1967) Vol. XII, 728.

his friend, declaring that Emerson in his life was pleasing to God. Eugene McCarthy added, "He was also pleasing to men." A memorial Mass was offered simultaneously at St. John's Abbey in Collegeville.

In his relatively short lifetime, Emerson Hynes was a voice for our world. His profound insights, schooled in Benedictine tradition, examined human life and linked our happiness and well-being to the unique treasure of family and community, to the simple balance of meaningful work and prayer, to the re-union of land and nature for human artistic inspiration and spiritual energy, to justice and hospitality. In a word, to *conversatio*.

Emerson Hynes, man of peace, be our guide into the new millennium that dearly desires "the way to life" (*RB* Prol.).

15

St. Benedict and the Maritains

Lucie R. Johnson, OBL.S.B.

"Living in the world, deprived of the help that monks and nuns find in their rules and their vows, . . . we must make up by inner fervour and by poverty of spirit for what we lack in outer supports." These are Raïssa Maritain's words, part of a little Rule of Life she composed in 1923. She carefully penned three copies in leaflet form: one for her sister Vera, one for her husband Jacques, and one for herself.[1] Raïssa, Jacques, and Vera formed one household. All three were Benedictine Oblates. All three were converts to the Catholic faith. In 1963, three years after Raïssa's death (four years after Vera's passing), Jacques still kept this Rule of Life in his Book of Hours.

Jacques, Raïssa, and Vera

Jacques Maritain and Raïssa Oumançoff came into the world fourteen months, six days, and a whole world apart. Raïssa was born September 12, 1883, in Rostoff-on-the-Don, part of a Russian-Jewish family. Jacques was born in Paris on November 18, 1882,[2] from a Catholic father, a Protestant mother, and an influential maternal grandfather, Jules Favre. Jules Favre was known for his strong sense of justice and democracy (which involved a good dose of anticlericalism), and for the most difficult

[1] Raïssa Maritain, *Raïssa's Journal: Presented by Jacques Maritain* (Albany, N.Y.: Magi Books, 1974) 154. The original French edition was published in 1963 by Desclée de Brouwer.

[2] Jacques Maritain, *Carnet de Notes* (Paris: Desclée de Brouwer, 1964) 19. ET: Jacques Maritain, *Notebooks,* trans. Joseph W. Evans (Albany, N.Y.: Magi Books, 1984).

task of negotiating the Bismarck agreements of 1871 in a way that would safeguard at least some of the honor of France. Raïssa also was strongly attached to her maternal grandfather, whose particular gentleness, compassion, and holiness stemmed from his Hassidic roots.[3] His Russian neighbors had nicknamed him "Solomon the Wise" and warned him of upcoming pogroms, that he might stay inside and keep his family safe.[4]

Vera, younger than Raïssa by almost three years, was born in Marioupol, Russia, July 2, 1886,[5] near the sea of Azoff, where the family had moved. Until they were eight and ten and a half years, respectively, they played an imaginary game which filled much of their childhood. In it, Vera was Mimo, the mother, and Raïssa was Pifo, her mischievous little boy. Theirs was an elaborate imaginary world from which they took special care to exclude anything evil or mean—even the words for good were barred because they implied their opposites.[6] Vera, in a sense, always remained Raïssa's mother, and adopted Jacques. She saw the task of watching over Raïssa and Jacques as her calling, and she found joy in it. She was the practical one. She enjoyed dealing with the outside world. Her health, like that of Raïssa, was frail at times. She was an encourager and a helper, and did whatever needed doing. Though she was an intimate part of Jacques and Raïssa's lives, her individual journey is hidden to us, except for its landmarks,[7] because she destroyed her journals, notes, and letters. She could be fiery (as a child she was nicknamed "little spark"), but she was most often very quiet. She brought to Jacques and Raïssa—who were intense people— a unique lightness of heart. Vera died December 31, 1959, after a two-year battle with cancer.[8] The following September Raïssa had a stroke and, a few weeks later, a premonition of her own death.[9] She died November 4, 1960, at the age of seventy-seven.[10] Jacques lived another thirteen years. He died suddenly of a heart attack on April 28, 1973,[11] as a Little Brother of Jesus (a religious order founded by Charles de Foucauld.)

---

[3] Raïssa Maritain, *Les grandes Amitiés* (Paris: Desclée de Brouwer, 1949) 16–18.

[4] Ibid., 18. The image of the cross prominently processed during the pogroms remained a very vivid memory for Raïssa's mother, and was for many years an obstacle to her conversion.

[5] Jacques Maritain, *Carnet de Notes*, 106.

[6] Raïssa Maritain, *Les grandes Amitiés*, 20–1.

[7] Much of what we know about Vera comes from a chapter dedicated to her in Jacques Maritain's *Carnet de Notes*, 186–219.

[8] Julie Kernan, *Our Friend, Jacques Maritain* (Garden City, N.Y.: Doubleday, 1975) 160.

[9] Jacques Maritain, *Carnet de Notes*, 334.

[10] Kernan, *Our Friend, Jacques Maritain*, 163.

[11] Ibid., 186.

Reluctant Agnostics

They were seventeen and eighteen when they met in the hallways of the Sorbonne, outside of Mr. Matruchot's plant physiology classroom. Jacques already had a license in philosophy. Both were agnostic, in search of foundational, absolute truth, and were looking to science to provide it. The young Parisian approached the Russian emigrée for the first time as he was seeking support for a petition protesting the mistreatment of Russian socialist students in tsarist Russia, and together they gathered many signatures and letters in France's intellectual and literary circles. This was the beginning of their friendship; after that, they never parted. Despite background and temperamental differences, there immediately was between them deep harmony and great trust.[12]

So, it was not much of a surprise that they became engaged two years after they met, and were married the following year. What was unusual was their common passion: the urgent need to rethink together the entire universe.[13] Raïssa and Jacques were painfully reluctant agnostics. They wanted a solid theory of knowledge, but discovered that their professors did not want to speak about truth and were leery of the term itself. This stance, in Jacques and Raïssa's eyes, led to relativism, intellectual skepticism, and moral nihilism; to an absurd and thus intolerable human life. Such were their musings one day during a walk in the Jardin des Plantes. Before leaving the garden they made a solemn promise: to face radically and fully this universe of which skepticism and relativism seemed the only light. They decided to trust the unknown and hope that, in Raïssa's words, "in response to our vehement appeal, the meaning of life would be unveiled, and new values would reveal themselves so clearly they would result in our full assent, and deliver us from the nightmare of a sinister and unneeded world."[14] If their quest failed, they planned to commit suicide, as a protest against the absurd. This is when, said Raïssa, the mercy of God led them to Henri Bergson.[15] Through his teaching, they found enough truth to make life worth living. The last time Jacques visited Paris, in January 1973, a few months before his death, Desclée de Brouwer, his publisher, wanted to take his picture. Jacques chose the Jardin des Plantes, and

---

[12] Raïssa Maritain, *Les grandes Amitiés,* 54–6.

[13] Ibid., 55: *"Il fallait repenser ensemble l'univers tout entier."*

[14] Ibid., 90: *"dans l'espoir qu'à notre appel véhément, le sens de la vie se dévoilerait, que de nouvelles valeurs se révèleraient si clairement qu'elles entraineraient notre adhésion totale, et nous délivreraient du cauchemar d'un monde sinistre et inutile."*

[15] Henri Bergson (1859–1941): French philosopher reacting against the reductionistic empiricism of his contemporaries. His epistemology stressed the primacy of intuition. Nobel Laureate (1927).

stood in the very spot of their initial bold promise to search for truth.[16] It had shaped their lives.

The Threshold of Faith

Henri Bergson taught at the College of France, across the street from the Sorbonne. He contrasted the limitations of the rational intellect with the ability of intuition to directly perceive reality. He spoke about spirit and life. He opened for his students new possibilities of thought, and thus much hope. It is while she was studying Plotinus under Bergson that Raïssa for the first time had a sense of the presence of God. She found herself kneeling, her heart burning.[17] It took Jacques another year to pray "God, if you exist, and if you are the truth, make me know it," and then kneel and say the Lord's prayer.[18] In the entrance hall of their first home, to reflect his willingness to question everything, Jacques hung from the mouth of a gargoyle a sign that said: "To the Absolute. Enterprises demolished."[19]

It was not, however, their studies and reflections that finally made them cross the threshold of faith: it was their encounter with the unusually intense and prophetic French writer Léon Bloy, whose book *The Woman Who Was Poor*[20] touched them deeply. Léon Bloy was a man who believed deeply and lived a faith marked by a burning zeal for justice. He viewed his writing as a calling from God, and lived with his family a life marked by poverty, and—as a last resort—dependence on his friends. "There is only one sadness," said Bloy, "it is of not being saints."[21]

The Maritains became part of Bloy's circle of friends. Another one of his books, *Salvation through the Jews*,[22] which highlighted the teachings of Romans 9–11 and John 4:22, was helpful particularly for Raïssa to whom the book offered a way to link the Old and New Testaments. Witness the following quote from Bloy: "One passes from one to the other[23] through Christ. He himself said this; he, the Salvation, he comes from the Jews."[24] In their many talks together, Bloy did not use apologetics—that

---

[16] Kernan, *Our Friend, Jacques Maritain,* 185–6.

[17] Raïssa Maritain, *Les grandes Amitiés,* 109.

[18] Jacques Maritain, *Carnet de Notes,* 34; Raïssa Maritain, *Les grandes Amitiés,* 157.

[19] Raïssa Maritain, *Les grandes Amitiés,* 116: *"À L'ABSOLU. DÉMOLITIONS D'EN-TREPRISES."*

[20] *La Femme pauvre.*

[21] Raïssa Maritain, *Les grandes Amitiés,* 119.

[22] *Le Salut par les Juifs.*

[23] From the Old to the New Testament.

[24] Raïssa Maritain, *Les grandes Amitiés,* 135: *"On passe de l'un à l'autre par le Christ. C'est lui-même qui le dit; lui, le Salut, il vient des Juifs."*

did not even occur to him. Rather, he talked to his young friends about mystics, holy men and women, often with tears. They read Angela de Foligno, Ruysbroeck, and Catherine Emmerich.

Le Catechisme Spirituel by Fr. Sorin, a seventeenth-century Jesuit, brought them a more systematic understanding of the contemplation for which they were yearning.[25] They had come to see faith as a superior gift of intuition, a way to perceive absolute truth. If this was the case, then human intelligence could engage that truth as well, and human knowledge could attain the real. The world was not absurd.[26] In a somewhat paradoxical fashion, the existence of faith, the transformative encounter with God in contemplation, was the root of any valid human knowledge. For the Maritains, prayer, contemplation, and the way they lived the dailyness of life were foundational.

They were baptized, Jacques (conditionally), Vera, and Raïssa, on June 11, 1906, one year after they had met Bloy, at St. John the Evangelist in Montmartre.[27] It was, said Jacques, a desert time. They received baptism in the hope that, through it, they would receive faith. They were not disappointed. A couple of months later they found themselves in Heidelberg, where Jacques had received a two-year fellowship in biology to study with Hans Driesch, a proponent of dynamic vitalism. Though biology was no longer Jacques' primary interest, their stay in Heidelberg provided them with the flexibility to more fully assimilate their conversion and its interface with their professional and personal lives.

Neophyte Enthusiasm

Raïssa and Jacques plunged into Christianity with unbridled enthusiasm. They read Scripture and the mystics as Léon Bloy, their godfather, had instructed them. The medieval Benedictine mystic Gertrude of Helfta and Teresa of Avila (mostly through her autobiography) became dominant influences. They considered St. Gertrude as their spiritual guide, and viewed themselves as a semimonastic community living in the world but not of the world.[28] The household set up a quasi-monastic horarium including daily Mass, the Liturgy of the Hours, times for work, meals, music, conversation, and reading.[29] A bit later, they added a rotating abbot system (weekly Captain whom the others needed to obey—they found the

---

[25] Ibid., 165.
[26] Ibid., 161.
[27] Jacques Maritain, *Carnet de Notes,* 44.
[28] Ibid., 75.
[29] Ibid., 64.

practice very useful)[30] and a daily chapter.[31] They tried to put into practice all that they learned, sometimes a bit too much at one time. In that first year, in addition to their adjustment to being new Christians, they went through the Ignatian Exercises (but without much benefit) and, while on pilgrimage at Our Lady of La Salette, consecrated themselves to Mary, in the tradition of Grignon of Montfort.[32]

This was also the year of Jacques' first visit to the Abbey of Solesmes (then in exile on the Isle of Wright), where he had gone on behalf of Charles Péguy. While there he spoke to Dom Delatte, the abbot, about the household's need for spiritual direction. In Raïssa's words, "at that time they thought perfection would be easy if someone would just show them how."[33] Dom Delatte was of the opinion that very few people needed spiritual directors, and that their young neophyte enthusiasm would settle down. They should pray and discern, and consider the matter in a year. After the waiting period was over, he sent them to Fr. Humbert Clérissac, a Dominican, who was to have a most significant influence on their lives, though he would die prematurely five years later, at the age of fifty.[34] During this time also, Raïssa and Vera were in correspondence with Madame Cécile Bruyère, Abbess of Saint-Cécile in Solesmes, who encouraged Raïssa to pursue a contemplative life within the parameters of her station in life.[35]

It was Father Clérissac who introduced the Maritains to the *Summa Theologica,* which Raïssa was the first to read. In so doing, she fell in love with Thomas Aquinas, with his brilliant mind, but also with his contemplative and prayerful spirit. At the time, Jacques was working for Hachette, compiling encyclopedias. He had declined the opportunity to teach in France's public schools because of the atheistic atmosphere there. A year later, when Jacques also started to read the *Summa* (at the same time as he was reading St. Gertrude), he too was enthralled. Thomism allowed one to be rational, and human reason could be trusted. Under Father Clérissac's tutelage and critique, Jacques started writing philosophy[36] and the Maritains moved to Versailles to be close to him.

[30] Ibid., 73.
[31] Ibid., 97.
[32] Ibid., 58.
[33] Raïssa Maritain, *Les grandes Amitiés,* 231.
[34] Ibid., 233, 235.
[35] Jacques Maritain, *Carnet de Notes,* 87.
[36] Kernan, *Our Friend, Jacques Maritain,* 42–3.

Encountering Benedict

Though a Dominican, Fr. Clérissac liked Benedictine spirituality, its balance, simplicity, and its non-self-absorbed nature. He encouraged the Maritains in that direction. Dom Jean de Puniet, a monk from Solesmes, was then abbot of St. Paul Abbey, a foundation of Solesmes in Oosterhout, Holland. On May 10, 1911, he came to see them and invested them as novice oblates of St. Paul Abbey. They were now, said Abbot de Puniet, a very small branch of St. Paul Abbey, and their lives were their work. There was no need to seek for extra things to do. On September 29, 1912, they went to Oosterhout and made their final oblation, Jacques as Placid, Vera as Agnes, and Raïssa as Gertrude.[37] In those days also they met another pair of Léon Bloy's godchildren: Pierre and Christine van der Meer, who became close friends[38] and Benedictines as well (both of their children became monastics, and Pierre entered St. Paul in Oosterhout after his wife's death).

From Teaching to Thomist Circles

At about the same time, Jacques was offered a teaching position at St. Stanislas, a prestigious boys' school of fifteen hundred students. He accepted and gave up with joy his work at Hachette. Now he was free to pursue philosophy in a more concentrated and also a more public way. He gave a series of lectures at the Institut Catholique on "The Philosophy of Bergson and Christian Philosophy." He was a charismatic speaker and young people flocked to his lectures.[39] Shortly thereafter, Jacques started to write his *Introduction to Philosophy,* and in 1920, together with Raïssa, *Art and Scholasticism.*

It might seem to an observer that Jacques' career then blossomed. But the term "career" did not apply to Jacques. Work, for both him and Raïssa, was simply an actualization of one's spirituality and obedience to God. The other aspects of life were every bit as important: their home life, hospitality, family, prayer, reading. For twenty years Raïssa's mother lived with them. They were faithful to their friends and opened their home to many. To the best of their ability they walked with God. Their friends, relatives, and students were touched by the lived authenticity of their faith. Many of them converted, many were renewed in their faith, many were grateful. One of those was Pierre Villard, who had come to Jacques for assistance, and who was killed in the war in 1918. To his great surprise,

---

[37] Raïssa Maritain, *Les grandes Amitiés,* 446.
[38] Ibid., 262.
[39] Kernan, *Our Friend, Jacques Maritain,* 44.

Jacques found himself the heir of half of Villard's considerable estate.[40] True to form, Jacques no longer took a salary for his teaching, and started Thomist Circles, which met in their house. The monthly seminars grew in size, so that by the 1930s, forty to fifty people were coming to the monthly meetings and the seminars evolved into a more systematic Thomist Society of which the renowned Dominican, Father Garrigou-Lagrange, became director.

The vision of the Maritains for this Society was not just intellectual. Raïssa especially wanted to emphasize the spiritual dimension as well, and ask of the members that they practice silent contemplative prayer.[41] To that effect, in 1922 they wrote, at first in private edition, a little book entitled *Prayer and Intelligence*.[42] The paper jacket of the English edition reads: "This little book shows what the life of Prayer can be for those whose way of life is intellectual."[43] The section on the spiritual life—a strong endorsement of contemplative prayer—starts with a quotation from the Rule of St. Benedict (Prol. 19). Gertrude, Hildegard, Anthony, and Cassian are cited as well—along, of course, with Thomas Aquinas, Teresa of Avila, John of the Cross, and others. The practice of *Lectio Divina* is explained (in the words of Dom Delatte's commentary on the Rule). This little book (fifty-six small pages) offers an unusual insight into the core of the Maritains' spirituality, into what they considered most important to convey. What is striking in their writing is their passionate love for God, and the honesty and earnestness of their search for ultimate Truth.

Spirituality and Politics

Yet this very openness to spiritual guides is not without its risks. Under the influence of Father Clérissac, his spiritual director, Jacques had let his socialist tendencies and his "liberalism" be critiqued, and out of obedience, even after Father Clérissac's death, Jacques supported (though he never joined) the "Action Française"—a nationalist, monarchist movement—and its leader Charles Maurras.[44] When in 1926 Rome condemned the movement, and forbade Catholic participation in it, Jacques was relieved, immediately obeyed, and wrote in 1927 *La Primauté du Spirituel*,[45] his first systematic reflection on the relationship between spiritual and temporal power. His continued thinking on the subject led him to be a seminal

---

[40] Ibid., 56.

[41] What is called in French *oraison,* simply being silent before God.

[42] The French title is *La Vie d'Oraison.*

[43] Jacques and Raïssa Maritain, *Prayer and Intelligence* (New York: Sheed & Ward, 1943).

[44] Raïssa Maritain, *Les grandes Amitiés,* 400ff.

[45] The English translation is entitled: *The Things That Are Not Caesar's.*

influence upon Vatican II's formulation of the role and status of the laity, the values of the individual conscience, the dignity and rights of the human person, and the value of democracy[46] reflected in such documents as *Lumen Gentium* and *Gaudium et Spes.* He was formally consulted about those matters, and Paul VI called himself "a disciple of Maritain."[47]

Even though she disliked the political arena and avoided it, the controversy was painful for Raïssa as well. Friendships were broken. They lost Dom Delatte, but gained Dom Florent Miège, a Carthusian, whose friendship, said Jacques, more than compensated for any hatred he encountered. They questioned the nature and limits of spiritual direction and of one's obedience, and saw more clearly that directees need to form their conscience, not abandon it.[48]

As painful as it had been, the Action Française incident made Jacques free to expand his thinking along the lines of social justice, leading him to publish in 1936 *True Humanism,* a book which, according to Julie Kernan, could be considered a charter for social action. At this time, Jacques had started to give courses at the Institute of Medieval Studies in Toronto, and gave lectures at the University of Chicago and at Catholic University. He spoke against anti-Semitism, and took an anti-Franco stance. His social ideas caused him to be poorly received at first even at Notre Dame,[49] where he was to return many times to lecture and where the Maritain Center (which now houses most of Jacques and Raïssa's writings) was constituted in 1958.

The Maritains in the United States

World War II broke out as the Maritains were spending the summer near the Benedictine abbeys of Solesmes and Fontgombault.[50] Still hopeful of French victory, they left for the United States in January 1940. Shortly thereafter, the French having been defeated, they found themselves exiled in the United States, cut off from French financial resources. Jacques, of necessity, engaged in a heavy schedule of writing and lecturing, and Raïssa worked on her memoirs, as they settled for the duration of the war in an apartment on Fifth Avenue in New York. Despite their own anguish and their work, the Maritains' home became again a center of hospitality. Once more, people were attracted to Catholicism through them, and they had a number of adult godchildren.

---

[46] Kernan, *Our Friend, Jacques Maritain,* 172.

[47] Ibid., 173.

[48] Raïssa Maritain, *Les grandes Amitiés,* 412.

[49] Kernan, *Our Friend, Jacques Maritain,* 93.

[50] Ibid., 119.

In 1945, when the war was over, Jacques was named French ambassador to the Vatican. He accepted, but resigned after two years. In 1947 he was offered a resident professorship at Princeton, in the philosophy department, to teach a graduate course in ethics based on Thomist principles. He accepted in 1948, and the household settled in Princeton for twelve years.[51] In addition, Jacques taught at New York's Hunter College, and each year went to lecture at Notre Dame, as well as at the University of Chicago.

Final Years

In the early fifties, Fr. René Voillaume, first prior of the Little Brothers of Jesus, asked Jacques to help organize a body of philosophical studies suitable for the formation of the Little Brothers.[52] This was the beginning of a long association. After Raïssa's death in 1960, the Little Brothers offered him a home. He then disposed of his material goods and lived among them. In 1969, at the age of eighty-four, he made his novitiate in Toulouse[53] and became formally one of them. He lived four more years as a Little Brother, died in Toulouse in 1973, and was buried next to Raïssa in Kolbsheim.[54]

The years before Raïssa's death had been difficult, painful years for them. The troubles started with Jacques' heart attack in March 1954, from which he took about six months to recover.[55] Then, in 1957, Vera became ill with breast cancer. After an apparent recovery and remission, the cancer reappeared the next year and, after a long illness, she died on New Year's Eve 1959. Seven months later, Raïssa had a stroke while on vacation in France. She died November 4, 1960.[56]

Still, during the time of Vera's illness, Jacques and Raïssa wrote *Liturgy and Contemplation*. Julie Kernan calls this book "the best key to the spiritual ideals which the Maritains tried all their lives to attain themselves."[57] It is also a rather Benedictine book. Two main influences are credited in the first chapter: Dom Virgil Michel, of St. John's Abbey, Collegeville, Minnesota, and Madame Cécile Bruyère, Abbess of Sainte-Cecile in Solesmes.[58] Contemplation, for the Maritains, is something to

---

[51] Ibid., 148.

[52] Ibid., 151.

[53] Ibid., 185.

[54] Ibid., 187.

[55] Raïssa Maritain, *Raïssa's Journal: Presented by Jacques Maritain*, 324.

[56] Ibid., 334.

[57] Kernan, *Our Friend, Jacques Maritain*, 159.

[58] Jacques and Raïssa Maritain, *Liturgy and Contemplation*, trans. Joseph W. Evans (New York: P. J. Kenedy & Sons, 1960).

which every Christian is called. Liturgy leads to contemplation. Though individual contemplation may seem to be the most personal thing in the world, the one thus engaged "is a member of the Church, more than ever, and by highest right."[59] Contemplation connects one to the prayer of the Church.

The death of Raïssa left a great void in Jacques' life. Though she stayed more in the background of his professional work, she read all that he wrote and gave him feedback. She, of course, was also a writer in her own right. Her contemplative spirituality nourished his. He always missed her, though he felt very much at home with the Little Brothers.

The Maritains' story is an unusual story of love and faithfulness. They were two people in love with God and with each other, two people about whom one could truly say that they loved each other in God. Though at times they became well-to-do and successful, they did not grasp for status or power, but kept their aim true. They were faithful their entire life to their young resolve in the Jardin des Plantes. They opened their lives and home to the needs of others. They loved the Church. In an important sense, they were Benedict's children, obedient and faithful listeners, whose lives stayed fully open to transformation until their very last days.

[59] Ibid., 23.

16

Walker Percy: The End of His Beginning[1]

Edward J. Dupuy

What we call the beginning is often the end
And to make an end is to make a beginning.

—T. S. Eliot

Four Quartets

When Walker Percy became a Benedictine oblate of St. Joseph Abbey on February 16, 1990, he was already very near the end of his life. His prostate cancer had metastasized, and it finally subdued him on May 10, 1990—less than three months after his final oblation.

Very much aware of the seriousness of his illness, he wrote in July of 1989 to his lifelong friend, Shelby Foote (the noted novelist and Civil War historian):

> We're headed for Mayo's tomorrow—on the strength of a new drug combo (something called interferon and 5FU) said to be promising in some cancers.
>
> The worst thing is the traveling and hospitals. Flying around the U.S. is awful and hospitals are no place for anyone, let alone a sick man.
>
> I'll tell you what I've discovered. Dying, if that's what it comes to, is no big thing since I'm ready for it, and prepared for it by the Catholic faith which I believe. What is a pain is not even the pain but the nuisance. It is a tremendous bother (and expense) to everyone. Worst of all is the indignity. Who wants to go to pot before strangers, be an object of head-shaking for friends, a lot of trouble to kin? . . .
>
> Seriously, and now that I think of it, in this age of unbelief I am astounded at how few people facing certain indignity in chronic illness make an end to it. Few if any. I am not permitted to.[2]

---

[1] The author wishes to thank Fr. Raphael Barousse, o.s.b., of St. Joseph Abbey, for his assistance.

[2] Jay Tolson, ed., *The Correspondence of Shelby Foote & Walker Percy* (New York: Doubletake/Norton, 1997) 302–3.

This sobering letter heralds not only the end but also the beginning of Percy's life as a writer. In it he touches on the issues and questions that face all of his protagonists in what he often called this "post-Christian age."

Early Years

Born in Birmingham, Alabama, on May 28, 1916, Walker Percy came from a family of wealth and privilege. His grandfather, also named Walker Percy and a prominent member of Birmingham society, married into the DeBardeleben family, who were central to the burgeoning steel industry. Grandfather Walker's marriage brought together two of the wealthiest families of the state. Yet wealth and responsibility had a shadow side. Bertram Wyatt-Brown has shown how such privilege, especially in the South, often brought with it a stifling sense of honor, duty, and obligation that could lead to depression, despair, and suicide.[3] Grandfather Walker committed suicide on February 8, 1916—three months before Walker Percy's birth, on May 28, 1916. Thirteen years later Percy's father, LeRoy, took his own life. Two years after that, Percy's mother was killed in an automobile accident. Percy and his two brothers were taken in and raised by his cousin, William Alexander Percy, a lawyer, poet, and memoirist from Greenville, Mississippi, whom Percy called "Uncle Will."[4] Will, who had thought of religious life in his early years, was a lapsed Catholic. He provided Percy and his brothers with an active literary household, a good dose of Southern Stoicism, and ethical Christianity, which gave them some mooring in what must have seemed a random world. The boys were Presbyterian by birth, and though they attended Sunday school and services, it may be safe to say that they were more impressed by the presence of their "fabled relative," as Percy put it in his introduction to *Lanterns on the Levee,* than they were by any presence at Sunday services. It is glib to say that the tragedies of his early life and his upbringing by Uncle Will marked the future writer, but how could they not?

A Thematic Struggle

In one of his many interviews, Percy acknowledges that suicide is a leitmotif throughout his works and that it is consciously so—used to ex-

---

[3] See Bertram Wyatt-Brown, *The House of Percy: Honor, Melancholy, and Imagination in a Southern Family* (New York: Oxford University Press, 1994).

[4] Will Percy's most famous book is *Lanterns on the Levee: Recollections of a Planter's Son,* originally published by Knopf in 1941 but reprinted by Louisiana State University Press in 1973, with an introduction by Walker Percy.

plore a certain state of being left unexplored in the literature of the South or of the nation at large. In his first novel, *The Moviegoer,* he created Binx Bolling, possibly his most well-known character, in part as a foil to Quentin Compson, perhaps the best-known character of the best-known Southern writer, William Faulkner: "I would like to think of starting where Faulkner left off, of starting with the Quentin Compson who didn't commit suicide. Suicide is easy. Keeping Quentin Compson alive is something else. In a way, Binx Bolling is Quentin Compson who didn't commit suicide."[5]

Although despair and the possibility of suicide loom large in many of Percy's works, it would be inaccurate to say that is his major concern as a writer. Rather, he tries to find a way beyond it—a way through the sometimes morbid sense of honor of his family history and his region (and the malaise of living death that has grown throughout American culture at large) to the possibility of redemption. It is accurate to say that possibility and meaning run throughout his works, and they, more than anything else, reflect Percy's interests as a writer. Note that the letter he wrote to Shelby Foote has echoes of possibility and hope beyond the despair that terminal illness can breed. Yet such possibility was neither won nor maintained easily.

When he wrote Foote in July of 1989, Percy had already published six novels, beginning in 1961 with the National Book Award winning *The Moviegoer,* a collection of philosophical essays on the nature of language and meaning, *The Message in the Bottle* (1975), and a serious yet comic book in the vein of Søren Kierkegaard's *Either/Or—Lost in the Cosmos* (1983)—which carries as its main subtitle *The Last Self-Help Book.*[6] He was working on another book about the philosophy of language even as he wrote to Foote toward the end of his life:

> Like I say, it's too damn much trouble, the running around looking for a cure. I'm content to sit here and try to finish *Contra Gentiles,* a somewhat smart-ass collection of occasional pieces, including one which should interest you—"Three New Signs, all more important than and different from the 59,018 Sign of Charles Sanders Peirce." You want a copy?[7]

Contra Gentiles never made it to a publisher, although a collection of Percy's occasional prose was edited posthumously by Patrick H. Samway, s.j., under the title of *Signposts in a Strange Land* (1992).

[5] Lewis A. Lawson and Victor Kramer, eds., *Conversations with Walker Percy* (Jackson: University Press of Mississippi, 1985) 300.

[6] Percy's other novels include *The Last Gentleman* (1966); *Love in the Ruins* (1971); *Lancelot* (1977); *The Second Coming* (1980); and *The Thanatos Syndrome* (1987). Except for *The Moviegoer,* which was originally published by Knopf, Percy published all of his works with Farrar, Straus, and Giroux.

[7] Tolson, *The Correspondence,* 303.

At a memorial ceremony held at St. Ignatius Church in New York City a few months after Percy's death, Eudora Welty said that Percy did not begin his literary life as a "wide-eyed dreamer." Instead she suggested that "he already knew the world, he already knew its literature and he must have early begun to heed and to explore what was already a trustworthy insight into himself the man." She went on to note that she suspects "that he had prepared for becoming a novelist for as long as he had lived."[8] Welty's insight may well be true, but it is given in the preterit, and it may not have been always apparent to Walker Percy himself. His path to a writing career, to faith in the Roman Catholic Church, and to oblation at a remote Benedictine monastery was circuitous at best.

Percy the Physician/Percy the Novelist

After graduation from Greenville High School, Percy attended the University of North Carolina at Chapel Hill, where he earned a degree in chemistry. He went from UNC to Columbia's College of Physicians and Surgeons, earning an M.D. Percy admired the scientific method for its rigor, certitude, and self-correcting nature. He was in many ways a man of his time, taken with the view proffered at Columbia—of the "mechanism of disease"—an epistemological method that posited order in the face of disorder. At this time in his life he had very little to do with the mysteries of any religion, let alone those of the Catholic Church. While working as an intern at Bellevue in New York City, Percy contracted tuberculosis, thus becoming a victim of the mechanism of a disease that he had studied only in others—and from a remove. Once diagnosed, he took up residence at Trudeau Sanatorium in Saranac Lake, New York, and there, like Hans Castorp in Thomas Mann's *The Magic Mountain,* he "took the cure."[9] He did return to Columbia to teach pathology for a time after his first "break" of tuberculosis, but a subsequent bout with it necessitated a stay at Gaylord Farm Sanatorium in Connecticut and virtually ended his medical career. Although he liked to quip later in his life that he was the happiest "failed

---

[8] This remembrance is taken from a monograph published by Farrar, Straus, and Giroux (Percy's publishers) after the memorial service. Other speakers at the service were Shelby Foote, Robert Giroux, Stanley Kauffmann, Patrick Samway, s.j., Mary Lee Settle, and Wilfrid Sheed. The monograph has no page numbers.

[9] See Patrick H. Samway, *Walker Percy: A Life* (New York: Farrar, Straus, and Giroux, 1997) 118ff. Percy's unpublished and lost apprentice novel, "The Charterhouse," borrowed from his time at Trudeau and, according to Samway, was largely Wolfean in style. His second apprentice novel, "The Gramercy Winner"—of which there is an extant typescript among Percy's papers at UNC—was a tribute to Mann's *The Magic Mountain* and borrowed even more directly from Percy's experiences at Trudeau.

doctor" there ever was, his time at Saranac Lake and Gaylord Farm, like the death of his parents, brought him to a "change of focus" in his life.

While taking the cure, Percy read. Always voracious in his appetite for books, he turned away from "McCleod's *Physiology* and Gay's *Bacteriology,* and took up the works of Søren Kierkegaard, Martin Heidegger, Gabriel Marcel, Jean-Paul Sartre, and Albert Camus."[10] Through his reading of the existentialists, he came to see that the scientific view, in which he had put so much stock, left a "huge gap" in the understanding of the world. Because science looks at "specimens" and "classes" of items, it has a tendency to discard the importance of the individual. Instead science looks at an individual only inasmuch as it relates and measures up to other specimens of a general class. The individual entity, that is, is lost in favor of its relation to the general. Such a condition may not seem perilous when dealing with pine trees or dragonflies. When applied to persons, however, its limitations become apparent. As Percy writes in a later essay:

> What did at last dawn on me as a medical student and intern, a practitioner, I thought, of the scientific method, was that there was a huge gap in the scientific view of the world. This sector of the world about which science could not utter a single word was nothing less than this: what it is like to be an individual living in the United States in the twentieth century.[11]

This insight, which Percy said had "all the force of a revelation" for him,[12] brought him to see novels as that art form capable of exploring this "huge gap." Novel-writing for Percy was a type of cognitive science, not the positive science (or scientism) that reduces individuals to a class, but science taken in its root sense of "knowing." Novels—a type of "indirect communication" Kierkegaard adopted[13]—provide an avenue to explore the individual, especially the individual consciousness.

By exploring an individual consciousness in words, Percy hoped to wake up the reader to the sense of loss he saw as a product of a "misapprehension of the scientific method."[14] In *The Moviegoer,* for example, Binx Bolling calls the "malaise" the "pain of loss. The world is lost to you, the world and the people in it, and there remains only you and the world and you no more able to be in the world than Banquo's ghost."[15] This "loss" Binx describes repeats closely what Percy said in one of his early

---

[10] Samway, *Walker Percy: A Life,* 126.

[11] Walker Percy, *Signposts in a Strange Land* (Farrar, Straus, and Giroux, 1992) 213.

[12] Ibid., 213.

[13] See Lewis A. Lawson, "Walker Percy's Indirect Communications," *Following Percy: Essays on Walker Percy's Work* (Troy, N.Y.: Whitston Publishing Company, 1988) 4–40.

[14] Percy, *Signposts in a Strange Land,* 210.

[15] Percy, *The Moviegoer,* 106.

essays, "The Loss of the Creature," published originally in the University of Houston *Forum* and later reprinted in *The Message in the Bottle*. In this essay, Percy follows Whitehead by calling the "loss" of malaise a consequence of the "fallacy of misplaced concreteness. It is the mistaking of an idea, a principle, an abstraction, for the real."[16] For Percy contends that the elevation of science (idolatry, he says in one place) bifurcates consciousness and persons into theorists or consumers, angels or beasts, afloat in the transcendent world or sunk in the everydayness of the immanent. How does one recapture the real—the immanent and transcendent—especially when one is unaware that it is lost in the first place? Percy's explorations of consciousness in his novels and essays seek to make readers aware of such loss and to bring them to a point of action.

It is important to note that "consciousness" derives from the Latin *conscio,* "to know with." For Percy, the novelist and the reader "know with" one another through the words of the novel. The novelist is a "namer" of a peculiar disorder of consciousness in the postmodern age. Percy thus corrects what he sees as an errant view of consciousness that has lingered since Descartes, who saw the conscious mind separated from the world (*res cogitans* separate from *res extensa*). This view remained in Sartre, who posited a sort of free-floating consciousness, one that is simply "there." Percy argues instead for an "intersubjectivity," a knowing with one another through language.[17] I know this is a chair, for example, because of the word "chair" and because you are there with me to accept and validate the thing and the word. Percy would repeat and expand upon this "revelation" that changed his focus in various ways throughout his life and, to my mind, it cannot be separated from his eventual entry into the Catholic Church and oblation to the Benedictine expression of that faith at St. Joseph Abbey. The emphasis of the Church on the dignity of the individual human person and the view of life espoused by monastic profession—an individual pilgrimage of faith in community—both find expression in Percy's linguistic basis of consciousness.

St. Joseph Abbey, Beginnings as a Writer, Conversion, and Oblation

The Abbey of St. Joseph, which became so important to Percy, was founded in 1889 in Gessen, Louisiana, by a handful of monks from St. Meinrad Abbey in Indiana. The abbey took its name from one of the

---

[16] Walker Percy, *The Message in the Bottle* (New York: Farrar, Straus, and Giroux, 1975) 58.

[17] See "Symbol, Consciousness, and Intersubjectivity," *The Message in the Bottle,* 265–76. See also Mary Deems Howland, *The Gift of the Other: Gabriel Marcel's Concept of Intersubjectivity in Walker Percy's Novels* (Pittsburgh: Duquesne University Press, 1990).

founding monks' favorite saints. Fr. Luke Gruwe, O.S.B., had a strong devotion to St. Joseph, and he wanted to name the new town after him. A St.
Joseph, Louisiana, already existed, however, so he "named the place
'Gessen,' after the land in Egypt which Pharaoh gave to the people of an
earlier Joseph."[18] The monastery endured the difficult beginning years and,
with the support of Archbishop Francis Janssens of New Orleans, it looked
to a prosperous future. Janssens' death in 1897, prolonged periods of ex-
treme weather, and an outbreak of malaria, however, all contributed to the
monks' realization that they had to begin again—and in a new place. They
purchased twelve hundred acres of land near Covington, Louisiana, on
November 20, 1901, and two years later the foundation was granted the
status of an independent abbey.[19] They would undergo hardships in Covington—including a fire in 1907 that completely destroyed their build-
ings—but they endured and thrived. It is this foundation in Covington that
made possible the convergence of Benedictine history with Walker Percy's
history a half century later.

While the monks of St. Joseph Abbey prayed for world peace and for
the safety of three of their own priests who served in the armed forces during World War II, Walker Percy faced the necessity of another period of
"the cure" in 1945. After a 136-day stay at Gaylord Farm Sanatorium,
Percy was scheduled to teach pathology in the fall at Columbia, but illness
prevented him from doing so. Patrick Samway reports that Percy later told
Robert Coles he "wanted to go home, but [he] had no home."[20] He returned
to Greenville to live for a while with his brother and sister-in-law (Uncle
Will had died in 1942), and in the summer of 1946 he and Shelby Foote
left Greenville for Santa Fe, New Mexico, where they took up temporary
residence at Rancho La Merced. Bothered by the sense that he had "not
emerged from his illness with a career or even prospects for a family life,"
Percy telegrammed Mary Bernice Townsend (Bunt), whom he had dated
from time to time and who was working in New Orleans: "I need you to
be my wife. I am neurotic as hell. I need you to get me out of my state. I
love you."[21] They married in New Orleans at the First Baptist Church on
the corner of St. Charles Avenue and Delachaise on November 7, 1946.

After a prolonged stay at Brinkwood, Will Percy's house in the Tennessee hills near Sewanee, and after Percy began concentrated work on
what would become his first apprentice novel, the Percys moved to New

[18] See *A Century of Grace: A Pictorial History of St. Joseph Abbey and Seminary* (St.
Benedict, La.: St. Joseph Abbey, 1989) 3.

[19] Ibid., 8–10.

[20] Samway, *Walker Percy: A Life,* 136.

[21] Ibid., 140–1.

Orleans. There, they both took instruction to become Catholics. Always reticent to speak of the reasons he converted—"How to write about conversion if it is true that faith is an unmerited gift from God? How to describe, let alone explain it, if this is the case? When it comes to grace I get writer's block?"—Percy was asked to do so outright by Clifton Fadiman for a book Fadiman published in 1990.[22] He acknowledges his own reticence on the topic and relates it to the writer's business of indirection and not straightforward prose:

> [One] reason for reticence is that novelists are a devious lot to begin with, disinclined to say anything straight out, especially about themselves, since their stock-in-trade is indirection, if not guile, coming at things and people from the side so to speak, especially the blind side, the better to get at them. If anybody says anything straight out, it is apt to be one of their characters, a character, moreover, for which they have not much use.[23]

Later in the essay, Percy does speak somewhat directly about his turn to Catholicism, and he relates it to the misapprehension of the scientific method—and its creation of the theorist/consumer split—already discussed: "The scientific method is correct as far as it goes, but the theoretical mindset, which assigns significance to single things and events only insofar as they are exemplars of theory or items for consumption, is in fact an inflation of a method of knowing and is unwarranted."[24] He goes on to say that the reasons for his conversion to the Catholic Church "can best be described as Roman, Arthurian, Semitic, and semiotic."[25] The romantic broadsword tradition of Richard I in *Ivanhoe* recalls an earlier tradition—the stoicism of Marcus Aurelius. And both later find incarnation in R. E. Lee, the person about whom so many Southern romantics wax eloquent. The Jews, for their part, find a peculiar semiotic place in Percy's thought. For him, they are that sign that cannot be subsumed by theory: "In this desert . . . of theory and consumption, there remains only one sign, the Jews. By 'the Jews' I mean not only Israel, the exclusive people of God, but the worldwide ecclesia instituted by one of them, God-become-man, a Jew."[26]

[22] See Walker Percy's foreword to Dan O'Neill, ed., *The New Catholics: Contemporary Converts Tell Their Stories* (New York: Crossroad Publishing Company, 1987) xiii. Percy wrote "Why Are You a Catholic?" in 1990 for Clifton Fadiman, ed., *Living Philosophies: The Reflections of Some Eminent Men and Women of Our Time* (New York: Doubleday, 1990) 165–76, reprinted in *Signposts in a Strange Land*.

[23] Percy, *Signposts in a Strange Land,* 304.

[24] Ibid., 313.

[25] Ibid.

[26] Ibid., 314.

It is not very surprising, then, that when Walker and Bunt moved to Covington in the late 1940s, they were excited about having a Benedictine monastery nearby. The Benedictines tapped into Percy's romantic roots of faith. Like Marcus Aurelius, they must have seemed stoics and individualists. And like the Jews he admired so much, they, too, stood outside the theorist/consumer dilemma posed by the misapprehension of the scientific method. In *Pilgrim in the Ruins: A Life of Walker Percy,* Jay Tolson writes that "the solemnity and purpose of the brothers at the abbey struck a deep chord [in Percy]; their commitment represented an ideal of single-minded devotion and sacrifice that Percy hoped to emulate in his own work and life. And the monastic life had a powerful aesthetic appeal as well."[27] If it is true, as Dom David Knowles says, that Benedictines foster a "double polarity in the religious life—of other-worldliness and detachment, and of this-worldliness and attachment," then Percy would have felt even more at home with the monks of St. Joseph Abbey. For such a "double polarity" seems to correct the theorist/consumer, immanent/transcendent split he saw as dividing the consciousness of the denizens of the postmodern age.[28] Knowles goes on to say that the Benedictine takes "things as they are . . . not forcing them into categories or looking upon them as elements in a pre-arranged scheme, and it is this that gives him his independence."[29] What better attitude could Percy seek for recapturing the loss of the individual?

During his years in Covington, Percy, Bunt, and their two girls (Mary Pratt and Ann) befriended any number of the monks. Percy eventually taught a course at St. Joseph Seminary College, the monks' primary apostolate. In 1983, Percy was invited by Fr. Pius Lartigue, O.S.B., President-Rector of the seminary college, to deliver the commencement address. The original typescript of this address is framed in a portion of the campus library dedicated to Walker Percy, and it is reprinted in *Signposts in a Strange Land* as "A Cranky Novelist Reflects on the Church." Walker and Bunt were especially close to Fr. Andrew Becnel, O.S.B., and Fr. James Boulware, O.S.B. The two could not have been more different in character or outlook. Father Andrew was a canny Cajun, steeped in St. Thomas Aquinas, the patristics, and the divines. Father James was a modern, a sociologist who not only knew his sociology but who was also very well read in contemporary theology and literature. James knew his way around a tool shop, and he could often be found rewiring a building, tending to a

---

[27] Jay Tolson, *Pilgrim in the Ruins: A Life of Walker Percy* (New York: Simon and Schuster, 1992) 214.

[28] Dom David Knowles, *The Benedictines: A Digest for Moderns* (St. Leo, Fla.: The Abbey Press, 1962) 41.

[29] Ibid., 41–2.

broken air-conditioning unit, or making furniture. As a student at the college in the late 1970s, I saw the two men walking through the halls of the classroom building in animated conversation. I had no idea of either man's depth or stature.

Percy and James corresponded for a time before James left the abbey after the fall semester of 1980. In a letter to James dated September 22, 1979, Percy first broached the idea of teaching a course at the seminary college:

> My motives are a bit shady. It's not the munificent salary I'm interested in but a chance to grow closer to the Benedictine life and a Benedictine community. There is this vague hunch at the back of my mind that St. B may have as much to tell this sorry century as he did the 6th.[30]

Two weeks later, Percy followed up this letter with: "I have not been able to envision myself performing a valuable function teaching at St. Joseph's—yet. The truth is—what was in the back of my mind was a hankering to become a Benedictine—which ain't exactly practical." He goes on to say that he's not sure if the hankering is a result of "(1) writer's neurosis . . . (2) male menopause (3) true vocation (4) none of the above."[31] Six months later, Percy wrote James again, asking him to become his "spiritual advisor" and outlining an array of "paradoxes, axioms, questions that engage[d]" him.[32] In his response, James tried to assure Percy that some of the questions he posed were ones that still gnawed at him. He also tried to deflect some of the "romance" he saw in Percy's view of monasticism and the Church. Years later, Boulware told Jay Tolson that it was clear to him that Percy

> wanted the church to keep the world from going down the tubes. . . . He heard from me a much more liberal—and cynical—interpretation of the church than perhaps he was always comfortable with. I talked about the inner machinations of the hierarchy, and I would say that the American hierarchy needed to face the issues of the day. . . . He was reluctant to take the valuable and throw out the rest. He didn't do that with his life; so he couldn't do it with his faith.[33]

Perhaps it was this "all or nothing" character that Percy espoused in his life that so attracted him to the Benedictine way. Or perhaps it is the everyday blend of work and prayer that he so admired. When Percy did not speak of Roman, Arthurian, Semitic, and semiotic roots of his conversion, he said that Kierkegaard, more than anyone else, had much to do with his turning to the Catholic Church. I would like to think that Percy's attraction

---

[30] Unpublished letter from Walker Percy to James Boulware, September 22, 1979.

[31] Unpublished letter from Walker Percy to James Boulware, November 6, 1979.

[32] Unpublished letter from Walker Percy to James Boulware, May 20, 1980.

[33] Tolson, *Pilgrim in the Ruins,* 368.

to the Benedictine life has to do with Kierkegaard's "knight of faith," perhaps a continuation of a romantic view of religious life, but valuable nonetheless. For Kierkegaard makes no distinction in outward appearance between the knight of faith and a regular denizen of the modern world. In this view, the everydayness Binx finds so troublesome gives way to the mystery of the everyday. Always a proponent of the Catholic Church's (and the Benedictine's) emphasis on the incarnation, Percy found in the complex writings of this Protestant philosopher/theologian a vehicle for naming the bifurcated consciousness of the postmodern world and for an entry back into the mystery of being.

In *Fear and Trembling,* Johannes de Silentio describes the knight of faith:

> Here he is. The acquaintance is made, I am introduced to him. The instant I first lay eyes on him, I set him apart at once; I jump back, clap my hands, and say half aloud, "Good Lord, is this the man, is this really the one—he looks just like a tax collector!" . . . I examine his figure from top to toe to see if there may not be a crack through which the infinite would peek. No! He is solid all the way through. . . . He belongs entirely to the world; no bourgeois philistine could belong to it more. . . . He attends to his job. To see him makes one think of him as a pen-pusher who has lost his soul to Italian bookkeeping, so punctilious is he.[34]

Like Kierkegaard's knight of faith, Benedictine monks belong entirely to "the world," and they do most of the things that everyone else does—but for altogether different reasons. They bear witness to the grace of incarnation by recognizing grace in the everyday circumstances of their lives.

Kierkegaard used to stroll through the streets of Copenhagen so that people thought he was an "idler"—all the while writing some forty odd volumes of work. Persons in and around Covington, Louisiana, often described Walker Percy as a "regular" guy—even as he produced a body of fiction and essays that have spawned much inquiry and hope. While it may be almost impossible to speak of another's religious convictions (as Percy recognized), perhaps he saw in the monks of St. Joseph Abbey a solidity to counter his own perceived lack of definition, an avenue to unite the infinite and the finite, a way to overcome the split between consumer and theorist. Percy's end as a Benedictine oblate stretches back to his beginnings as a child of an honorable, melancholic family. His writing bears testimony to the hope that is always and already available in everyday life and in the mystery of death—an end which is yet another beginning.

---

[34] Søren Kierkegaard, *Fear and Trembling/Repetition,* ed. and trans. Howard V. Hong and Edna H. Hong (Princeton, N.J.: Princeton University Press, 1983) 38–9.

17

Faithful to the Very End:
Oliver Plunkett, Irish Martyr and Archbishop

Jem Sullivan

Introduction

The life of St. Oliver Plunkett, archbishop and martyr, is a mid-seventeenth-century tale of courage in the face of rank injustice, steadfast faith in the midst of severe religious persecution, and boundless hope in the life that is to come. Martyred at Tyburn, England, on July 1, 1681, during a renewed wave of religious persecution, Oliver Plunkett's life exemplifies the heroic virtues witnessed to by the Church's martyrs through the ages. His life is also the story of a memorable and unique Benedictine oblate.

Typically one becomes a Benedictine oblate during the course of a formal ceremony at which the candidate makes his or her final oblation. For some, that moment in time marks a new beginning. For others, it serves to confirm an existing spiritual path. Still others profess their oblation as the culmination of a lifelong journey. Oliver Plunkett's oblation is unique because it took place during the final days of his life while he was preparing for martyrdom in prison.[1] Consequently, he was not, strictly speaking, affiliated to a particular monastery. Instead, Oliver Plunkett considered himself under a form of obedience to a fellow prisoner, Dom Maurus Corker, president of the English Benedictine Congregation, to whom he referred all decisions during the last days of his life. This uncommon form of oblation made at the hands of Dom Corker, to whom he also bequeathed his body, is the basis for his inclusion in this volume, and it can be argued

---

[1] *The Book of Saints: A Dictionary of Servants of God,* comp. the Benedictine monks of St. Augustine's Abbey, Ramsgate (Wilton, Conn.: Morehouse Publishing, 1989) 422.

that the fact of Oliver Plunkett's oblation is based on a rather loose inter-
pretation of the events surrounding his final days. However, in spite of
possible questions concerning his atypical oblation, the circumstances of
Oliver Plunkett's extraordinary life and his martyrdom bear ample witness
to a life lived in the spirit of the promises typically made by an oblate of
St. Benedict.

Life Story

The life of Oliver Plunkett may be divided into three successive
stages beginning in Ireland, followed by almost two decades he spent as
an "exile" in Rome, first as a student, and later on as a professor, and culminating in his return to and martyrdom in Ireland.[2]

Oliver was born to John and Thomasina Plunkett, a prominent Irish
family, on All Saints Day, November 1, 1625. Of his childhood very little
is known beyond the fact that his early education was entrusted to his uncle,
a young Cistercian, Doctor Patrick Plunkett. A few years later this uncle
was appointed Abbot of St. Mary's, Dublin, where he is credited with re-
building part of the ancient abbey. In time, he would be appointed Bishop
of Ardagh and Meath. Under his uncle's guidance, Oliver's education included reading, writing, and grammar. But as one biographer notes,
Oliver's education was not limited to pedagogical training alone, for "during these formative years the wise teacher did not neglect the spiritual training of his young pupil."[3] Consequently, in the early 1630s Oliver Plunkett
was introduced, at a rather young age, to monastic spirituality as he began
his education, possibly with the monastic community of St. Mary's at Kil-
cloon. Undoubtedly, this early spiritual influence had a formative impact on
his life's journey, and his heroic embrace of his eventual martyrdom.

Having completed his elementary education at the age of sixteen,
Plunkett was ready to begin higher studies in Ireland. But this was not to
be, for, by the end of 1641, all of Ireland was in a state of rebellion. Oliver
remained with his uncle and monk, Patrick Plunkett, who hoped instead to
send him to Rome for further studies. Once again we learn of the formative
influence the monk had on young Oliver's life in the words of Emmanuel
Curtis, who writes,

---

[2] Since 1975, the year of Oliver Plunkett's canonization, there has been a steady stream
of literature devoted to the life and the writings of this saintly martyr and archbishop. For
succinct biographies see Emmanuel Curtis, *Blessed Oliver Plunkett* (Dublin: Clonmore &
Reynolds Ltd., 1963), and Tomás Ó Fiaich and Desmond Forristal, *Oliver Plunkett* (Hunt-
ington, Ind.: Our Sunday Visitor, Inc., 1975).

[3] Curtis, *Blessed Oliver Plunkett,* 14.

hitherto he had taught him to read books and to con their meaning; now he had to teach him the more difficult art of reading men. Such an experience would broaden his outlook and give him a sense of proportion . . . of his own personal worth, of his own personal integrity.[4]

In the midst of the growing political turmoil of 1642, at the young age of seventeen, Oliver Plunkett decided on a vocation to the priesthood. To this end, he would have to leave Ireland and pursue his studies at an Irish college abroad. He was fortunate, a year later in 1643, to meet Fr. Pier Francesco Scarampi, an Oratorian priest, sent to Ireland as the Papal Envoy of Pope Urban VIII. Father Scarampi would also exert a profound influence on young Oliver's life, for in mid-February 1647 Oliver Plunkett, together with four other Irishmen and Father Scarampi, left Ireland for Rome. It was a perilous sea and land journey made even more dangerous, in those days, by lurking pirates, bands of roving robbers, and ocean storms. The company eventually reached Rome on May 15, 1647. For the next two decades the Eternal City would be Oliver Plunkett's temporary home.

At the turn of the mid-seventeenth century, the city of Rome was being prepared for the Jubilee Year of 1650 in which the young Irish pilgrim fully participated, as we learn from his letters. However, the state of turmoil in Ireland resulted in a severe lack of funds for student priests at the Irish College. While relying on the generosity of Father Scarampi who provided him with monetary assistance and temporary lodging, Plunkett was forced to wait for three years before his formal entrance into the Irish College. His days at the Irish College in Rome passed quickly and he distinguished himself as a "gifted and exceptional student." Then, on New Year's Day 1654, Oliver Plunkett was ordained a priest. Now he longed for the day when he would return home, but once again the political and social circumstances in Ireland prevented his immediate departure.

In 1654 Catholic Ireland was in the throes of the Cromwellian persecution. Consequently, in one of the earliest letters which still survives in his own hand, the young priest petitioned for permission to stay in Rome while stating his willingness to return to Ireland whenever his superiors saw fit. He would avail, once again, of the hospitality of the Oratorian Fathers of San Girolamo della Carità. It was during these years of his continued exile in Rome that Plunkett obtained doctorates in canon law and in theology. On Father Scarampi's recommendation he was appointed professor of theology, and for some twelve years taught speculative and moral theology. In his spare time he devoted himself to works of charity, especially to the care of the sick, the abandoned, and the poor of Rome. An Oratorian priest would

[4] Ibid., 16.

later recall that Plunkett frequented the sanctuaries of the early Christian martyrs and took time to care for the infirm and the lonely. On one such visit, the Prior of the Santo Spirito Hospital in Rome declared to Plunkett, "You are now going to shed your blood for your faith."[5] His humble response speaks volumes: "I am unworthy of it; yet help me with your prayers, that this my desire may be fulfilled."[6]

In July 1669, his twenty-two year exile in Rome would come to a sudden end when he was appointed by Pope Clement XI to the See of Armagh. On the First Sunday in Advent, December 1, 1669, at the age of forty-four, Oliver Plunkett was consecrated archbishop of Armagh, Ireland. The third and final phase of his life was about to begin, and the episcopal and political challenges that lay ahead of the young archbishop were daunting. One indication of the gravity of the political situation in Ireland was the occasion of his consecration ceremony, which was conducted in strict secrecy in a private episcopal chapel in Brussels. Another equally telling sign was the fact, recorded in his letters, that the first few months of his return to Ireland were spent in disguise. The newly appointed archbishop of Armagh was forced to assume a false identity under the name of "Captain Brown," and carry with him the appropriate martial attire of swords and pistols!

On his return to Ireland as archbishop of Armagh, Oliver Plunkett also faced innumerable challenges in his pastoral work among the Irish laity and religious who were still suffering from the ruthless suppressions of the Cromwellian decade. While it is well beyond the scope of this essay to describe what one author refers to as the "shattered fabric of the Irish Church" in the mid-seventeenth century, suffice it to say that the steady flow of letters from the newly appointed Archbishop to the Holy See paint a rather dismal picture.[7]

For example, the numbers of dioceses far outweighed the ranks of Irish bishops to the extent that "although there were thirty-four dioceses in Ireland there were only six bishops." Emmanuel Curtis vividly describes the disheartening situation when he observes that "without doing anything else, it would take them all their time to administer the Sacrament of Confirmation to the faithful." In a report of December 1673 Oliver Plunkett would write: "During the past four years I confirmed forty eight thousand, six hundred and

---

[5] Ibid., 30–1.

[6] Ibid.

[7] Today an ever growing corpus of literature provides us with vivid descriptions of the state of the Irish church after the Cromwellian decade. For Plunkett's own description of the conditions in the Irish church of his time refer to John Hanly, ed., *The Letters of Saint Oliver Plunkett: 1625–1681* (Dublin: The Dolmen Press, 1979).

fifty five!"[8] As "pastor of souls," Plunkett's determination against the odds are well attested to in the following description of his untiring pastoral work:

> He [Plunkett] saddled his horse and continued his round of the northern dioceses. There was plenty of work, plenty of work to be done, for some districts had not seen a bishop in forty years. The young Primate took it all in his stride. Kilmore, Clogher, Derry, Dromore, Down, and Conor—all had been visited by the end of September. Considering the difficulty of travel in those days, the journeys alone must have called for real feats of physical endurance. Yet the labours and fatigues of the road were but the prelude to the real work of this tireless apostle. . . . He was indefatigable, therefore, in instructing the people, to whom he preached both in English and in Irish. There were times, as he was forced to confess, when he could scarcely stand with fatigue. . . . Oliver had one consolation on his journeys—the companionship of his friend and servant, James McKenna.[9]

Time and time again the archbishop of Armagh and Primate of Ireland found himself in the midst of bitter disputes and deep divisions among prelates, clergy, religious, and laity. Predictably this situation played directly into the hands of the King's Viceroy, the Earl of Essex, who is reported to have declared that "one of the most important things I could do is to keep these men divided, or if they were united to break them again."[10] Plunkett's repeated attempts to resolve various intra-Church disputes sowed seeds of hostility and revenge among a few disgruntled clerical parties. Years later, at Plunkett's trial, these men would betray their longstanding grudges against the archbishop by willingly and falsely testifying against him.

In March 1673 the English government demanded the expulsion of all bishops and clergy from Ireland and enforced a ruthless suppression of religious houses. By mid-November 1673 this renewal of religious persecution forced Plunkett and his fellow bishops into hiding, into what he would later refer to as a fifteen-month-long "severe noviciate." He describes their plight in these words:

> Catholics are so afraid of losing their property that no one with anything to lose will give succour to bishop or regular. The priests give nothing to the bishop, so that sometimes I find it difficult to procure even oaten bread. The hut in which we are is thatched with straw. When we go to bed, we can see the stars through the opening in the roof, whilst every slightest shower refreshes us. For all that, we are determined to die from hunger and cold rather than abandon our flocks.[11]

[8] Curtis, *Blessed Oliver Plunkett,* 59.
[9] Ibid., 63–4.
[10] Ibid., 102.
[11] Ibid., 110.

By the end of the following year, a period of temporary calm was restored and bishops and priests came out of hiding. But before long, in late 1678, the same edicts were again enforced. Bishops and priests were banished, convents and religious houses were suppressed, and Catholic schools were destroyed. This time, Oliver Plunkett sensed a more personal and imminent danger that would prompt him to write, "I am morally certain that I shall be taken, so many are in search of me. Yet in spite of danger I will remain with my flock, nor will I abandon them till they drag me to the ship."

In early November 1679 Oliver Plunkett received news of his uncle's failing health. So as Patrick Plunkett, his childhood mentor and spiritual guide, lay deathly ill, Oliver set out to comfort his dying kinsman. As he had done on previous occasions, Plunkett disguised himself and changed his name. By the month's end, Patrick Plunkett was dead. His trusted nephew, now archbishop Oliver Plunkett, mourned him, and then prepared for the perilous trip home. But this particular journey would be cut short, for as he attempted to return home the archbishop was captured on December 6, 1679, and taken prisoner in Dublin Castle.

Once in custody, Plunkett was held prisoner on charges that implicated him in the so-called "Popish Plot," the supposed attempt of those who were seen as subverting the King's government by fomenting a revolt that would lead to the establishment of the "Popish religion." As his various trials proceeded, the specific charge being brought against him was his alleged and direct role as archbishop in a "conspiracy to overthrow king and government in order to establish the Catholic faith and uproot Protestantism." The final stage of his life would unfold over a period of eighteen months as the captured archbishop endured persecution and calumny while in prison, at his trial, and ultimately at his martyrdom.

As a political prisoner, Plunkett was subject to a series of trials beginning in Dundalk, Ireland, and culminating with his appearance in the docket of Westminster Hall, London, on May 3, 1681.[12] He was given only five weeks to prepare his defense and obtain the needed witnesses and made to face an English jury which did not need to abide by laws of evidence. Hearsay evidence, not permitted by English jury law, was admitted at Plunkett's trials, adding to the injustices against him. Moreover, while ensuring that no documentation against their witnesses were easily obtained, his accusers gathered a formidable, albeit timorous, group of ex-

---

[12] For an engaging account of Plunkett's trials refer to Alice Curtayne, *The Trial of Oliver Plunkett* (New York: Sheed and Ward, 1953). A small sheet of paper, preserved in Downside Abbey, contains Plunkett's notes of the points and a list of documents he intended to use in his own defense.

friars, suspended priests, and convicted criminals to testify against him. Their testimony was meant to establish that Oliver Plunkett was made Archbishop of Armagh and Primate of Ireland in order to revive Irish Catholicism and overthrow the king's government. Emmanuel Curtis points to the absurdity of the trials against the archbishop when he notes that "it has been admitted by all authorities that in the Popish Plot trials, English legal practice reached its lowest level. The trials themselves have been described as 'the most astounding outburst of successful perjury which has occurred in modern times.'"[13]

On April 29, 1681, Oliver Plunkett was found guilty of high treason, to which his humble response was "Deo gratias." The prosecution had successfully established the two "facts" of his case: first, that a general plot against the king existed in Ireland; second, that Oliver Plunkett was intricately involved in it! A week later, the condemned prisoner was brought back to receive his sentence of death. His own words capture the serenity and fearlessness with which he faced this ultimate falsehood as he wrote:

> Sentence of death was passed against me on the 15th, without causing me any fear, or depriving me of sleep for a quarter of an hour. I am innocent of all treason as the child born yesterday. As for my character, profession, and function, I did own it publicly, and that being also a motive for my death, I die most willingly. And being the first among the Irish, I will teach others, with the grace of God, by example, not to fear death. But how am I, a poor creature, so stout, seeing that my Redeemer began to fear, to be weary and sad, and that drops of his Blood ran down to the ground? I have considered that Christ, by His fears and passion, merited for me to be without fear.[14]

Now as a condemned man, the archbishop would spend the concluding weeks of his life in Newgate Prison, London, and the unfolding of these final days provides us with a moving account of his unique oblation in the presence of a fellow prisoner. The prisoner was none other than Dom Maurus Corker, a Benedictine monk of the Abbey of Lambspringe in Germany. Earlier he, too, had been condemned to death for his alleged involvement in the "Popish Plots," but his sentence had yet to be carried out. In 1680 he was elected president of the English Congregation, and the installation ceremony was performed in his cell.

It is reported that Dom Maurus Corker continued an active spiritual ministry among the prisoners at Newgate. Among his many fruitful apostolic encounters was the instant friendship and deep spiritual bond that

---

[13] Curtis, *Blessed Oliver Plunkett,* 151.
[14] Ibid., 172.

instantly developed between the Benedictine monk and Oliver Plunkett.[15] As one writer notes:

> their spiritual intimacy makes their correspondence one of the most inspiring chapters in all prison literature . . . most of the archbishop's other surviving letters are official reports in Latin or Italian to his superiors in Brussels or Rome, but in the letters to Maurus Corker, which are in English, he poured out his heart.[16]

Although the two condemned men exchanged a series of letters, they would meet face to face only once. It was the moment when the archbishop would make his confession, and place himself under a form of obedience, his oblation, at the hands of the Benedictine monk.[17] A few days after Plunkett's death, Dom Corker would write of their meeting in these words:

> After he certainly knew God Almighty had chosen him to the crown and dignity of martyrdom, he continually studied how to divest himself of himself, and become more and more an entire, pleasing and perfect holocaust. To which end, as he gave up his soul with all its faculties to the conduct of God, so for God's sake he resigned the care and disposal of his body to unworthy me, and this in such an absolute manner that he looked upon himself to have no further power or authority over it.[18]

Dom Corker also made the needed arrangements so that Plunkett had the opportunity to celebrate the Eucharist daily for the last week of his life, including on the morning of his execution.

Finally, on July 1, 1681, Archbishop Oliver Plunkett was led out of Newgate Prison to be hanged, drawn, and quartered at Tyburn in London, England. Those who witnessed the unfolding of this gruesome event were struck by his fearless calm and his embrace of death. He delivered his final speech from a horse cart on which he was mounted, and the following description vividly captures his life's final moments:

> He recounted the circumstances that had brought him to Westminster, summarized the charges made against him, and one by one refuted them. Fol-

---

[15] Most of what we know of these final prison days comes to us from the archbishop's prison letters. For a collection of these letters refer to Hanly, ed., *The Letters of Saint Oliver Plunkett,* and Dom Ethelbert Horne, "Blessed Oliver Plunkett: His Prison Letters," *Downside Review* 39 (July 1921) 98–111.

[16] Tomás Ó Fiaich, *Oliver Plunkett: Ireland's New Saint,* 97.

[17] What we know of their brief meeting comes to us from a letter of Dom Maurus Corker to Mrs. Elizabeth Sheldon, written only days after Plunkett's martyrdom. In it, the Benedictine monk gives an account of the archbishop's life in prison, their meeting, and his last hours. A reprint of this letter may be found in Curtis, *Blessed Oliver Plunkett,* 178–82.

[18] Desmond Forristal, Oliver Plunkett: In His Own Words, 248.

lowing the example of Saint Stephen, he begged the Lord to grant true repentance to those who had sworn falsely against him. From his heart he forgave the judges, the witnesses and all who had concurred in his condemnation. Lastly, he asked forgiveness of anybody he had ever offended by thought or word or deed. For a while longer he prayed; then handing his rosary beads to McKenna, he indicated that he was ready. The white cap was drawn down over his head. Jack Ketch knotted the heavy rope and the horse was urged forward. Oliver was still alive when they cut him down and the butchery began.[19]

Such was the manner in which his exemplary and selfless life was brought to an end at the age of fifty-six. Born on All Saints Day, Oliver Plunkett, Archbishop of Armagh and Primate of all Ireland, now joined that heavenly company as one of the Church's martyrs. The fruit of his martyrdom was palpable almost immediately, for the very next day the people of England rejected the "Popish Plot" as a malicious falsehood, and turned against its originators, many of whom were themselves later imprisoned. St. Oliver Plunkett would be the last Catholic martyr to die for his faith in England.

How Plunkett's Life Was Influenced by His Oblation

Given the circumstances of Plunkett's oblation we are left only to consider how this unique oblation served as a fitting conclusion to an entire life lived in wholehearted service of God. It can be said, without doubt, that although his Benedictine oblation took place at the very end, Plunkett's entire life was inspired by the spirit of the promises made by oblates of St. Benedict.

In speaking of the manner of Plunkett's death, Desmond Forristal applies the phrase *Finis coronat opus,* the "ending crowns the work." This phrase is just as true of Plunkett's Benedictine oblation which was the crowning moment in his spiritual life. Throughout his Rule, St. Benedict urges his monks to prepare their hearts and bodies for the battle of holy obedience and joyful perseverance. Oliver Plunkett's life bears witness to his heroic "battle of holy obedience" that culminated in his "baptism by blood." The martyr's own final words in a letter to the Benedictine Maurus Corker bear repeating here: "Happy are we who have a second baptism, nay a third; water we have received, the sacrament of penance we got. And now we have . . . the baptism of blood." Plunkett's consolation was the Gospel conviction he shared with St. Benedict who writes in the concluding

---

[19] Curtis, *Blessed Oliver Plunkett,* 176.

lines of his Prologue that those who "through patience share in the sufferings of Christ deserve also to share in his kingdom."

Benedictine House with Which Plunkett Is Associated

Since Oliver Plunkett's oblation was made in prison at the hands of Dom Maurus Corker, then President of the English Benedictine Congregation, he was, strictly speaking, not affiliated with a single Benedictine monastery. Plunkett's body was placed in two tin boxes and buried alongside five Jesuits who had died before him. On his release from the Newgate Prison two years later, Dom Maurus Corker had the remains moved to a Benedictine monastery in Lambspringe, Germany. Some two hundred years later, in February 1883, Plunkett's body was transported to Downside Abbey, England, where it is still enshrined today. His head is preserved in St. Peter's Church at Drogheda, Ireland. Nearly three hundred years after his death, Oliver Plunkett was beatified by Pope Benedict XV on May 23, 1920, and canonized on Sunday, October 12, 1975, in St. Peter's, Rome.[20]

Importance of Plunkett for Contemporary Oblates and Benedictine Monastics, for Christianity and Contemporary Culture, and for This Author

By definition, an oblation is an act of offering oneself to God. Few of us, however, are called to the martyr's ultimate offering of life itself, as Oliver Plunkett was. But we are called as Benedictine oblates and monastics to witness to a life that is daily offered in humble service of God and one another. In imitation of this saintly witness to faith, we too are called to partake of the triumph of Christ's cross.

The stability of heart, mind, and body that so characterizes the monastic journey is reflected in Plunkett's decision to remain in Ireland in the face of certain death, instead of seeking the continued comfort and safety of temporary exile. His prison letters and final speech reflect his fearlessness and total self-abandonment to what he knew would be an unusually cruel death. This final self-abandonment could only spring from the cumulative fruitfulness of his daily abandonment to the will of God, a challenge for contemporary oblates and Benedictine monastics even today. In the ordinary and extraordinary moments of his life, Plunkett accepted suffering and tirelessly climbed the steps of St. Benedict's "ladder of humility" (RB 7), offering to oblates and monastics alike an outstanding example

---

[20] The text of Pope Paul VI's homily during canonization ceremonies for Oliver Plunkett may be found in *Origins* 5:20 (November 6, 1975) 313–5.

of a life lived in the freeing and exhilarating power of daily conversion, *conversatio morum.*

In reading about Plunkett's life, this author was particularly struck by the severe conditions and hardship in seventeenth-century Catholic Ireland under which Oliver Plunkett, "pastor of souls," served the Church. Never giving up and always encouraging his flock in the face of innumerable obstacles, injustices, and ultimate betrayals, Plunkett's resolve reminds this author of the truth of St. Benedict's urging to "not be daunted immediately by fear and run away from the road that leads to salvation" (RB Prol. 48).

Finally, a few reflections on the importance of Oliver Plunkett for contemporary Christianity and culture. "The blood of the martyrs is the seed of Christianity," wrote Tertullian in the second century. His words ring true even as we stand at the dawn of a new century and a new millennium. The last century has witnessed a fresh wave of Christian martyrdom such that Pope John Paul II has observed that, "at the end of the second millennium, the Church has once again become a Church of martyrs" (On the Coming Third Millennium, *Tertio Millenio Adveniente,* 37).

Moreover, he notes that "perhaps the most convincing form of ecumenism is the ecumenism of the saints and of the martyrs . . . which speaks louder than the things which divide us" (*Tertio Millenio Adveniente,* 37). For in the lives of the martyrs, the Church venerates Christ himself, who is the origin of their strength in the face of martyrdom. Plunkett's martyrdom fueled by the bitter religious conflicts and divisions of seventeenth-century Ireland reminds us of the necessity of ongoing religious dialogue and a firm Christian commitment to ecumenism.

In an age that continues to offer new waves of ethnic cleansing, religious conflicts, persecutions, and even martyrdom, the "veneration of the saints establishes among the faithful a marvelous exchange of gifts in virtue of which the holiness of one benefits others in a way far exceeding the harm which the sin of one has inflicted upon others" (John Paul II, On the Mystery of the Incarnation, #10). Some three centuries later, Oliver Plunkett's virtues of self-sacrifice and holiness in life and in death are marvelous gifts to contemporary Christianity, to Benedictine oblates and monastics, and to women and men of good will everywhere. For the witness of this unique oblate, contemporary Benedictine oblates and monastics can confidently join in St. Oliver Plunkett's humble prayer, *Deo Gratias.*

18

Denys Prideaux: The Oblate Abbot

Charles Preble

William Charles Gostwick Prideaux, Benedictine oblate who later became Abbot Denys Prideaux of the Benedictine community which he assisted into being, is as intriguing as he was self-effacing.

> No life of this remarkable character has been written. It is only a very skilled professional biographer who would dare to undertake such a task. The least of his difficulties would be that horror of the limelight, alternating with an outspoken longing for it—not for himself for a moment but for his community—which characterized the life of [Denys Prideaux].[1]

Denys was a "remarkable" character and the more I have studied him the more I have been moved by who he was and what he did. At the same time I have been frustrated that he has not revealed more of himself to other writers. Still, I have come to know him somewhat and have found him a wise and holy companion.

An intellectual yet unassuming person, Denys Prideaux was often reclusive with few of the skills and talents for leadership, administration, or public relations. In many respects he might have been the least likely to gather around him men to establish, amidst much hardship and controversy, a monastic community which would grow to form an Anglican Benedictine abbey. In comparison to those who had gone before and attempted to establish Benedictine communities (such as Aelred Carlyle, who was called by his biographer Peter Anson "Abbot Extraordinary"),

---

[1] *The Jubilee Book of the Benedictines of Nashdom: 1914–1964* (London: Faith Press, 1964) 46.

Denys was an understatement, absolutely self-effacing. He seems to have felt no call within to become a professed monk, but as an oblate he made an oblation in the fullest sense. He offered himself readily, obediently, and wholeheartedly to God's call. It was through his ready obedience to God's call that a Benedictine abbey now exists.

Denys Prideaux was born on September 16, 1864. He was raised within the Anglo-Catholic faith and practice. He was the eldest of five children. Educated in universities in England, Geneva, and Leipzig, he received a degree in classics and literature from Clare College, Cambridge. He studied theology at Cuddesdon Theological College and was ordained a priest in the Church of England in 1892.

To understand Fr. Denys's story, one must comprehend the Catholic revival within the Church of England, for Denys was very much a product and proponent of this movement. This revival began in the early- to mid-nineteenth century. After several centuries of Protestant and anti-Catholic emphasis, the Catholic revival sought to restore the Catholic heritage to the Church of England. The proponents of this movement thought of themselves not as Protestants, nor as Roman Catholics, but as truly Catholic. The reforms under Henry VIII in the sixteenth century initially were more political and economic than religious, unlike the continental reformation of Calvin and Luther. Henry believed that the English Church should be free of the pope. He also believed that all property and wealth of the Church should be under the authority of the crown. Henry was not trying to start a new church, but to give the church which already existed independence and self-determination. Later, the influence of the continental Reformation had a strong effect on the Church of England, but in the midst of that the Church continued to possess what was believed to be the essential elements of the Catholic Church: the ecumenical creeds, Scripture, ministry of bishops, priests, and deacons in apostolic succession, and the sacraments. During the periods of the strongest Protestant influence, none of these were discarded even if some remained in the background. Through much of the history between Elizabeth I (1570, the date when Pope Pius V excommunicated her and released her subjects from their allegiance to her) and Victoria (1837, the year she was crowned queen), England had distrusted almost anything associated with Roman Catholicism. In the mid-nineteenth century a change occurred. The Catholic revival of that time was a movement within the Church of England to reclaim the fullness of its Catholic heritage. The supporters of the movement believed they were claiming what already belonged to the Church of England. One result of this revival was the women's and men's monastic communities founded within the Church of England during the mid- and late-nineteenth century. However, these foundations did not occur without controversy, opposition, and overt conflict. Many of the Church of England still feared what they saw to be Roman Catholic faith and practice, and their opposition was often severe. To be an "Anglo-Catholic" often meant disfavor, if not persecution.

Following his ordination, Denys served curacies in several Anglo-Catholic parishes which were in the midst of this conflict during the years 1892 through 1906. One parish was St. Margaret's, Liverpool. There he experienced a health breakdown in 1904, perhaps because of the Protestant-Catholic tensions in the parish and that area. The parish was often harassed by Protestant agitators, and the rector himself had actually been jailed for some of his "Romish" practices.

From Liverpool Denys went to St. Cuthbert's, Philbeach Gardens. It was at St. Cuthbert's that Fr. Denys met Dom Aelred Carlyle, a charismatic preacher with a magnetic personality and abbot founder (1896) of the Anglican Benedictine community on Caldey Island just off the coast of Wales near St. David's. Abbot Aelred preached for the feast of the parish dedication on November 24, 1906, and his meeting with Prideaux proved to be a tremendous consequence both for the life of Prideaux and for the Benedictine community at Caldey.

The Benedictine community which had moved to Caldey was initially formed in 1896. Caldey had been the seat of a monastery in the fifth century. In 1902 the Archbishop of Canterbury, Frederick Temple, confirmed the election of Aelred Carlyle as abbot of the Benedictine community. In 1906 Aelred's community, Anglican Congregation of the Primitive Observance of the Holy Rule of St. Benedict, was established there on the ancient church ruins.

The Caldey site seemed perfect for the monastery. Monsignor Ronald Knox said:

> There was a faint air of make believe about the old Caldey. This, I think, contributed something to its charm. The island itself was a fairy-story island; those caves, those little combes, those wide beaches. . . . You had the sense, when you went there, of having left the real world of inadequate compromises and jarring controversies behind you; there was an enchantment in the stone walls and the fuchsia hedges; you were projected, not into some revival of a Gothic past, but into a world of the imagination, in which there was neither Roman nor Anglican, High Church nor Low Church—no echoes carried across the bay. It was a dream world.[2]

The establishment of a Benedictine community on Caldey was hailed by members of the Catholic revival as a great sign that the Church of England was returning to the fullness of her Catholic heritage. The Benedictines

---

[2] *Pax* (March 1914) 84–5. Quoted in Peter Anson, *The Call of the Cloister* (London: SPCK, 1955) 171.

of Caldey drew directly from the fourteenth-century Roman monasticism
for their inspiration in faith and practice. Abbot Aelred saw his community
as fully Catholic and hoped they would be in communion with both Canterbury and Rome. However, Bishop Charles Gore, then visitor for the
community, wanted the Benedictines of Caldey to be accountable to the
Church of England's discipline and practice.

Aelred invited Denys to come to Caldey Island as chaplain and Denys
arrived in 1906. Caldey must have been a fair haven for Denys, isolated as
it was from so much of the Catholic-Protestant conflict of the Church.
Denys became an oblate of the Caldey community, but there is no indication that Denys had a sense of a monastic calling. During Denys's six-year
residence in the "Catholic" paradise there is no indication that he desired
to be anything other than what and where he was. He was content and performed his work simply as chaplain, occasionally saying Mass for the
community in the absence of Dom Aelred. As an intern oblate, Denys was
also guest-master and apologist for the Benedictine community within the
Church of England.

For Denys Prideaux, the apologist for the revival of Benedictine monasticism within the Church of England, to be Catholic was paramount.
He sought a Catholicity which would be definitely Anglican. For Denys
the Catholic Church was person centered. It was the person of Christ who
filled the Church and would bring it to fruition. Denys's thoughts on
Benedictine monasticism are part of his understanding of the nature of the
Church. Denys believed that it was Christ himself who would bring Benedictine monasticism to full expression within the English church. It was
the person of Christ who would bring Anglican Benedictinism to its own
fruition and integrity.

Denys Prideaux wrote of Benedictine monasticism:

> Other monastic systems [apart from Benedictines] are closed corporations
> with a line of succession, and they did not exist in the early church. Bene-
> dictinism was founded in the early church, without a line of succession, as
> an independent form, based upon the enactments of an Ecumenical Coun-
> cil, and was first made into a closed corporation or "order" by Pope Inno-
> cent III, in 1215. At the Reformation this corporation form was absorbed
> into the Roman Catholic Church, but this does not prevent a return to the
> original independent form of Benedictinism, which, as belonging to the
> whole Catholic Church, belongs also to the English Church. If the Papacy
> is indeed of the essence of the church, independent Benedictinism has no
> validity. But has the Pope the power to forbid St. Benedict's original scheme
> (which existed for some hundreds of years unchanged) to be adopted, at the
> present day, under episcopal sanction, based upon the enactments of an
> Ecumenical Council? That is the question. Not whether Benedictinism can

be revived in the two particular provinces of Canterbury and York, geo-graphically constituting the Church of England.[3]

But trouble was brewing. Bishop Gore wanted the Caldey community to give up some of its practices, such as the use of the Roman Catholic Latin *Monastic Breviary,* and to use the Church of England's *Book of Common Prayer* to bring themselves more within Anglican tradition. He also wanted them to drop the practice of Benediction of the Blessed Sacrament, which Bishop Gore believed had no place within the tradition of the Church of England. He stated that the practices which Dom Aelred believed to be truly Catholic, and therefore was unwilling to give up, "cannot be justified on any other than a strictly papal basis of authority." Dom Aelred thought that the demands were too much and did not wish to change. Caldey was a perfect copy of a fourteenth-century English Benedictine monastery with Mass and Offices in Latin. Aelred could see no need for any post-Reformation changes in their Benedictine practices. Lord Halifax, a strong advocate for the Catholic revival within Anglicanism and a friend of the community, tried to intervene. His hope was that Caldey would be a great example of Catho-lic monasticism within the Church of England. It would help prove that the Church of England was truly Catholic. He said, "It was the chief dream of my life realized." Aelred and his community believed that they could not continue their practice and devotion according to Bishop Gore's proposed changes and that they had no alternative other than to seek recognition by Rome. Twenty-two of the thirty-three were received into communion with Rome and left Caldey in 1913.

For those who were suspicious of the practices of Caldey, the submis-sion to Rome was good riddance. The Roman Catholic press saw it as the beginning of a great tide of conversions to Rome. Lord Halifax saw it as a tragic event, yet he worked for a new opportunity. As an article in the *Church Times* prophetically related, "The research which has been the re-sult of the attempt [to revive the Benedictine life in the Church of England] has proved conclusively that it only awaits a founder possessed of stability of character and with sufficient knowledge of history and theology, to see what really constitutes catholicity."[4] That "stability of character with suffi-cient knowledge of history and theology" describes Denys Prideaux.

In the end there were only ten monks of Caldey who went to the Roman Catholic monastery of Prinknash. It is difficult to really understand clearly what effect the Caldey debacle had on Denys. It could have been

---

[3] "Benedictinism," *Pax* (December 1911) 497. Quoted in Anson, *The Call of the Cloister,* 165.

[4] Ibid., 183.

devastating. He had given six years of his life to the community and its abbot, and here it all ended. He had no desire to go to Rome. He remained a stalwart Anglican, continuing to live out the faith he had expressed in his apologetic work during his time at Caldey. Lord Halifax was very disappointed but not defeated. He now saw Denys as the new hope to establish a Benedictine community in the Church of England. He knew Denys as an excellent apologist for Benedictine monasticism and its place in the Church of England. He also saw that he had the stability of character and the courage for the job. Denys was encouraged and helped by Lord Halifax and others to begin anew. And that is what they did. It took a great deal of faith. They were not stymied by the collapse of Caldey.

This turn of events gives us some real insight into Denys's character. There was a strong stability, patience, and courage in him, even more stability than in the community of monks to which he had made an oblation. Denys's character is even more pronounced when we compare him to the character of the "Abbot Extraordinary," Dom Aelred Carlyle. With all of Aelred's magnetism and dynamic personality, he could not listen to anyone except himself. He was able to attract many to him, but he seems to have had to be the one in charge with no room for compromise. When he faced Bishop Gore's demands he lacked any patience. In comparison, Denys was persistent, stable, consistent, patient, and self-effacing.

In 1914 Denys would have been fifty. He had established himself as an excellent apologist for the Catholic revival. He could have gone back into work as a parish priest. Instead, Fr. Denys and one fully professed lay monk moved to Pershore to begin anew. This was not viewed as a continuation of Caldey, but as an entirely new effort to establish Benedictine life within the Church of England. Lord Halifax had brought together a committee of people to encourage the beginning of a new Benedictine community. It was this committee that helped so much to find a new location and provided the finances to begin anew. It has been suggested that Lord Halifax himself was a Benedictine oblate. In any case, it was his determination and work for a Benedictine community that gave the real support to the founding of the new community.

On May 1, 1914, a house at Pershore was solemnly blessed with two in residence, Fr. Denys and the lay monk. There was some press in the local papers, but little in the paper of London. However, a "Wickliffe Preacher" from Birmingham staged a protest and was finally convinced to depart from the scene. At this time Fr. Denys was appointed warden and chaplain of the new foundation. The one fully professed lay monk from Caldey who had not gone to Rome was named superior. This arrangement of one person as superior and Denys as warden did not work out well, and the monk finally sought to be received at Prinknash with the others from Caldey. Fr. Denys was alone.

During this trying period Lord Halifax and a group of twelve others continued working to support this new beginning at Pershore. There is no evidence of anyone having been professed; however, some were intern oblates. At one point there were possibly five persons in residence. The war years (1914–18) were terribly bleak. Many of the brightest and best of England were serving in the military. One man who clearly wanted to try his vocation at Pershore ended up being killed in the war. It was only after 1918 that more began to come. During this time Denys wrote optimistically of what was happening at Pershore, but so little really was happening that it had to be disappointing.

Little information exists about what happened at Pershore between 1915 and 1921. This may have been because Denys kept no records or the records were destroyed in a basement flood. The one document we do have comes from *A Statement of an Appeal* in 1916. It states: "The Community is at present quite small: it consists as yet of five members only, but its numbers are increasing and its applications are being received from both priests and laymen who feel that they have a vocation to the religious life as it is lived at Pershore."[5] In 1919 Bishop Yeatman-Biggs was followed as diocesan bishop by Dr. Ernest Pearce. Where Bishop Yeatman-Biggs had encouraged the community at Pershore, the new bishop was downright hostile to the Pershore foundation. The *Times* of December 4, 1934, printed the following description of this period:

> Of the privations and loneliness of those four years 1914–1918 it is impossible now for anyone to speak. Fr. Denys, as he was then known, alone endured the whole period, and he could never be induced to give more than fragmentary hints of the difficulties encountered. The rare guests who knew the Abbey House at that time have said a little more, but the full story of his great courage and tenacity at that time will never be known in this world.[6]

One description of Denys Prideaux by a monk who was at Pershore and Nashdom provides this picture:

> [Abbot Prideaux is] a mysterious presence brooding over the community, inspiring the juniors and novices with feelings of respect and even of awe. His learning was prodigious if somewhat uncoordinated. He was a very fine classical scholar, able to read and write verse or prose with the utmost ease in either Greek or Latin. He had the very rare gift of being able to remember the exact reference to anything which might have struck him in the

---

[5] *The Jubilee Book,* 16.
[6] Ibid., 18.

course of reading. His linguistic ability was exceptional, for he could speak most European languages and not a few Eastern ones fluently and idiomatically. Like Moses, he viewed the promised land from a distance, to which he guided others without being able to enter it himself.[7]

While Denys oversaw the day by day life of the Benedictine community at Pershore, he did not at this time believe he was called to monastic profession. According to the *Jubilee Book of the Benedictines of Nashdom: 1914–1964:*

> During all these years Father Denys had shut himself up as far as possible in his book-lined study, only emerging when it could not be avoided. . . . All accounts, as well as one of his letters, which has been preserved agree that from the first he had no intention of entering the Religious Life, feeling called only—in the absence of any one else available and better qualified than himself—to watch over the attempt at a reconstruction after the Caldey debacle. His eventual change of mind was slowly forced upon him by the pressure of outward circumstances reinforced by encouragement from without in the persons of Lord Halifax and the other notables of the Pershore Helpers Committee: and all this he naturally interpreted as being the Will of God for him.[8]

Finally, however, in 1921 Denys, still an oblate, was convinced by several friends of the venture that he ought to be the abbot. Denys, who had only intended to be the nursemaid of the venture, decided to take their advice and to actually agree to the abbatial call even before he had made monastic profession. At a meeting in the autumn of 1921 Denys was elected the first abbot of the Benedictine community of Pershore. The election was accepted grudgingly by Bishop Pearce of Worcester. On February 18, 1922, Father Denys made his profession. On March 21 two novices made their professions, and there were then three life-professed monks. Since three life-professed monks were required for a Benedictine foundation, Denys could then be installed as abbot.

As abbot Denys remained very much in charge. The abbot made necessary decisions. He decided who should be accepted and when. It was he who decided if a person was to become professed. He kept the finances himself with relatively little knowledge of bookkeeping. He also was the confessor to all members of the community both at Pershore and Nashdom. It is said that he ruled through the confessional, but never abused the role or the sacrament. What is recorded is that even in that circumstance he was an excellent confessor and an extremely perceptive spiritual director.[9]

---

[7] Quoted in Anson, *The Call of the Cloister,* 186.
[8] *The Jubilee Book,* 16–17.
[9] Ibid., 28–9.

The years immediately following 1922 brought change and there were a significant number of applicants wishing to enter the religious life at Pershore, so much so that the quarters there became inadequate and a new facility was needed. In 1926 Abbot Denys chose to move the community to Nashdom, a fine mansion which was close to London. Denys continued his work as abbot, taking on more work rather than delegating. He was often away for engagements outside of the abbey. He did this to raise money for the community as well as to spread the word about the community. His vision of their life was that Benedictinism was essentially contemplative and that the cenobitic life was important as it helped each grow into spiritual maturity. It was the Rule of St. Benedict itself to which he and the community continued to return for guidance as to how they were to live. Bishops and others in authority pressured them to conform their lives more to the basic discipline and practice of the Church of England, e.g., to not use the Latin liturgies and to use the English *Book of Common Prayer* for the Eucharist. This was by and large unheeded by the monks. Although the community was clearly recognized by the authority of the Church of England, they continued to find their own unique way of living the Rule of St. Benedict as they were given guidance by their own discernment of God's will. Always they were decidedly Anglican in their affiliation and loyalties, even if they challenged the Church of England to expand its understanding of the Church, monasticism, and to broaden Anglican inclusiveness.

In his later years Abbot Denys had doubts concerning his choice to allow himself to become a professed monk and made an abbot. There is a hint that he believed that it may not have been God's call after all. Perhaps he suffered from depression. He continued his reclusive life while at Nashdom and remained self-effacing, not burdening others with his own difficulties or doubts. Denys never considered himself the founder of this community, which could not have come into being without his oblation of himself for its work. Abbot Prideaux died at Nashdom Abbey on November 29, 1934.

Abbot Denys succeeded where others had not in establishing a male Benedictine monastic community within the Church of England. That community continues today in England, having also helped establish St. Gregory's Abbey, an Episcopalian Benedictine foundation in Three Rivers, Michigan. In England the monks have moved from Nashdom and are now the monks of Elmore Abbey. They continue on with a beautiful spirit, and I believe they remain a community with which Abbot Denys would be pleased. I asked Abbot Basil, the current Abbot of Elmore, "What would Denys think of you now?" He smiled and said, "That's a good question; I haven't thought of that before. I believe he would say, 'You're doing fine. Keep on doing what you are doing!'"

I was touched by my visit to Elmore. I think Denys Prideaux would find himself at home with this community. It is a community which seeks God through the inspiration of the Rule of St. Benedict. The professed monks' lives are living proof of the essential Catholic nature of Benedictine monasticism in the Church of England.

Even though the community at Elmore is small, they have an extensive oblate program. Their manual for oblates[10] would be helpful for oblates of any Benedictine community. The manual describes the Benedictine charism in terms of the life of St. Benedict, the Rule of St. Benedict, professed Benedictine monks and the role of oblates within the Benedictine community. The life and work of the oblates of Elmore Abbey are seen to be equally as important as the life of the professed monks. In their ministry to oblates the monks of Elmore Abbey are presenting an offering of thanksgiving for the oblation of Denys Prideaux, who gave his life to the work of establishing their community. That the role of oblates in their monastery is so prominent is perhaps the natural outcome for this community which probably would not exist had it not been for an oblate who had a vision, and who had the courage and the stability to put his life on the line for it.

[10] Dom Augustine Morris, *Oblates: Life with St. Benedict* (Elmore Abbey, 1992).

19

H. A. Reinhold:
Architect of the Liturgical Movement
in America

Julia Upton, R.S.M.

God never asks of us anything for which we have not been carefully prepared. That preparation characteristically precedes our conscious awareness of it and only comes into full view when we look back with sustained reflection. So it was for Hans Emil Alexander Reinhold, born in Hamburg, Germany, on September 6, 1897. While southern Germany at that time was predominantly Catholic, its northern cities like Hamburg were predominantly Lutheran. As a result both Catholics and Jews in that area were treated as outcasts. Educated in Hamburg's public schools from the fourth grade on, Reinhold and his Jewish classmates, for example, were excused from the Lutheran catechism classes, thus throwing them together in an unusual alliance. During those years, Reinhold began to develop lifelong interests in languages and history, art and architecture. In time, those interests and relationships would both save and shape his life.

Persuaded by government propaganda that Germany had been attacked, the very day he became eligible for service in 1914 Reinhold joined the field artillery of his Royal Highness, the Grand Duke of Mecklenburg, expecting that military life would satisfy him for the rest of his days.[1] Injured several times in battle and left for dead twice, Reinhold was repeatedly sent back to the front until May 1917, when a shell exploded near his dugout smashing his right leg. Hospitalized until October of that year, when he was finally released from the hospital military authorities deemed him unfit for front-line service. Instead, Reinhold applied for

[1] H. A. Reinhold, *H.A.R.: The Autobiography of Father Reinhold* (New York: Herder and Herder, 1968) 23. [Hereafter cited as *Autobiography*.]

admission to interpreter school, hoping to be assigned to army intelligence after training. His language skills were so good, however, that he passed the examinations for English, French, and Italian and was immediately assigned to intelligence work. Although Reinhold found the work ingenious and fascinating, he was also continually confounded, for while it was obvious to him that the German front was collapsing, leaders of government, commerce, and industry seemed to be successful in perpetuating an illusion that Germany was winning the war. This conflict forged in him a basic instinct of distrust in government.

While recovering from his wartime experiences, Reinhold studied philosophy in Fribourg during the spring and summer semesters of 1919. He would assist the priest at Mass each morning, take long walks in the pinewoods on the edge of the city, and on free days go mountain climbing on the outskirts of the Black Forest with friends. "It was a great emotional release for all of us after the restraining years of the war. I found peace here." At that time Reinhold also discovered Romano Guardini's *The Spirit of the Liturgy,* which further enhanced his peace and gave him "not so much new insight into the liturgy as a positive attitude towards Catholic teaching."[2]

When the student chaplain suggested that he consider becoming a priest, Reinhold admitted that, although he had considered that possibility in his youth, he did not now think that he was cut out to be a priest—that he lacked the "strength of will, the character, the ascetic requirements, and so on." Still he mulled this over in his mind for a short period of time and then decided to try his vocation. Upon the chaplain's recommendation, Reinhold enrolled at Innsbruck the following year. Although he enjoyed his studies there, he left the seminary at the end of the academic year because, in his own mind, he believed that he would serve the Church best in the South Tyrol, where he had regularly vacationed with his family and where his best images of the Church had been forged. The bishop of Trent, ecclesiastical superior of South Tyrol, accepted him as a candidate and sent him to Bressanone, where German-speaking members of his clergy were trained.

Reinhold was not to stay there long either, for the next great idea to seize him was the desire to be a religious—a Benedictine! To this end, he visited the Abbey of Maria Laach in the Rhineland. Reflecting on this visit almost fifty years later, he admitted that the approach to the Abbey was "forbidding."

> The abbey is located in the crater of an extinct volcano, now filled with a rather large lake rimmed by a dense forest. If you couldn't call this setting gloomy, you would probably choose the word austere. But the spirit inside

[2] Ibid., 38.

the abbey was full of life—young life. A great number of novices gave pulsating impetus to the monastic traditions of Maria Laach.[3]

Growing up in Hamburg, Reinhold was acquainted with the name of Maria Laach and associated it as a center of culture and learning. Reinhold immediately recognized that Abbot Ildefons Herwegen was an extraordinary man, and under his leadership "an air of charity suffused the abbey." The next morning in the crypt under the main altar, Reinhold was to have his first experience of a dialogue Mass, celebrated by the Abbey's Prior, Fr. Albert Hammenstede, facing the assembly. The experience moved him deeply, and within the hour Reinhold was transformed. Not only was he "sold" on the concept of the dialogue Mass and Mass celebrated facing the assembly, he was later to become its apostle.

Benedictine Roots

Reinhold entered Maria Laach as a novice in April 1922 and was given the name Ansgar in honor of the patron of the city of Hamburg and of his home parish. "Most of what I learned of the liturgy and the way of thinking of the liturgical apostolate was given to me in that year," he would later write.[4] "While the liturgical efforts of Maria Laach were directed to the intellectual and the scholar, the intention was that eventually the apostolate of the liturgy would be taken up by the people and their pastors."[5] The tower of learning in the house at that time was Dom Odo Casel,[6] who had just developed the theology of *mysterium,* which he discussed at great length with the novices. Although Reinhold left the official formation process at Maria Laach a year later, he never really left the community. He became an oblate of Maria Laach in 1925 and again took the name Ansgar. All of his later correspondence with the community is signed Fr. Ansgar, OBL.S.B. Thus, he retained his Benedictine identity for the rest of his life, and the relationships with both friends and teachers that began forming in that year at Maria Laach continued to be developed over the course of his lifetime. More importantly for us, however, in that year Reinhold had so thoroughly absorbed the liturgical mission of Maria Laach that he continued its work for almost fifty years in a variety of ministries as pastor and author on both sides of the Atlantic and both coasts of the United States, among thousands of people, through hundreds

[3] H. A. Reinhold, "Maria Laach Revisited," *Commonweal* 78 (August 23, 1963) 497–500.

[4] Ibid., 498.

[5] *Autobiography,* 47.

[6] Cf. H. A. Reinhold, "Dom Odo Casel," *Orate Fratres* 22 (1948) 366–72.

of articles, and in several important books. Wherever he went, Reinhold formed community and empowered the laity through the liturgy.

Reflecting on the meaning of being a Benedictine oblate twenty years later he wrote:

> I think a Benedictine oblate should realize that however close he is to his abbey and however often he returns to it to be refreshed and built up, he should be in this world and not a sort of frustrated monk tangled up in his own network of little rules and observances. He should be an active member of his parish and not via the monthly meeting of oblates only.
>
> An oblate's mind should be large and wide, a thing which can only be achieved by historical reading. It will make him immune against the chicken hearted sectarianism so rampant in our time.[7]

On December 18, 1925, Reinhold was ordained to the priesthood at Osnabrück and the following day sang his first Mass at the Ursuline convent chapel there. Before beginning his first assignment, Reinhold spent a few days' vacation at the Monastery of the Holy Cross at Herstelle, where Dom Odo Casel served as chaplain to the Benedictine nuns. There Reinhold celebrated his first dialogue Mass, when the chaplain relinquished his right to preside in favor of the newly ordained. "He treated me as a younger brother," Reinhold observed, "and was always very kind and affectionate towards me. He also regarded me as a disciple, and read to me excerpts from his forthcoming book, and gave me articles and book reviews of his to read."[8] It was a place to which Reinhold was to return time and again over the years, whenever he could take time off to rest and restore himself in spirit.

In the summer of 1928, Reinhold was selected to return to Rome and resume his archaeological studies at the Pontifical Institute of Archaeology. A few months later, however, the bishop asked that he interrupt these studies to take on a special assignment as bishop's secretary for the seaman's apostolate, responsible for the entire coastal area of Germany. He was expected to set up a foundation to support the work and establish a number of seaman's clubs in port cities. Headquartered in Bremerhaven, Reinhold embarked upon his new assignment with fervor if not instant enthusiasm.

Although the seaman's apostolate had been established in Germany in 1925, its effectiveness was not ensured until Reinhold's appointment as *Seemannspastor.* Peter Anson, who has written extensively about the seaman's apostolate, described Reinhold's holistic approach to the ministry.

---

[7] H. A. Reinhold "The Oblates of St. Benedict: A Letter," *Benedictine Review* 1:1 (January 1946) 36–40.

[8] *Autobiography,* 56

During a visit to Bremerhaven shortly after Reinhold had begun his work there, Anson described his conversations in which

> Fr. Reinhold expounded his views on the nature of the Catholic sea aposto-
> late. I discovered that they went much deeper than those of the average
> priest and were based just as much on a profound study of philosophy and
> theology, not to mention liturgy, as to an immediate sense of the need for
> purely religious and social work.[9]

Today we would say that Reinhold established "base ecclesial communities" among the seaman.

Nazi Threat

Although Adolf Hitler had not yet come into power when Anson visited Father Reinhold in Bremerhaven in1929, Anson noted that Hitler's
"Party" was often spoken about and "one was conscious of a feeling of acute
pessimism in the air."[10] "Everything in Germany was in turmoil at this time,"
Reinhold observed. "Hitler's power was growing, communism was taking
root, and the moderate parties had lost control of the government. . . . I
was greatly alarmed by the evident progress of Nazism and communism in
Germany, and foresaw either a civil war or terrible revolution."[11]

Reinhold drew up a plan in which Catholics would seize the initiative
and restore balance in the German government. "The Church would sur-
render all properties which were of no direct social use; mansion-like rec-
tories would house the poor; convent schools would educate the children
of the poor; and the bishops would lead their people in this act of sacrifice
by donating large sums of money to impoverished areas."[12] Such idealism
and gospel consciousness cast upon Reinhold a cloak of suspicion; while
the government initially took covert action to get Reinhold out of Germany, its tactics intensified over time and eventually resulted in his expulsion from the country.

> It was perhaps the saddest day of my life when this hard job after exactly 6
> years of up-hill work was taken out of my hands by 5 agents of the secret
> political police on 30 April 1935 and I had to sit down at my own desk to
> sign the receipt of the decree banishing me from all contacts with the sea

---

[9] Peter F. Anson, *Harbour Head: Maritime Memories* (London: John Gifford Limited, 1944) 176.

[10] Ibid.

[11] *Autobiography,* 66–7. See also Jay P. Corrin, "H. A. Reinhold: Liturgical Pioneer and Anti-fascist," *The Catholic Historical Review* 82 (July 1996) 436–59.

[12] *Autobiography,* 67.

and her men "according to Section I of the Law of the Reich President for the Protection of People and State" under which I had to leave the coast that very afternoon.[13]

Father Reinhold was instructed to leave the city at once, by way of a particular bridge that would head him toward Munich which, he was instructed, was to be his next place of residence. He was given a two-hour reprieve, however, to bid farewell to his mother. On his way out of the office, the Gestapo officer placed a packet containing Father Reinhold's passport and visa on the secretary's desk. The secretary interpreted this as a merciful hint to leave the country immediately. The secretary, a British citizen, served as a protection while Father Reinhold first visited his mother and then drove to Osnabrück to meet with his bishop, who immediately contacted the Gestapo.

Within a few days and with the help of a few brave friends, Father Reinhold was able to cross the border into Holland and begin his escape to England, with only a toothbrush and a fountain pen. He spent the next few months in England under the protection of friends from the ICAS (International Seaman's Apostolate) while he determined where to settle more permanently. Ultimately he wanted to go the United States, but advisors suggested that refugee priests were not readily accepted by American society.

Father Reinhold took a position as a curate in a parish in Interlaken, Switzerland, for one year while he continued his efforts to emigrate to the United States. On August 20, 1936, that dream finally became a reality when, aboard the S. S. America, Father Reinhold docked in New York harbor. Freedom at last!

Missioned to America

While we would like to think that Father Reinhold, after being hounded, harassed, and hunted by the Nazis, received a warm welcome in "the land of the free and the home of the brave," quite the opposite was the case, just as he had been advised. Within a week of his arrival, for example, the Chancellor of the Archdiocese of New York forbade him to give any public lectures. Although he was permitted to say Mass, permission extended no further than that because the Chancellor incorrectly concluded that Father Reinhold was a Spanish Loyalist. It would be two years before Father Reinhold would find a permanent residence and ministry in the United States.

---

[13] H. A. Reinhold in an interview with Warren Bovee, Archives, Marquette University.

In the meantime, God was preparing him for the next phase of his mission, for during those two years Father Reinhold made friendships that would endure through his life. He took up residence within the Diocese of Brooklyn, in St. Margaret's Parish in Middle Village. This put him right in the center of a German-speaking community and with easy access to the educational resources of New York City. His credentials from the University of Munster enabled him to be matriculated at Columbia University, where he began studies toward a doctorate in history. He also became an integral part of the Catholic intellectual circles in New York and established close bonds with the Catholic Worker Movement and *Commonweal.*

The following year Father Reinhold taught at Portsmouth Abbey, a Benedictine prep school near Providence, Rhode Island. In addition to providing him with productive employment and a monastic community, this opportunity also gave him relatively convenient access to Boston's rich scholarly resources. Harvard's Widener Library, for example, was one of his most treasured discoveries. In addition, he also formed relationships with many of the people of New England who were involved in the Liturgical Movement. One day, in the sacristy of St. Peter's Church in Cambridge, he met Fr. Emeric Lawrence, o.s.b., from St. John's Abbey in Collegeville, Minnesota, who was studying at Harvard. Father Reinhold was familiar with St. John's Abbey through the work of Fr. Virgil Michel, whom he deeply admired. It was natural, then, that Reinhold and Lawrence would develop a long and fruitful relationship.[14]

Liturgical Apostolate

When Father Reinhold had heard that Gerald Shaughnessy, bishop of Seattle, was looking for a priest who would establish a seaman's apostolate in his diocese, he applied for the position, and in the fall of 1938 traveled across America to take up residence in Seattle. On this cross-country journey he stopped to spend a few days at St. John's Abbey in Collegeville, to spend some time with Emeric Lawrence and the Benedictine community there. Father Reinhold had contributed a few articles to *Orate Fratres,* but when Fr. Virgil Michel died unexpectedly that following year, Father Lawrence proposed that Father Reinhold succeed him as writer of the "Timely Tracts," a popular feature of the magazine originally penned by Fr. Virgil Michel. Father Reinhold would continue in this ministry for a remarkable fifteen years.

---

[14] Emeric A. Lawrence, "H.A.R.—Death of a Friend," *Commonweal* 87 (March 8, 1968) 686–8.

Father Reinhold's arrival in Seattle on a drizzly day in October of 1939 was unheralded, and from the outset he was regarded with suspicion by the bishop and his fellow clergy. In those days his credentials as a refugee from Hitler and opponent of Franco were enough to brand him as a leftist and communist sympathizer. Before assigning Father Reinhold to the seaman's apostolate in his diocese, Bishop Shaughnessy decided to try him out as a parish assistant to get an idea of what kind of man he was. Staying at the cathedral rectory, with few duties and much free time, Father Reinhold seized the opportunity to write articles and become active in the liturgical apostolate. Perhaps to stem that activity, the bishop finally gave Father Reinhold permission to establish a seaman's club in Seattle the following spring.

Suspicion, however, continued to hound Father Reinhold, and he was both treated and investigated as a Nazi spy. Despite having to live under this dark cloud, he went about his work among the seamen with enthusiasm, and at the same time became actively involved in the national liturgical apostolate, writing, giving retreats and talks throughout the country, and regularly teaching summer sessions in several liturgical programs and institutes.

In October of 1941 Father Reinhold was transferred to Yakima, a city in central Washington, about two hundred miles from the coast, but suspicion followed him there and, once the United States entered the war two months later, he became a virtual prisoner of the rectory. Regarded as an enemy alien, immigration authorities restricted him to a five-mile radius of Yakima, and between dusk and dawn he was not permitted to leave the rectory. Since much of the parish at that time extended eighty miles east into the Cascade Mountains, Father Reinhold's ministry as a parish priest was virtually halted.

After enduring this trial for eighteen months, Father Reinhold requested a leave from the diocese. In the spring of 1943 he returned to New York and settled into Corpus Christi Parish as the guest of its pastor. There, in the shadow of Columbia University, he was able to do the kind of parish work from which he had been prevented all the years he had been in Seattle. During that year he also completed work on an edited volume of spiritual writings, *The Soul Afire,*[15] which had been commissioned by Kurt and Helen Wolff, editors and publishers at Pantheon, who wanted to publish an anthology of mystical writings similar to the German anthology edited by Deitrich von Hildebrand.

---

[15] H. A. Reinhold, *The Soul Afire: Revelations of the Mystics* (New York: Pantheon Books, 1944).

Freedom at Last

The following year, much to his surprise and delight, he received a telegram from the federal courthouse in Yakima informing him that he had finally been accepted as an American citizen. As you might expect, Father Reinhold's return trip to the West Coast was as exuberant as his journey eastward had been labored. Immediately following the naturalization ceremony, he drove to Seattle to see Bishop Shaughnessy, who was exceedingly surprised at this turn of events. Every false rumor about Father Reinhold had found its way to Bishop Shaughnessy's desk but, after carefully examining the citizenship papers, he offered Father Reinhold a pastorate in Sunnyside, Washington.

Today Sunnyside lies in the heart of Wine Country in the Yakima Valley, known for its magnificent fruit orchards. When Father Reinhold arrived there on Labor Day afternoon in 1944, however, it gave all the evidence of being a little village on the edge of nowhere. Father Reinhold was to remain as pastor in Sunnyside for twelve years, until 1956, although during the summers he usually took a leave of absence to conduct a school of liturgy on campuses across the country. The parishioners knew of this interest and some also knew of his writings in *Commonweal* and *Orate Fratres*. It was this, Father Reinhold believed, that gave an "air of respectability" to the innovations he introduced into the parish, which might otherwise have been regarded simply as the "whims of a liturgical avant-gardist."

Father Reinhold's interests and concerns were not only liturgical. From the very beginning he saw the essential connection between worship and justice. Just as he had with the seamen, Father Reinhold formed an educated Catholic community in Sunnyside. He brought together people of like interests and needs, met with them, prayed with them, taught them, and challenged them. For example, he brought together young couples in mixed marriages, and met with them regularly to discuss the particular challenges that were theirs. He worked with teenagers on faith formation and took them on trips into the wilderness, just as other pastors had done in Germany when he was young. When large numbers of Mexican migrant workers moved into the area later, he formed groups of adults and teens among them as well, and involved other parishioners in caring for their physical and spiritual needs. Rather than establish these groups entirely by himself, however, he employed another strategy. First, he identified a leader in the community itself, invited that person to use his or her gifts for the community and then empowered the person to bring others together. Thus he developed lifelong leadership in them from which the state of Washington still benefits today.

Even today, more than forty years after he left the parish and more than thirty years after his death, the people of Sunnyside remember Father Reinhold as a quintessential preacher, who never failed to challenge or inspire them. When faced with a moral decision they still ask themselves, "What would Father Reinhold say?"

Diagnosed with Parkinson's disease in the mid 1950s, continually plagued by difficulties with the local bishop, and wanting to devote more time to writing, Father Reinhold asked to resign from his parish responsibilities. After several months of negotiation, Father Reinhold left Sunnyside on May 1, 1956, hoping to devote his remaining time and energy to writing and teaching.

Summing Up

Father Reinhold's most important contribution to liturgical life in his adopted homeland can be found in his "Timely Tracts," referred to earlier.[16] In 1953, after fifteen years, Father Reinhold retired as monthly columnist for *Worship,* although he continued to publish occasional pieces there and elsewhere. How he was able to prepare a monthly column for fifteen years, covering a broad range of topics, is truly amazing. When you consider that he did this while engaging in full-time pastoral ministry, teaching regularly in summer programs at institutions such as the University of Notre Dame, Mundelin, and St. Xavier College among others, and playing a leading role in the Liturgical Movement in the United States, the full force of his energy and dedication is immediately evident.

In writing about Father Reinhold's contribution to *Worship,* its long-time editor Fr. Godfrey Diekmann, O.S.B., wrote:

> With sure instinct he has ranged over wide fields, and with incisive pen he has helped many to distinguish between essential and peripheral. One of the most appreciated facets of his writing was his ability to keep readers informed of the main currents of creative thinking, more especially as this appeared in European journals and books.[17]

His was not a quiet tenure as columnist. Rather he both incensed and inspired. "Timely Tracts are not meant to give solutions," he wrote in one of his first columns, "but to stir up problems and help us face facts."[18] His

---

[16] An annotated bibliography of these columns can be found in Sandra L. Lindsey, "Accents of Candor and Courage: H. A. Reinhold in the American Liturgical Movement" (master's thesis, University of Portland, 1992) 113–43.

[17] Godfrey Diekmann, "H.A.R.'s Sabbatical Leave," *Worship* 27 (1953) 569–70.

[18] H. A. Reinhold, "More or Less Liturgical," *Orate Fratres* 13 (March 1939) 213–8.

approach, therefore, was intentional—"a natural by-product of sowing the seeds of a more broadly based perspective among American Catholics."[19]

Looking back twenty-five years later, Father Reinhold wrote[20] that he was "deeply satisfied" with the accomplishments of the liturgical reform of Vatican Council II, but emphasized that what had been achieved to that point was only what affects the congregation. "The inner reform is yet to come . . . the visible and audible field of expression will reshape our concepts."[21]

Father Reinhold spent the end of his days trying to do just that. Incardinated into the Diocese of Pittsburgh in 1961, he resided at the Cathedral Rectory and served on the Liturgical Commission there as long as he was able. He continued to write pastoral articles for a wide variety of Catholic periodicals despite the continuing advance of Parkinson's disease. He died at Mercy Hospital in Pittsburgh on January 26, 1968. At the funeral liturgy, which was celebrated at St. Paul's Cathedral in Pittsburgh, Father Reinhold's gift to the Church was expressed well by the homilist, Fr. William C. Clancy:

> What we celebrate here today and give thanks for is a public life, a public ministry, and a public example—a life, a ministry, and an example that taught many in our generation and will teach many for generations to come. But . . . many of us come also to pay a debt—the greatest of all debts, the debt of faith itself. Because Hans Ansgar Reinhold taught us (some of us when we were very young, some of us when we were older) to see in a way we had not seen before, in a way we had not suspected was possible before we read him or knew him. He taught us to see the very things we celebrate today—the mystery and the joy of the church, that is, the mystery and the joy of the resurrection and the glory of Christ Jesus.[22]

His earthly remains lie beneath a statue of the Good Shepherd in the oblate cemetery at Mount Saviour in Elmira, New York. We can only hope that his spirit remains with us, urging us to celebrate well the mystery of faith around the table of the Lord and in deeds of justice. Writing about his dear friend, Fr. Emeric Lawrence, O.S.B., noted:

> Father Reinhold never rested in his life. He would not want to rest now. For him life has changed, it has not been taken away. And of one thing I am sure: he knows now, as he may not have known while he was with us, that it has all been enormously worthwhile.[23]

[19] Joel Garner, "The Vision of a Liturgical Reformer: Hans Ansgar Reinhold, American Catholic Educator" (Ph.D. dissertation, Teachers College, Columbia University, 1972) 157.

[20] H. A. Reinhold, "A Liturgical Reformer Sums Up," *New Blackfriars* 46 (1965) 554–61.

[21] Ibid., 560.

[22] William C. Clancy, "In Memoriam: H.A.R.," *Worship* 42:3 (March 1968) 130.

[23] Lawrence, "H.A.R.—Death of a Friend," 688.

20

Rita Sorg's Life of Joyful Hope: Remembering the Transfiguration on Tabor

Donald S. Raila, O.S.B.

Oblate Rita Mary (Krellner) Sorg of St. Marys, Pennsylvania, lived her whole life in the Catholic Benedictine atmosphere of her home town. Although she became an oblate late in life, when in her sixties, she was immersed in Benedictine values throughout her life span, and she lived her whole life in close affiliation with the Benedictine motherhouse in St. Marys and with St. Vincent Archabbey. Rita's inherited connections with Benedictines and the Catholic Church through family and parish led her to far broader interests. Gifted with a warm, personal style of writing, Rita authored articles that shed new light upon the rich history of the St. Marys area. In addition, she became known for her many editorial contributions to local publications. Blessed with a heart that empathized with the loneliness and suffering of others, she became editor-in-chief of a newsletter that was sent out worldwide to soldiers who were local high-school alumni. Called to bear with the hardships of raising a special-needs child, Rita became an articulate advocate for the cause of special-needs people throughout northwestern Pennsylvania. She pursued all these endeavors with strong faith and joyful hope.

Story of Rita's Life[1]

Rita Mary Krellner was born on July 23, 1919, to John B. and Rosa Werneth Krellner in St. Marys, Elk County, Pennsylvania, in the foothills

---

[1] Unless otherwise indicated, the quotations in this essay are taken from Rita's writings, from the Sorg family's private documents, from letters by Leonard and Rita Sorg, from public documents citing Rita Sorg for her achievements, or from interviews conducted with the Sorg family and with a close friend of Rita.

of the Allegheny Mountains. She was the youngest of nine children. The Krellner family belonged to St. Mary's Church and were very active in the parish. Influenced by the Benedictines who staffed St. Mary's, Rita's brother Raymond, the future Fr. Justin Krellner, left home for the arch-abbey in 1919 to enter the ninth grade at St. Vincent Scholasticate and ul-timately to become a monk and a priest. As Rita wrote in 1994, "My brother left for St. Vincent when I was only six weeks old; so all my early life was entwined with St. Vincent trips and visits."

Even closer to Rita's daily experience were the Benedictine sisters at St. Joseph's Convent right in her home town of St. Marys. This was the place and the community that marked the historic beginning of Benedictine convent life on this continent in 1852. One of Rita's sisters, Sr. Rose Mary Krellner, entered that community and was at one point elected its prioress.

Rita's father, John, was a coal miner and a part-time farmer, a man whom she described as "short but mighty." When she was only nine years old he was stricken with glaucoma, causing him blindness for the remain-ing twenty years of his life. In order to support her husband and nine chil-dren, Rita's mother, Rosa, opened a store and gasoline station on the grounds of the family's rural home on Bucktail Road. She ran the store, pumped gasoline, and sold groceries, tobacco, penny candy, and inciden-tal items. Since Rosa and John had very little time or energy to care for the household, it fell to young Rita to do the housekeeping, baby-sit her nieces and nephews, and take care of the greenhouse attached to the home, which was an additional source of income. In the course of her family's hard-ships, Rita learned early to bear the burdens that fell to her and to accept them patiently out of loving concern for others.

Episodes during World War II

Rita attended Central Catholic High School and was graduated as salutatorian in 1936. She had some desire to study journalism in college, but her family had come to depend on her at home. As the United States became involved in World War II and large numbers of men were drafted into military service, the Krellner family allowed Rita to go to work as a shipping clerk for Keystone Carbon Company, which was experiencing a shortage of male employees. About 1941 she was moved to the company's chemical lab and then became its head for about four years. Despite their initial discomfort at having women as co-workers, the men began to ap-preciate Rita's practical wisdom and compassionate heart.

Probably the most memorable contribution that Rita made during World War II was her editing of a newsletter called *The Alumni Crusader.* Rita later reminisced,

Early in the war, Father Boniface [Buerkle, O.S.B.,] of St. Mary's Church, moderator of our Alumni of Central Catholic High School, had conceived the idea of a monthly newsletter for our men and women in the service. I got the job, and the newsletter continued to the end of the war.

The monthly publication was sent to every alumnus of the high school in the military service. It had a circulation of almost one thousand and featured a "Walkie Talkie" column, which published letters written by the troops themselves so that they were able to contact one another through the newsletter.

Rita's Marriage and Family

While employed at Keystone's chemical lab, Rita worked alongside Leonard G. Sorg, a product-development engineer who had worked there since 1933 and who knew her brother Joseph. Rita and Len began to develop a friendship, which through prayerful discernment led to their wedding on August 6, 1946, at St. Mary's Church. At the time of their forty-ninth anniversary, Rita reminisced, "We purposely picked August 6, the [feast of the] Transfiguration, that in the Calvaries of our life we might remember Tabor." Rita's good friend of sixty years reflected that it rained in torrents on their wedding day; so that little taste of "Calvary" motivated the new couple to look forward to a brighter "Tabor" even from the start.

At the time of her marriage Rita terminated her work at Keystone Carbon, and soon afterward, in 1947, she began to raise their children; this vocation of child-rearing would continue for the remaining fifty years of her life. A better term might be "child-formation," since Rita strove to incorporate her lively faith into every dimension of her relationships with her children. For one thing, each of her nine children received a baptismal name that had some form of spiritual significance.

Her philosophy of raising children might be summarized as giving them abundant loving attention and, at the same time, entrusting everything to God. She made it clear to them that they were destined for eternal life with Christ and all the saints. Rita and Len found the strength to provide much loving care not only to their own children but also to the children living in their neighborhood. In fact, they became known as the "neighborhood sitters." Despite their many expenses there was always enough food to go around for extra guests. The Sorgs' freezer normally contained five-gallon tubs of ice cream, and the neighborhood children delighted in gathering at their home to enjoy such generous offers of hospitality. As their own children outgrew cribs and baby blankets, Rita and Len would donate them to the St. Vincent de Paul Society or provide them to needy families. Sometimes the Sorgs felt called to give away even currently used items. Rita often reminded her children, "Our gifts are to be shared." Since their income was often stretched to the limit, she would joke, "God would always give us enough money—but never any extra!"

Christmas celebrations at the Sorg home gave Rita's children and all their friends a taste of the true meaning of Christmas. On Christmas Eve Rita would organize a procession to the family creche, with biblical readings and Christmas hymns, and the event would end with a singing of "Happy Birthday" to Jesus. All this, in Rita's mind, helped "to take the edge off Santa Claus" and to counteract the secularistic customs that obscured the genuine significance of the Incarnation.

The Gift and Blessing of Timothy Sorg

One of the greatest influences on the Sorgs' family life was the condition of the fourth child, Timothy, who became the focal point of Rita's energies for many years. Born in 1950, Tim at first seemed normal, but he did not talk until the age of three. Only at the age of four, when Len and Rita took Tim to a doctor in Philadelphia, was he diagnosed with autism. Rita always saw her special child as a precious gift and blessing. She spent endless hours teaching Tim to write. When it was clear that he was not performing well at regular schools, Rita and her sister, Sr. Rose Mary Krellner, O.S.B., of St. Joseph Convent, then the mother superior, together formulated a plan to establish a school for mentally handicapped children in the basement of the convent. Another Benedictine Sister offered to teach the classes. The new institution, named "Our Lady's Special School," attracted about fifteen pupils.

Part of the gift and blessing of Tim's handicap was that it opened Rita's heart to assist other children with problems. Rita believed that the stirrings of the Holy Spirit were especially powerful when tragedies struck, and she kept herself alert to these stirrings. One such event occurred in the late 1950s when the Sorgs met a lawyer in Wilcox, Pennsylvania, who had a handicapped child of his own. Almost immediately Rita and Len began to work with him to establish what became the Elk County Association for Retarded Children, or ARC. Rita was a charter member and the publicity director of the organization. For twenty-five years she served as editor and writer for the association's newsletter, which had a circulation of several hundred. Rita enlisted the help of all her children to fold the newsletters and stuff envelopes. The work of ARC ultimately influenced the Commonwealth of Pennsylvania's initiatives to establish programs for "special education."

Rita's concern for special-needs people found new expressions as Tim grew older. Realizing that these young people would need specialized assistance after the completion of their formal education, she collaborated with others to establish a center where they could make crafts that could be sold. This effort gradually evolved into the Elk-Cameron County Vocational Rehabilitation Center, often called ELCAM, established to provide work skills for handicapped people, including those with physical disabilities and speech defects. Rita's daughter Rose Mary explained that ELCAM, a sheltered workshop that employs special-needs adults, was started through the efforts of the ARC of Elk County. As a key figure in its development from inception to completion, Rita was given the title of a charter and founding member. In the year 2000, ARC was doing over a million dollars of business annually and was providing employment and other opportunities for many special-needs clients. Rita's interest in the welfare of special-needs adults also led her to assist in the establishment of group homes in the St. Marys area so that these adults could live and work together under supervision. As of this writing, Tim continues to live in one of these group homes.

Rita's Ongoing Service

Queen of the World Parish in St. Marys was also fortunate to be a recipient of Rita's almost boundless energy. Active in the founding of the parish in 1956, she and Len sacrificed many evenings to participate in organizational meetings, serve on committees, and assist with the physical building of the church, rectory, and school. Rita donated homemade candy, baked goods, and other items to be sold or raffled at fund-raising events and often did the writing to publicize them. The annual Queen of the World Festival, a citywide event meant to build community and raise funds for the parish, was dear to Rita's heart, and she served as its publicity chairperson from its inception. The feature articles that she wrote for the local magazine *Roaming in Elk County* from 1976 to 1981, most of which were stories concerning "old time memories," were compiled into a booklet during St. Marys' sesquicentennial in 1993, and the publication was sold for the benefit of the parish festival. Rita and Len also served the parish as eucharistic ministers to the homebound and served the local community as hospice volunteers until a year before she died.

Rita was also known for her "parking-lot conferences," situations that arose when people would approach her informally in supermarkets and parking lots for emotional and spiritual counseling. She had the patience to accept many such spontaneous requests and the gift of saying what people needed to hear. She responded wholeheartedly because she perceived God's call in such interruptions.

Rita Becomes an Oblate and Faces Old Age and Death

With all these accomplishments behind her, Rita decided to become an oblate at the age of sixty-four. She had been close to Benedictine monks and sisters all of her life and had consistently lived by the motto *"ora et labora."* After the children were grown, she and Len regularly prayed an oblates' version of the Liturgy of the Hours together. When the local oblate group was being reactivated, Rita decided to be invested as an oblate novice of St. Vincent Archabbey along with others on March 20, 1984, the Vigil of the Solemnity of St. Benedict.

St. Vincent Archabbey, the first Benedictine monastery in the United States, was founded in 1846 from St. Michael's Abbey in Metten, Bavaria. Soon after Fr. Boniface Wimmer began the community by investing eighteen newly-arrived monks, it grew rapidly and began to make other foundations, many of which became independent abbeys, the first two being St. John's Abbey in Collegeville, Minnesota (founded in 1856), and St. Benedict's Abbey in Atchison, Kansas (founded in 1857). St. Vincent became an abbey in 1855 and was raised to the rank of archabbey in 1892. The monastery has been the "mother house" of the American Cassinese Congregation since 1855. Currently, its main apostolates include the operation of St. Vincent College and St. Vincent Seminary and the staffing of some twenty-five parishes. The community also has foreign missions in Brazil and Taiwan, staffs a priory and military preparatory school in Savannah, Georgia, and provides Catholic chaplains to Penn State University in State College, Pennsylvania. Among the earliest apostolates of the community was the staffing of St. Mary's Church in St. Marys, Pennsylvania, beginning in 1852.

Rita subsequently made full oblation on April 9, 1985. She commented, "My husband Len, who has been an oblate since 1936, became involved [in the St. Marys group], and so did I. And I could almost feel my beloved big brother's [Fr. Justin's] satisfaction that I was becoming a 'Benedictine.'" In May of 1986 the couple decided to attend the first oblate retreat at St. Vincent Archabbey. During that retreat Rita had a profound spiritual experience. She later reflected, "We were sitting in the choir stalls praying with the monks, and all at once I seemed to be aware of Fr. Justin's presence saying, 'I'm here. I'm still here. You haven't lost me.' And it was true, and once again the Abbey is dear and familiar." (Fr. Justin had died in 1949.) This experience seemed to confirm her prayerful decision to become an oblate.

Rita continued to serve the Church and her community right up to her rather sudden death on June 10, 1997. Although Rita did not easily accept the diminishments of old age, she made light of her ailments, such as two knee replacements and two cataract surgeries, and she frequently alluded to her readiness for death. Only when she suffered a slight heart attack about 1995 did she realize that she had a weak heart. Shortly after she was hospitalized in June of 1997, she died with Len at her side.

Significance of Rita's Life

The life of Rita M. Sorg was a journey from the crucifixion at Calvary to the Transfiguration at Tabor, seen as a foretaste of the Resurrection. Like St. Benedict, one of her patron saints, she knew that "the life of a monk [or of any Christian] ought to be a continuous Lent" (RB 49:1),[2] especially if one was to give one's life in sacrificial loving service to others. At the same time, Rita could, even on this earth, regularly "look forward to holy Easter with joy and spiritual longing" (*RB* 49:7). The anticipation of "Tabors," both of this life and of eternal life with Christ and all the saints, was an inherent dimension of Rita's life amid the various crosses that she bore.

Like the Benedictine Order itself in its historical progression, Rita's early life did not seem destined to have any profound impact on society, and yet her persistent practice of faith and charity bore fruits that had significant influence throughout much of northwestern Pennsylvania. She lived the Benedictine values of simplicity of life and dedication to service that would glorify God. Her editing of *The Alumni Crusader,* her efforts to build Queen of the World Church and School, and her initiatives in founding several institutions for special-needs people all reflected her great love for people and her trust that the time and strength she received from God were intended to further Christ's kingdom on earth.

Despite her lack of formal training, Rita was a natural journalist, poet, and playwright. She used these literary gifts freely to express her maternal love and wisdom and to bring other people together to work for the kingdom. The plays and poems that she wrote affirmed people, lifted their spirits, and brought them closer to God. Some of her inspirational poems brought comfort to individuals and families in need of consolation, and others added to the joy of special events or landmark occasions as Rita penned verses about the persons being honored. After Rita became an oblate, she naturally took on the task of writing to the local newspaper about oblate events. Her homespun wisdom often found expression in her writings. In *A Collection of Old Time Memories* she combined factual historical accounts with such bits of advice as, "Cherish life, hold it close. Tell people you love them while the lamp still glows!"

---

[2] RB here refers to *RB 1980: The Rule of St. Benedict in English,* ed. Timothy Fry, (Collegeville: The Liturgical Press, 1982).

St. Benedict exhorts his monks, "Yearn for everlasting life with holy desire. Day by day remind yourself that you are going to die" (*RB* 4:46-47). Rita lived these precepts to the fullest. She believed in preparing for death at all times and strove likewise to prepare others, even children, for good, holy deaths. She often spoke of looking forward to life after death, and she passed on this attitude to her children and grandchildren. Rita's own death seemed to fulfill her own hope-filled attitude toward death and eternal life. The Sorg children's narration about a cut poppy bud which surprisingly began to bloom on top of Rita's coffin shortly before the funeral Mass interpreted this event as an extension of her humor and a reminder of her faith in resurrection.

Conclusion

The life of Rita Sorg contained many "Calvaries." Her upbringing in relative poverty, her father's blindness, her early assumption of household duties, the stressful raising of a special-needs son, and the weaknesses that she endured in old age were burdens that were heavy but not remarkable. They were like the crosses that many others have had to carry. However, Rita's way of bearing these crosses was truly significant. Amid her various sufferings she developed the gift of her faith by focusing and refocusing on Christ and on the "Tabor" to come. She thus found in Christ the peace and strength to serve others with joy-filled energy and to share in others' sufferings in his name. By participating in Christ's Passion and finding joyful hope in him, Rita had arrived at "that perfect love of God which casts out fear" (RB 7:67). May her example help us to envision Tabor amid our Calvaries and look forward "with joy and spiritual longing" (RB 49:7) to our eternal Easter with Rita, with all the saints, and with our merciful God who encourages us to live in joyful hope.

Contributors

Roberta C. Bondi, D.Phil., a graduate of Oxford University, is a professor of Church history at the Candler School of Theology, Emory University in Atlanta, Georgia. She is the author of nine books, among them: *To Love as God Loves: Conversations with the Early Church* and *Memories of God: Theological Reflections on a Life.* She is a United Methodist and an oblate of St. Benedict's Monastery in St. Joseph, Minnesota.

Mary Ruth Coffman, O.S.B., a member of Sacred Heart Monastery in Cullman, Alabama, earned a master's degree in English from The Catholic University of America and a master's degree in library science from Peabody Library School (now merged with Vanderbilt University in Nashville, Tennessee). She is the author of *Build Me a City: The Life of Father Harold Purcell, the Founder of the City of St. Jude* (1984) and *On Good Ground: Benedictine Women of Alabama* (1993).

Margaret Colleton is a native of South Bend, Indiana. She graduated from the University of Notre Dame's Program of Liberal Studies. She was a Benedictine volunteer at Mount St. Scholastica in Atchison, Kansas, and participated in the Monastic Living Experience at St. Benedict's Monastery in St. Joseph, Minnesota.

Patty Crowley is an oblate of St. John's Abbey in Collegeville, Minnesota. She and her husband, Patrick, were the co-founders of the Christian Family Movement, an international organization based on the Inquiry Method of Joseph Cardijn, through which laity became more active in the Church. In 1957 they were awarded the church's Pro Eclesia et Pontifica medal in recognition of their work with this group. Patty also served, with her husband, as one of only three married couples on the pontifical commission to reevaluate the Church's stance on birth control in the 1960s.

Edward J. Dupuy is the newly appointed senior vice president for academic affairs at Our Lady of Holy Cross College in New Orleans, Louisiana. He served as academic dean, director of communications, and chair of the Division of Language Skills, Literature, and Music at St. Joseph Seminary College (operated by the monks of St. Joseph Abbey) before moving to New Orleans with his wife and three children. He earned an M.A. (1989) and Ph.D. (1993) in English from Louisiana State University. He is the author of *Autobiography in Walker Percy: Repetition, Recovery, and Redemption,* published by LSU Press in 1996, and he has published several articles and reviews on autobiography and southern literature.

Hugh Feiss, o.s.b., is a monk of the Monastery of the Ascension in Jerome, Idaho. Born in Lakeview, Oregon, educated at Mt. Angel Seminary (M.A., M.Div.), Catholic University (S.T.L., Ph.L.), Sant'Anselmo (S.T.D.), he has been teaching theology and philosophy and researching medieval religious thought for over thirty years. He contributes regularly to the *American Benedictine Review* and authored *Essential Monastic Wisdom* (HarperCollins, 1999) and several articles in the forthcoming *Encyclopedia of Monasticism* (Fitzroy Dearborn), in addition to translating a number of Latin works.

Lucie R. Johnson, obl.s.b., is an oblate of St. John's Abbey, Collegeville, Minnesota. Originally from Belgium, she is a graduate of the Catholic University of Louvain, and received her doctorate from the University of Minnesota. She is a professor of psychology at Bethel College in St. Paul, Minnesota.

Susan Anderson Kerr earned a doctorate in English literature and currently teaches English to international students at the University of Texas at Austin. A convert from the Lutheran Church, she writes about art and Catholic spirituality. She is an oblate of St. Scholastica Priory in Petersham, Massachusetts.

Ann Kessler, o.s.b., holds a Ph.D. in history from Notre Dame University. She is a professor emeritus of Mount Marty after serving as professor of social science (instructor in history and political science) for thirty-seven years before retiring in May 1999. She has lectured throughout the United States and Canada and served as a retreat director for Carmelite men in formation and monks of Mt. Michael Abbey. She is the author of *Benedictine Men and Women of Courage:*

Roots and History published in 1986, now out of print. Sister Ann prepared a series of lectures on reform and renewal given to monks of a Trappist Abbey in Virginia in July 2001.

Linda Kulzer, O.S.B., a member of St. Benedict's Monastery in St. Joseph, Minnesota, holds a Ph.D. in education with a minor in religion and culture from Syracuse University. She is co-editor of and contributor to *Medieval Women Monastics: Wisdom's Wellsprings* and *Purity of Heart in Early Ascetic and Monastic Literature*. She has had a long-term interest in monastic history.

Owen Lindblad, O.S.B., a member of St. Benedict's Monastery at St. Joseph, Minnesota, was an educator in the St. Cloud Diocese for thirty years. She has served as editor for Japanese writer/poet Toshimi Horiuchi for fifteen years. She has written many historical and biographical articles for local newspapers and magazines and several books of local history. Sister Owen is the author of *Full of Fair Hope* (Waite Park, Minn.: Park Press, 1997), the history of St. Mary's Mission on the Red Lake Indian Reservation of northern Minnesota.

Paschal A. Morlino, O.S.B., is a monk of St. Vincent Archabbey Latrobe, Pennsylvania, and an archimandrite of the Melkite, Greek-Catholic Church. Father Paschal is presently pastor of St. Benedict Church in Baltimore, Maryland. He has worked extensively in pastoral work, on the college level, in prison ministry, and is the founder and director emeritus of Adelphoi Village, an agency that cares for troubled youth. Being a retreat master and facilitating parish renewal programs over the years has been a steady part of his ministry.

Charles Preble is an oblate of St. Benedict's Monastery, St. Joseph, Minnesota, husband, father, and a full time artisan in wood, designing, and hand making furnishings for homes and sanctuaries. He is currently at work on a book about contemplative practice.

Donald S. Raila, O.S.B., is a monk of St. Vincent Archabbey, Latrobe, Pennsylvania. He professed his first vows in 1978 and was ordained a priest in 1983. Since 1988 he has been the monastic community's director of oblates, and since 1991 he has served as an assistant organist for the monastery.

Jem Sullivan and her husband, Scott, currently reside in Washington, D.C. She and her husband have been Benedictine oblates of St. Anselm's Abbey, Washington, D.C., since 1995. Having earned a doctorate in religious studies from The Catholic University of America, Washington, D.C., Jem has served as an adjunct faculty member at The Catholic University of America, the Education for Parish Service located at Trinity College, and the Pontifical Faculty of the Dominican House of Studies. She contributes articles to publications such as *Share the Word* and *Homily Service,* and is a scriptwriter for a nationally distributed Lectionary-based video program, *Sunday to Sunday.* Jem is the editor of the St. Anselm's Abbey oblate newsletter.

Phyllis K. Thompson, born and raised in the United States, has her B.A. from Rosary Hill College and her M.A. from Canisius College, both in Buffalo, New York; her area is English. She also did doctoral course work in English at the University of Wisconsin, Madison. In 1970 she moved to Canada, where she taught at the University of Saskatchewan for sixteen years. She taught a further five years at the college attached to St. Peter's Abbey in Muenster, Saskatchewan, also serving as campus minister there. Additionally, Phyllis served for fifteen years as the senior Catholic member of the ecumenical pastoral care team at the 238-bed facility for the chronically and terminally ill. She retired in 1998 and now lives on Vancouver Island in the Pacific. Phyllis has been an oblate of St. Peter's Abbey since 1993.

George C. Tunstall is currently an associate professor of German and classical languages in the Department of Modern Languages at Kansas State University in Manhattan. In January 1996 he took his first oblation at St. Benedict's Abbey in Atchison, Kansas, and his final oblation in January 1997. In addition to teaching German, Latin, and Greek at KSU, he is currently Catholic chaplain to the Mercy Hospitals in Manhattan and assists in coordinating the three-day oblate retreat held at St. Benedict's Abbey each Lent.

Rita McClain Tybor is an oblate of St. Bede Abbey, Peru, Illinois. Married to David and the mother of Dave, Julia, and Rachel, she writes from her home in Henry, Illinois. Rita holds a master's degree in counseling and has worked in education, public relations, and the mental health field. Also active in community service work, she is a parishioner of St. Mary's in Henry, Illinois.

Julia Upton, R.S.M., a member of the Institute of the Sisters of Mercy of the Americas, has been an oblate of Mount Saviour Monastery for twenty years. She holds a doctorate in theology from Fordham University and is researching a book-length biography of Fr. Reinhold. A full professor in the Department of Theology and Religious Studies at St. John's University in New York, she currently serves the university as interim provost. Her most recent book is *A Time for Embracing: Reclaiming Reconciliation* (The Liturgical Press, 1999).

Mary Anthony Wagner, O.S.B., a member of St. Benedict's Monastery, St. Joseph, Minnesota, died before the publication of this book. She was the Oblate Director at St. Benedict's for thirty years. She taught theology at the College of St. Benedict, and was for a time dean of the Graduate School of Saint John's Univesity, Collegeville, Minnesota. Her publications include *The Sacred World of the Christian: Sensed in Faith* (1993) and the editorship of *Sisters Today* (1979–2000). Sister Mary Anthony, together with Father Paschal Botz, O.S.B., Saint John's Abbey, Collegeville, began the Benedictine Institute of Sacred Theology at Saint Benedict's Monastery in 1958—later to become the School of Theology at Saint John's University, Collegeville.

Catherine Wybourne, O.S.B., was born in 1954. She was educated at Boscombe Convent and Girton College, Cambridge. After research and a few years in banking, she entered Stanbrook Abbey, Worcester, in 1981. Catherine is currently a printer. Her academic interests lie in Spanish history, especially Judaism and Cistercians.